Certification Study Companion Series

The Apress Certification Study Companion Series offers guidance and hands-on practice to support technical and business professionals who are studying for an exam in the pursuit of an industry certification. Professionals worldwide seek to achieve certifications in order to advance in a career role, reinforce knowledge in a specific discipline, or to apply for or change jobs. This series focuses on the most widely taken certification exams in a given field. It is designed to be user friendly, tracking to topics as they appear in a given exam and work alongside other certification material as professionals prepare for their exam.

More information about this series at `https://link.springer.com/bookseries/17100`.

Microsoft 365 Certified: Collaboration Communications Systems Engineer Associate Certification Companion

A Guide to Prepare for Exam MS-721

Fabrizio Volpe

Apress®

Microsoft 365 Certified: Collaboration Communications Systems Engineer Associate Certification Companion: A Guide to Prepare for Exam MS-721

Fabrizio Volpe
Burton upon Trent, UK

ISBN-13 (pbk): 979-8-8688-0517-2   ISBN-13 (electronic): 979-8-8688-0518-9
https://doi.org/10.1007/979-8-8688-0518-9

Copyright © 2024 by Fabrizio Volpe

This work is subject to copyright. All rights are reserved by the Publisher, whether the whole or part of the material is concerned, specifically the rights of translation, reprinting, reuse of illustrations, recitation, broadcasting, reproduction on microfilms or in any other physical way, and transmission or information storage and retrieval, electronic adaptation, computer software, or by similar or dissimilar methodology now known or hereafter developed.

Trademarked names, logos, and images may appear in this book. Rather than use a trademark symbol with every occurrence of a trademarked name, logo, or image we use the names, logos, and images only in an editorial fashion and to the benefit of the trademark owner, with no intention of infringement of the trademark.

The use in this publication of trade names, trademarks, service marks, and similar terms, even if they are not identified as such, is not to be taken as an expression of opinion as to whether or not they are subject to proprietary rights.

While the advice and information in this book are believed to be true and accurate at the date of publication, neither the authors nor the editors nor the publisher can accept any legal responsibility for any errors or omissions that may be made. The publisher makes no warranty, express or implied, with respect to the material contained herein.

Managing Director, Apress Media LLC: Welmoed Spahr
Acquisitions Editor: Smriti Srivastava
Development Editor: Laura Berendson
Coordinating Editor: Kripa Joseph

Cover image designed by eStudioCalamar

Distributed to the book trade worldwide by Apress Media, LLC, 1 New York Plaza, New York, NY 10004, U.S.A. Phone 1-800-SPRINGER, fax (201) 348-4505, e-mail orders-ny@springer-sbm.com, or visit www.springeronline.com. Apress Media, LLC is a California LLC and the sole member (owner) is Springer Science + Business Media Finance Inc (SSBM Finance Inc). SSBM Finance Inc is a **Delaware** corporation.

For information on translations, please e-mail booktranslations@springernature.com; for reprint, paperback, or audio rights, please e-mail bookpermissions@springernature.com.

Apress titles may be purchased in bulk for academic, corporate, or promotional use. eBook versions and licenses are also available for most titles. For more information, reference our Print and eBook Bulk Sales web page at http://www.apress.com/bulk-sales.

Any source code or other supplementary material referenced by the author in this book is available to readers on GitHub (https://github.com/Apress). For more detailed information, please visit https://www.apress.com/gp/services/source-code.

If disposing of this product, please recycle the paper.

Dedicated to my mother and father, whose love and sacrifices have paved the path I walk today.

Table of Contents

About the Author xv

About the Technical Reviewer xvii

Acknowledgments xix

Introduction xxi

Chapter 1: Introduction to Exam MS-721 1

1.1 Prepare for Your Microsoft Exam and MS-721 2

1.2 Book Outline 3

1.3 Introduction to Microsoft Teams 5

1.4 Microsoft Teams Licensing 7

1.5 Teams Admin Center and Teams PowerShell Module 10

    1.5.1 Teams Admin Center 10

    1.5.2 Teams PowerShell Module 10

Chapter 2: Teams Meetings 13

2.1 Introducing Meeting Types 14

    2.1.1 Meetings 16

    2.1.2 Webinars 19

    2.1.3 Live Events 20

2.2 Deploying Teams Meetings and Meeting Policies 20

    2.2.1 Meeting Scheduling 21

    2.2.2 Meeting Join & Lobby 23

    2.2.3 Meeting Engagement 24

    2.2.4 Content Sharing 25

    2.2.5 Recording & Transcription 27

TABLE OF CONTENTS

    2.2.6 Audio & Video 29

    2.2.7 Watermark 31

    2.2.8 Manage with PowerShell 31

2.3 Assigning Policies in Microsoft Teams 32

    2.3.1 Users' Effective Policy 32

    2.3.2 Ways to Assign Teams Policies 33

    2.3.3 Check Your Policy Assignments 34

2.4 Policy Packages in Microsoft Teams 35

    2.4.1 Custom Policy Packages 36

    2.4.2 Assigning Policy Packages 37

    2.4.3 Manage with PowerShell 39

2.5 Teams Webinars 39

    2.5.1 Creating a Webinar 40

2.6 Teams Premium Licensing and Features 42

2.7 Knowledge Check 45

Chapter 3: Configure and Manage Audio Conferencing and Live Events 47

3.1 Meetings Types and Features in Microsoft Teams 48

3.2 Introducing Teams PSTN Audio Conferencing 50

3.3 Configuring Audio Conferencing for Teams (Audio Conferencing Bridge, Dedicated and Shared Numbers, and User Assignment) 52

    3.3.1 Managing with PowerShell 56

3.4 Customizing Audio Conferencing in Meeting Invitations 56

    3.4.1 Managing with PowerShell 57

3.5 Setting Teams Live Events Roles and Policies 58

    3.5.1 Teams Live Events Roles 58

    3.5.2 Teams Live Events Policies 60

    3.5.3 Live Events Video Distribution Providers 62

    3.5.4 Managing with PowerShell 63

3.6 Create a Custom Meeting Template in Microsoft Teams	65
3.7 Meeting Themes	67
3.8 Meeting Options in Microsoft Teams	68
3.9 Live Events in Microsoft 365	70
3.10 Knowledge Check	73

Chapter 4: Introducing Teams Phone 75

4.1 Licensing for Teams Voice	76
4.1.1 Teams Usage Scenarios	80
4.2 PSTN Connectivity Options	81
4.2.1 Porting Existing Phone Numbers or Obtaining New Ones	82
4.2.2 Operator Connect	82
4.2.3 Teams Phone Mobile	84
4.2.4 Calling Plans and Transferring Phone Numbers to Microsoft	86
4.2.5 Communications Credits	88
4.2.6 Direct Routing	89
4.3 Teams Phone Devices	90
4.3.1 Personal Devices	93
4.3.2 Shared Space Devices	93
4.4 Teams Phone SIP Gateway	93
4.4.1 Preparing the Microsoft Teams SIP Gateway	94
4.5 Analog Devices with Teams Phone System	95
4.5.1 Integrate Using Analog Telephone Adapter	95
4.5.2 Integrate Using SIP Gateway	96
4.5.3 Integrate Using an Operator	97
4.6 SIP Handsets and SIP Devices	97
4.7 Deploying Compliance Voice Recording in Microsoft Teams	98
4.7.1 Managing with PowerShell	99
4.8 Integrating Third-Party Call Centers with Teams	100
4.9 Knowledge Check	102

TABLE OF CONTENTS

Chapter 5: Using Direct Routing with Teams Phone 105

5.1 Teams and the SBCs 107
5.1.1 Supported SBCs 107
5.1.2 Choosing Between a Cloud-Based SBC and an On-Prem SBC 108
5.1.3 Survivable Branch Appliance for Direct Routing 109

5.2 Configuring the SBC for Direct Routing 111
5.2.1 Deploying the SBC 112

5.3 Calls Flow in Direct Routing 113
5.3.1 Configuring the Call Flow for Direct Routing 114

5.4 Troubleshooting Direct Routing 115
5.4.1 Validate Direct Routing SBC Connectivity 116
5.4.2 Troubleshoot Firewall Issues for Direct Routing 117
5.4.3 Troubleshoot Certificate Issues for Direct Routing 117
5.4.4 Troubleshoot Direct Routing SBC Connectivity 117
5.4.5 Investigate and Diagnose Calling Issues by Using an SBC SIP Trace 119

5.5 Additional Configurations for Direct Routing 120
5.5.1 Design and Configure Location-Based Routing 121
5.5.2 Design and Configure Local Media Optimization (LMO) 122
5.5.3 Configure Trunk Translation Rules 125
5.5.4 Configure On-Network Conferencing for Direct Routing 126
5.5.5 Configure an SBA 127

5.6 Knowledge Check 129

Chapter 6: Configuring Teams Phone 131

6.1 Configure Teams Phone Policies 132
6.1.1 Teams Dial Plans 132
6.1.2 Configure Calling Policies 135
6.1.3 Configure Call Park Policies 138
6.1.4 Configure Caller ID Policies 139
6.1.5 Configure Call Hold Policies for Users 143
6.1.6 Configure Outbound Call Restrictions 145
6.1.7 Configure Inbound Call Blocking 148

TABLE OF CONTENTS

6.1.8 Configure Routing of Unassigned Numbers 150
6.1.9 Assign Voice Policies Through Policy Packages 151
6.1.10 Configure Compliance Recording Policies 154
6.2 Configure Dynamic Emergency Calling 156
6.2.1 Design Dynamic Emergency Calling Scenarios 156
6.2.2 Configure Emergency Calling Locations 158
6.2.3 Configure Emergency Calling Policies 159
6.2.4 Configure Networks and Locations (Location Information Service) 162
6.2.5 Validate Emergency Address and Emergency Calling from Teams Clients 164
6.2.6 Knowledge Check 165

Chapter 7: Call Queues, Auto Attendants, and Users 169

7.1 Configure Auto Attendants and Call Queues 171
7.1.1 Design Call Flows for Auto Attendants and Call Queues 171
7.1.2 Configure Auto Attendants and Call Queues 173
7.1.3 Configure and Manage Users for Teams Phone 189
7.1.4 Configure and Manage Calling Features for Teams Phone 193
7.1.5 Knowledge Check 203

Chapter 8: Teams Rooms and Devices 207

8.1 Plan and Design Teams-Certified Device Solutions 209
8.1.1 Recommend a Room Configuration Based on the Meeting Space 209
8.1.2 Recommend a Room Configuration Based on Customer and business requirements 211
8.1.3 Compare Capabilities and Features of Teams Rooms Basic and Teams Rooms Pro 211
8.1.4 Recommend a Teams Rooms Device Platform (Android vs. Windows vs. Surface Hub) 214
8.1.5 Recommend Teams-Certified Devices 220
8.1.6 Recommend Teams Rooms Certified Components 221
8.1.7 Recommend When to Use Coordinated Meetings 222
8.1.8 Recommend When to Use Cloud Video Interop (CVI) or Direct Guest Join 223
8.1.9 Recommend an Update Strategy for Teams Meeting Room Devices 224
8.1.10 Identify the Requirements for a Microsoft Exchange Online Resource Account 225

xi

TABLE OF CONTENTS

    8.1.11 Identify the Enrollment Requirements for Microsoft Intune 227

    8.1.12 Plan for Advanced Features on Shared Devices 229

  8.2 Maintain Teams Rooms and Devices 230

    8.2.1 Configure Device Settings 230

    8.2.2 Configure IP Phone Policies 232

    8.2.3 Configure Local Network Settings 233

    8.2.4 Configure Security and Updates 233

    8.2.5 Configure Conditional Access Policy MFA Exception for Resource Accounts 234

    8.2.6 Configure Meeting Room Settings by Using the Microsoft Teams Admin Center or the Local Teams Application Settings 235

    8.2.7 Create and Configure Device Configuration Profiles for Android Based Devices........ 240

    8.2.8 Manage Teams Rooms from the Microsoft Teams Rooms Pro Management Portal ... 240

    8.2.9 Configure Intune Policies for Teams Devices... 241

    8.2.10 Configure Intune Configuration Profiles (for Windows MTRs)................................. 243

    8.2.11 Enable Advanced Voice Capabilities for Shared Space Devices 244

    8.2.12 Enable Hotline for Shared Space Devices 244

    8.2.13 Configure Virtual Front Desk.. 244

    8.2.14 Deploy Common Area Phones, User Phones, Conference Phones........................... 245

    8.2.15 Create and Manage Teams Device Tags 246

    8.2.16 Deploy Android Devices Remotely 246

    8.2.17 Configure SIP Gateway 247

    8.2.18 Monitor Teams Device Health 248

    8.2.19 Troubleshoot Authentication Issues 249

    8.2.20 Troubleshoot Update Issues.. 251

    8.2.21 Troubleshoot Remote Provisioning Issues 252

    8.2.22 Troubleshoot Bluetooth Beaconing 253

  8.3 Knowledge Check 254

Chapter 9: MTRs Based on Windows and Surface Hub.. 257

  9.1 Configure and Manage Teams Rooms on a Surface Hub or Windows 258

    9.1.1 Configure the Authentication Type During a Surface Hub Out-of-Box-Experience (OOBE) Setup.. 258

    9.1.2 Configure Meeting Room Settings on a Surface Hub Device..................................... 259

9.1.3 Create and Validate a Surface Hub Provisioning Package 262

9.1.4 Assign a Provisioning Package to a Surface Hub 264

9.1.5 Specify Domain Group Policy Exclusions for Teams Rooms on Windows 265

9.1.6 Configure Custom Displays for Teams Rooms on Windows 266

9.1.7 Customize Meeting Room Settings by Using XML Files on Windows 267

9.1.8 Configure Settings for Peripherals for Teams Room on Windows 267

9.1.9 Monitor Surface Hub Health with Azure Monitor 267

9.1.10 Manage Surface Hub Updates via Update Rings 268

9.2 Configure Optional Features for Teams Rooms and Devices 270

9.2.1 Configure HDMI Ingest and Options 270

9.2.2 Configure a Content Camera 271

9.2.3 Configure Teams Casting 271

9.2.4 Auto Accept a Proximity Join 271

9.2.5 Allow Room Remote 271

9.2.6 Configure an Intelligent Speaker 272

9.2.7 Configure Direct Guest Join 273

9.2.8 Configure Hot Desking on Teams Shared Devices 274

9.2.9 Configure Hotline Phones 274

9.3 Knowledge Check 274

Chapter 10: Prepare the Network for Teams and Troubleshooting Calls 277

10.1 Prepare the Network for the Deployment of Teams 279

10.1.1 Perform a Network Analysis by Using the Microsoft Teams Network Assessment Tool 279

10.1.2 Determine Network Readiness for Teams 280

10.1.3 Determine Enterprise Content Delivery Network (ECDN) Requirements for Teams Live Events and Town Halls 280

10.1.4 Specify the Network Configuration for Certified Devices 281

10.1.5 Determine Network Requirements by Using the Network Planner for Teams 282

10.1.6 Specify the Optimal Network Architecture for Teams 283

10.1.7 Specify Teams Quality of Service (QoS) Requirements and Policies 284

10.1.8 Validate Local Internet Breakout Strategy for Client Media Optimization 287

10.1.9 Validate VPN Split Tunneling 287

TABLE OF CONTENTS

10.1.10 Validate DNS Resolves to the Nearest Point of Entry in Microsoft 365 288

10.1.11 Configure Teams for QoS 288

10.1.12 Configure Media Bit Rate (MBR) 290

10.1.13 Create and Assign a Network Roaming Policy 291

10.1.14 Configure the Network Topology 292

10.1.15 Configure Tenant Data Upload for the Microsoft Call Quality Dashboard 292

10.1.16 Configure Microsoft Power BI Reports for the Microsoft Call Quality Dashboard ... 292

10.1.17 Configure Reporting Labels for Call Analytics 293

10.2 Troubleshoot Call Failures and Session Quality 293

10.2.1 Troubleshoot a Missing Dial Pad 293

10.2.2 Troubleshoot Voice & Meeting Issues by Using Self-Help Diagnostics in the Microsoft 365 Admin Center 294

10.2.3 Troubleshoot Entra ID Sign-in Issues for Teams Phones 295

10.2.4 Interpret Teams Media Flows 296

10.2.5 Troubleshoot Tenant Dial Plans by Using Regular Expressions and PowerShell 297

10.2.6 Interpret E.164 Normalization Rules to Resolve Dialing Issues 298

10.2.7 Interpret Reverse Number Lookup to Resolve Caller ID Issues 298

10.2.8 Diagnose Call Failures 299

10.2.9 Troubleshoot Dynamic Emergency Address by Using Client Debug Logs 300

10.2.10 Troubleshoot Teams Client Media Issues by Using the Microsoft Remote Connectivity Analyzer for Teams 301

10.2.11 Troubleshoot Calls by Using Advanced Call Analytics 301

10.2.12 Troubleshoot Calls by Using the Microsoft Call Quality Dashboard 302

10.2.13 Inspect PSTN Usage Reports for SIP Call Failures 302

10.3 Knowledge Check 303

Index 307

About the Author

Fabrizio Volpe is an IT professional with more than two decades of experience in networking, security, and the Microsoft ecosystem, with a particular emphasis on Microsoft collaboration tools such as Microsoft Teams.

Fabrizio has contributed to the IT community by blogging, authoring several books, and giving speeches at industry conferences worldwide.

A passionate advocate for knowledge sharing and community engagement, Fabrizio plays a key role in organizing BeConnected day, a highly regarded community-driven conference in Italy that brings together IT professionals to explore the latest trends in technology.

In his professional capacity, Fabrizio serves as a senior consultant at Exponential-e, a leading British IT services company, where he specializes in delivering cutting-edge solutions in cloud computing, networking, and cybersecurity.

About the Technical Reviewer

Kapil Bansal is a PhD scholar and lead DevOps engineer at S&P Global Market Intelligence, India. He has more than 16 years of experience in the IT industry, having worked with Azure cloud computing (PaaS, IaaS, and SaaS), the Azure stack, DevSecOps, Kubernetes, Terraform, Office 365, SharePoint, release management, application lifecycle management (ALM), the Information Technology Infrastructure Library (ITIL), and Six Sigma. He completed the Advanced Program in Strategy for Leaders from IIM Lucknow & Cyber Security and Cyber Defense from IIT Kanpur.

He has worked with companies such as IBM India Pvt Ltd, HCL Technologies, NIIT Technologies, Encore Capital Group, and Xavient Software Solutions, Noida, and has served multiple clients based in the United States, the UK, and Africa, such as T-Mobile, World Bank Group, H&M, WBMI, Encore Capital, and Bharti Airtel (India and Africa).

Kapil also reviewed *Practical Microsoft Azure IaaS: Migrating and Building Scalable and Secure Cloud Solutions* and *Beginning SharePoint Communication Sites*, both published by Apress.

Acknowledgments

Whenever I start writing the "Acknowledgments" section of a book (and I've had to do this several times), I'm often tempted to think, "Well, many thanks to myself." Writing a book demands an immense amount of time—anywhere from several months to more than a year—and considerable effort. It requires choosing to write instead of engaging in other potentially less stressful activities.

But then, as always, I realize that I wasn't working in a vacuum. The people in my life who supported and contributed to this project were just as crucial as my own dedication in bringing this book to completion.

So, who am I talking about? I already expressed my gratitude to my parents by dedicating this book to them, but it bears repeating, as their daily support is invaluable. Equally important is my son Federico, who is nothing short of a blessing in my life. And then there's Heather, my partner, who knows just how to apply a bit of pressure when I start to lose momentum. I deeply appreciate her support and all the wonderful qualities she brings to my life.

I want to extend a heartfelt thank-you to the Modern Workplace team at Exponential-e, with special appreciation to my managers over the past two years—Stuart Fordham, Russell Sayer, and Kevin Watson—and to our CEO, Lee Wade. This is a company where individuals can thrive and grow, which is perhaps the highest compliment I can offer to any organization.

I cannot exclude from these acknowledgments all the other members of the board of the BeConnected day (`https://www.beconnectedday.it/`). This year we created a record-breaking community conference. So, kudos to Fabrizio Fabiani, Roberto Ferazzi, Alessio Giombini, Igor Macori, Paolo Pialorsi, Michele Sensalari, and Luca Vitali for being one of the best teams I have seen in many years.

Finally, a big thank-you to the team from Apress, especially Smriti Srivastava and Shonmirin P A, for the opportunity to write for their publishing house and for their support.

Introduction

The MS-721 exam syllabus covers a large part of the topics relevant to Microsoft Teams.

You could consider this good news (because what you learn for the certification has also real-world value) or bad news, because administering and configuring Teams means touching areas of information technology that, usually, are not managed by a single person (or group).

This exam covers different aspects of Microsoft Teams, and acquiring the required knowledge could be interesting for IT admins, IT professionals, IT support engineers, and (generally speaking) anybody who works with Teams and wants to understand some of the background mechanisms. With this book I hope to help you learn what you need and spare you from wasting time and effort.

Microsoft Teams works correctly and gives the best user experience when your connectivity to the Microsoft 365 tenant is optimized (which is the focus of Chapter 10).

That said, a Teams meeting (which is the feature your users will usually utilize most often) can be organized and accessed in different ways (with various formats depending on the number of participants and on the access and modalities used by them).
This is why I dedicated two full chapters (Chapter 2 and Chapter 3) to meeting and conferencing with Teams.

Looking at how the communication technology market has evolved in the past few years (accelerated by the COVID pandemic), Microsoft Teams has also replaced many legacy solutions as a phone system. PSTN connectivity, desk phones, Auto Attendants, and Call Queues are at least 30% of the knowledge required for the Collaboration Communications Systems Engineer exam.

Telephony in teams and the related features require some time to be understood, so a few chapters of the book have been set aside to give you as much information on these topics as possible to successfully take your exam (Chapter 4, Chapter 5, Chapter 6, and Chapter 7).

Finally, Microsoft Teams rooms (MTRs) have an important role for the certification (again, up to 30% of the whole exam score) and are also extremely relevant in the real world (even for companies that have completed their journey to Teams voice, a meeting

INTRODUCTION

room is an ever-evolving service). The two chapters dedicated to MTRs (Chapter 8 and Chapter 9) build on the information of the previous chapters and add all the additional details required to complete the exam syllabus.

Finally, I will talk about why (in my opinion) it made sense for me to write this book and for you (I hope) to read it. The knowledge required for the MS-721 certification exam is not hidden somewhere or secret. Every topic, at the end of the day, is based on the Microsoft official documentation and best practices.

Also, there are many different resources (many free) that could help you in your preparation effort. There are also many large language models (LLMs) or artificial intelligence apps that can give you answers in case you want to use them. So, what is the difference between browsing the Internet and buying this book (apart from the cost, obviously)?

Well, the main difference is that the content in this book is curated by somebody (me) who has deployed Teams for a few years now, working with some of the biggest organizations in the world. The value you get from this book (as with my previous works) is my ability to filter outdated information, documents that are not relevant, and explanations that are misleading or confusing (including the always present AI hallucinations) and create something that has logic and sense and flow. To better understand what I am talking about, please take one of the book chapters and try to find the relevant information for all the exam topics in it elsewhere. I am quite sure that a few hours could not suffice.

CHAPTER 1

Introduction to Exam MS-721

This book is an exam study guide based on the objectives of the new Microsoft 365 Certified: Collaboration Communications Systems Engineer Associate certification. The book's chapters have been designed to cover all the necessary knowledge for achieving a successful exam outcome for exam MS-721: Collaboration Communications Systems Engineer.

The new Microsoft 365 Certified: Collaboration Communications Systems Engineer Associate certification has replaced the previous Microsoft 365 Certified: Teams Voice Engineer Expert certification. And since March 2023, the exam MS-721: Collaboration Communications Systems Engineer has replaced the previous exam, MS-720: Microsoft Teams Voice Engineer.

MS-700: Managing Microsoft Teams and MS-721 are the only Microsoft exams focused on Teams, so if your work involves planning, deploying, administering, or troubleshooting Teams, these two exams are the easiest way to test and demonstrate your competence on Teams.

The ideal candidate for the two exams is slightly different. MS-700 is for Microsoft Teams administrators, while MS-721 is focused on communication specialists who will deploy and troubleshoot Teams Phone System, meetings, and devices (including Teams Rooms and Microsoft Surface Hub).

If you have already passed the MS-700 exam, a part of the knowledge you already have overlaps sometimes with MS-721 but in the latter exam the questions will be from a different point of view.

© Fabrizio Volpe 2024
F. Volpe, *Microsoft 365 Certified: Collaboration Communications Systems Engineer Associate Certification Companion*, Certification Study Companion Series, https://doi.org/10.1007/979-8-8688-0518-9_1

CHAPTER 1   INTRODUCTION TO EXAM MS-721

1.1 Prepare for Your Microsoft Exam and MS-721

MS-721 is a technical exam. All technical exams are presented on a scale from 1 to 1,000 with a passing score of 700 or higher (more details are available at *Microsoft Learn* (https://learn.microsoft.com/en-us/certifications/exam-scoring-reports)).

Like with other Microsoft exams, the testing is provided via Pearson VUE. The exam is available both online and in-person (if it is the first time you are taking a Microsoft certification exam, be sure to read all the requirements, especially for the online version (*About online exams with Pearson VUE* (https://learn.microsoft.com/en-us/credentials/certifications/online-exams)).

The exam contents are designed to suit the expertise of collaboration communications systems engineers (CCSEs) whose daily work requires them to work not only with Teams administrators and Microsoft 365 administrators but also with network engineers, security engineers, and device manufacturers.

The exam contents are divided into four main domains, each one with a different importance based on the expertise expected by an individual who has a CCSE role.

- Plan and design collaboration communications systems (30–35%)
- Configure and manage Teams meetings, webinars, and town halls (15–20%)
- Configure and manage Teams Phone (25–30%)
- Configure and manage Teams Rooms and devices (25–30%)

This book will offer you up-to-date information as much as possible, but it is a advisable to check the official study guide when starting your preparation to be sure you are considering last-minute changes: *Study guide for Exam MS-721: Collaboration Communications Systems Engineer* (https://learn.microsoft.com/engb/certifications/resources/study-guides/ms-721).

As a preparation tool, Microsoft offers two different learning paths.

- *MS-721: Plan and design Teams collaboration communications systems* (https://learn.microsoft.com/en-us/training/paths/plan-configure-teams-voice/)
- *MS-721: Manage Teams collaboration communications systems* (https://learn.microsoft.com/en-us/training/paths/manage-teams-voice/)

I suggest double-checking the information in the learning paths if you plan to use them, because part of them could be out-of-date.

A four-day instructor-led training is available too, and it covers the know-how required for the certification.

- Course MS-721T00-A: Collaboration Communications Systems Engineer (https://learn.microsoft.com/en-us/training/courses/ms-721t00)

1.2 Book Outline

The required exam topics are covered in this book, with chapters structured in the following way:

Chapter 1: Introduction to Exam MS-721

The chapter you are reading, Chapter 1 introduces the Microsoft certification exams and Microsoft Teams.

Chapter 2: Teams Meetings

This chapter covers the required skills to plan and design Teams meetings and the Teams policy package.

The contents of this chapter are relevant to prepare for the following exam objectives:

- Plan and design Teams meetings.
- Create and manage meeting policies.
- Configure and manage live events, webinars, and town halls.

Chapter 3: Configure and Manage Audio Conferencing and Live Events

This chapter covers the required skills to design and deploy Teams audio conferencing and live events, both for the initial configuration and for the customization.

The contents of this chapter are relevant to prepare for the following exam objectives:

- Plan and design Teams meetings.
- Configure and manage audio conferencing.
- Configure and manage calling features for Teams Phone.

Chapter 4: Introducing Teams Phone

In this chapter, you will acquire the basic knowledge required to deploy Teams Phone and PSTN connectivity.

CHAPTER 1   INTRODUCTION TO EXAM MS-721

The contents of this chapter are relevant to prepare for the following exam objectives:

- Plan and design Teams Phone and PSTN connectivity.

Chapter 5: Using Direct Routing with Teams Phone

In this chapter, you will acquire the skills to configure Direct Routing with Teams Phone.

The contents of this chapter are relevant to prepare for the following exam objectives:

- Configure and manage Direct Routing for Teams Phone.

Chapter 6: Configuring Teams Phone

In this chapter, the focus is on the exam skills to configure Teams Phone policies and features.

The contents of this chapter are relevant to prepare for the following exam objectives:

- Configure Teams Phone policies.
- Configure dynamic emergency calling.

Chapter 7: Call Queues, Auto Attendants, and Users

In this chapter, the focus is on deploying auto attendants and call queues in Teams.

The contents of this chapter are relevant to prepare for the following exam objectives:

- Configure auto attendants and call queues.
- Configure and manage users for Teams Phone.
- Configure and manage calling features for Teams Phone.

Chapter 8: Teams Rooms and Devices

This chapter is focused on Teams Rooms and devices, from the initial deployment to troubleshooting.

The contents of this chapter are relevant to prepare for the following exam objectives:

- Plan and design Teams-certified device solutions
- Maintain Teams Rooms and devices

Chapter 9: MTRs Based on Windows and Surface Hub

This chapter is dedicated to the configuration of Microsoft Teams Rooms (MTRs) based on Windows and Surface Hub.

The contents of this chapter are relevant to prepare for the following exam objectives:

- Configure and manage Teams Rooms on a Surface Hub or Windows
- Configure optional features for Teams Rooms and devices

Chapter 10: Prepare the Network for Teams and Troubleshooting Calls

This chapter is focused on optimizing your network for Microsoft Teams and troubleshooting.

The contents of this chapter are relevant to prepare for the following exam objectives:

- Prepare the network for the deployment of Teams
- Troubleshoot call failures and session quality

1.3 Introduction to Microsoft Teams

In this section, we will give a quick, high-level overview of Teams to create a starting point for the rest of the book's contents. If you are already extremely familiar with all the features of Teams, this section will probably contain information that you already know, so feel free to skim it.

Teams is part of Microsoft 365, which is a cloud-based productivity platform that includes apps such as Excel, Word, PowerPoint, Outlook, and OneNote but also the backend services that enable the apps, the identity infrastructure, and the tools required for security, compliance, and governance.

Teams is the tool meant to provide efficient teamwork and streamlined information sharing among individuals and groups, regardless of geographical locations.

The following is a short list of Teams' features:

- **Presence and Status:** Keep track of colleagues' availability and status, helping to determine the best time for communication or collaboration.
- **Chat and Messaging:** Engage in real-time conversations through one-on-one or group chats, enabling quick information exchange and discussions within the Teams interface.
- **Channels and Conversations:** Organize discussions into channels, which are dedicated spaces for specific topics or projects. Conversations within channels are threaded, allowing for focused collaboration and clear communication.

- **Video and Audio Meetings:** Initiate or schedule meetings with audio and video capabilities. Screen sharing, presentation mode, and recording enhance communication, making remote collaboration feel more personal.
- **Content Sharing:** Seamlessly share files and documents within conversations and channels. Preview files, provide feedback through inline comments, and collaborate on documents simultaneously.
- **Internal and External Collaboration:** Facilitate collaboration not only within your organization but also with external partners, clients, or guests by inviting them to collaborate in specific teams or channels.
- **App Integrations:** Extend Teams' functionality by integrating third-party and Microsoft apps directly within Teams. These integrations streamline workflows and centralize tools.
- **Microsoft 365 Integration:** Access and edit Office documents (Word, Excel, PowerPoint) within Teams. Integration with Outlook helps manage emails and calendar events without switching applications.
- **Mobile, Web, and Desktop Apps:** Use Teams on various devices, including smartphones, web browsers, and desktop applications.
- **Security and Compliance:** Ensure secure communication and collaboration with encryption, data protection, and compliance features to meet regulatory requirements.
- **User Customization and Organization Branding:** Tailor Teams to your organization's identity with customizable themes, branding, and background options.
- **Enterprise Management and Administration:** Centrally manage user access, permissions, and settings through the Teams admin center. Advanced controls and policies ensure smooth governance and adherence to organizational standards.

A large part of how these features work is based on the already mentioned Teams' channels, which are dedicated spaces for specific projects or topics for team members to share files, engage in threaded discussions, and collaborate on documents in real time. Teams channels integrate SharePoint and OneDrive to ensure a coherent content management experience, seamlessly uniting files, documents, and resources.

Teams presents a comprehensive set of administrative tools.

- The Microsoft Teams admin center (TAC) provides a centralized hub for administrators to orchestrate user provisioning, permissions, and security settings.

- The Microsoft Teams PowerShell module is a command-line tool that allows administrators to manage and configure various aspects of Microsoft Teams directly from the PowerShell interface.

- The Microsoft Teams Rooms Pro Management portal is an interface for configuring and fine-tuning MTRs.

In addition to those tools, as part of Microsoft 365, some configurations and settings that are relevant to Teams are performed using different administrative interfaces, including the ones for Entra ID (formerly Azure AD), Exchange Online, SharePoint Online, and Intune.

Teams has a deep integration with meeting room technologies, with the best example being the MTRs. MTRs transform meeting spaces into collaboration hubs, complete with HD video conferencing, audio, and seamless content sharing.

1.4 Microsoft Teams Licensing

It is important to understand how the different features in Teams are controlled by the different licenses. Some of the licenses will be mentioned when talking about meetings (Teams Premium) and auto attendants and call queues (Teams Phone Resource Account licenses). Table 1-1 summarizes them.

Note From the 1st of April 2024 new customers will have to buy a dedicated Teams Enterprise license to have access to the basic Teams features, because they have been removed from the E1/E3 and E5 license models. A similar situation applies to the Business and Frontline licenses that are now available with and without the Teams license. More information are available in the dedicated page `https://learn.microsoft.com/en-us/microsoftteams/teams-add-onlicensing/microsoft-teams-add-on-licensing`.

CHAPTER 1   INTRODUCTION TO EXAM MS-721

Table 1-1. *Teams Licensing*

License Name	Required For
Microsoft Teams Essentials	Basic Teams features such as group meetings, chats, and file sharing.
Microsoft 365 Business Basic	Same as Microsoft Teams Essentials, with some improvements to storage and email (Depending on the date the license was acquired, see the previous note).
Microsoft 365 Business Standard	Same as Microsoft 365 Business Basic, with desktop versions of Microsoft 365 apps and webinar hosting (Depending on the date the license was acquired, see the previous note).
Microsoft 365 E1 Microsoft 365 E3 Microsoft 365 Education A1 Microsoft 365 Education A3 Microsoft 365 F1 Microsoft 365 F3 Microsoft 365 G1 Microsoft 365 G3 Office 365 E1 Office 365 E3 Office 365 Education A1 Office 365 Education A3 Office 365 Enterprise G1 Office 365 Enterprise G3 Office 365 F1 Office 365 F3	Teams with all the standard features excluding Teams Phone (Depending on the date the license was acquired, see the previous note).

(*continued*)

Table 1-1. (*continued*)

License Name	Required For
Microsoft 365 Education A5 Microsoft 365 E5 Microsoft 365 G5 Office 365 E5 Office 365 Education A5 Office 365 F5 Office 365 Enterprise G5	Teams with all the standard features including Teams Phone (Depending on the date the license was acquired, see the previous note).
Microsoft Teams Calling Plans	This add-on license enables Microsoft as your PSTN provider and gives you a direct dial-in (DDI) phone number enabled to make PSTN voice calls (national or international, depending on the specific calling plan).
Microsoft Teams Phone (Phone System)	It's an add-on that enables Teams to work with the PSTN network (PBX capabilities hosted by Microsoft) including voicemail, call parking, and call forwards.
Microsoft Teams Premium	The Teams Premium license is an add-on that enhances customization and security. Some examples are advanced virtual appointments, custom meeting templates, and meeting sensitivity labels.
Microsoft Teams Shared Devices	This license is meant to be used on shared devices and includes Microsoft Teams, Microsoft Teams Phone, Microsoft Intune (Plan 1 and Plan 2), Entra ID (Azure Active Directory Premium) Plan 1, and Exchange Online Plan (voicemail only).
Microsoft Teams Rooms Basic	This license includes Microsoft Teams, PSTN audio conferencing, and a whiteboard. For each tenant, no more than 25 Teams Rooms Standard licenses can be used.
Microsoft Teams Rooms Pro	Rooms Pro includes all the features of the Basic license and adds Teams Phone, Microsoft Intune2, Entra ID (Azure Active Directory Premium) Plan 1, and access to the Pro Management Portal.

1.5 Teams Admin Center and Teams PowerShell Module

The Microsoft Teams admin center and the Teams PowerShell module are two tools for managing and configuring Microsoft Teams, each with its own unique capabilities and use cases.

1.5.1 Teams Admin Center

The Teams admin center provides a graphical user interface (GUI) that is intuitive and user-friendly, especially for users who prefer a visual method of management. It is accessible through a web browser and is designed for ease of use without requiring deep technical knowledge. The admin center allows administrators to manage Teams settings, users, teams, policies, and other configurations. It is particularly useful for common, everyday administrative tasks.

1.5.2 Teams PowerShell Module

The PowerShell module is a command-line interface (CLI) tool, offering more flexibility and control for users comfortable with scripting and command-line operations. It allows you to script and automate repetitive tasks, which can reduce the number of potential errors and save significant time. The PowerShell module is particularly efficient for bulk operations, such as applying a policy to multiple users at once or extracting detailed reports. Every time we explain PowerShell cmdlets in the book, the assumption is that you have the right administrative permissions in the tenant and that the PowerShell module for Teams is already available and connected with your credentials.

To import the PowerShell module for Microsoft Teams and connect to your Teams environment, you can follow these steps:

1. Install the Microsoft Teams PowerShell module.
   - The module should be installed with the CurrentUser scope, which means it will be installed only for the current user and doesn't require administrator privileges on the system.

CHAPTER 1   INTRODUCTION TO EXAM MS-721

2. Open PowerShell.

3. Run the following command to install the Microsoft Teams PowerShell Module for the current user:

    - `Install-Module -Name MicrosoftTeams -Scope CurrentUser -Force`

4. Import the Microsoft Teams PowerShell module by executing the following command:

    - `Import-Module MicrosoftTeams`

5. Connect to Microsoft Teams with this:

    - `Connect-MicrosoftTeams`

6. Enter the Microsoft Teams admin credentials. After successful authentication, you will be connected to Microsoft Teams in your PowerShell session.

Note   If you encounter any issues regarding execution policy (such as that scripts are not allowed to run), you may need to run the following command:

`Set-ExecutionPolicy -ExecutionPolicy RemoteSigned -Scope CurrentUser`

This allows running scripts that are signed by a trusted publisher.

CHAPTER 2

Teams Meetings

Microsoft Teams offers different options to organize a meeting: meetings, webinars, and live events. In this chapter, we will start with examining the differences between meetings, webinars, and live events within Microsoft Teams. Subsequently, we will talk about deploying Teams meetings and configuring the meeting policies required to enforce specific organizational guidelines and preferences.

The next topic will be Teams policy packages, used to encompass and simplify the distribution of a range of settings for meetings, messaging, calling, and more.

As part of the exam, you are required to understand Teams webinars (meetings where presenters and participants have fixed roles). Teams' webinars have additional registration management and event-oriented default meeting options.

The last topic of this chapter is Teams custom meeting templates that allow you to configure options that meeting organizers can change (or to lock them as required by your organization).

In this chapter, the following required skills and exam topics are described:

Plan and design Teams meetings

- Plan and design Teams meeting policies and settings.
- Compare capabilities and features of Teams Core and Teams Premium.
- Design Teams policy packages (includes meeting policies, calling policies, and live events policies).
- Recommend methods for assigning policies.

Create and manage meeting policies

- Configure meeting settings.
- Configure and manage Teams webinars.

CHAPTER 2   TEAMS MEETINGS

- Configure avatars for Teams meetings.
- Configure and manage Teams Premium meeting features.
- Create and manage Teams meeting templates and policies.

Configure and manage live events, webinars, and town halls.

- Configure the Live events settings.
- Create and manage live events policies.
- Configure meeting and event roles.
- Configure live events and town halls with Teams, Viva Engage, and Microsoft Stream.
- Configure in-org vs public town halls.
- Configure town halls with Teams Premium.
- Manage access to scheduling Teams webinars.
- Configure policies for Teams webinars.
- Configure in-org vs public webinars.
- Configure webinars with Teams Premium.
- Configure attendee interaction for webinars.

2.1 Introducing Meeting Types

Teams offers three different ways to organize a meeting (see Table 2-1). Each one has various features and limits.

Table 2-1. *Type of Meetings, Participants, and Interaction from Meetings, Webinars, and Live Events*

Type of Meeting	Number of Participants	Interaction	Registration Supported
Meetings	Up to 20,000*	Microsoft 365 Business Basic, Microsoft 365 Business Standard, Microsoft 365 Business Premium, and Microsoft Apps for Business plans: - You can host online meetings and video calls for up to 300 people using Microsoft Teams. Microsoft 365 E3/E5, Microsoft 365 A3/A5, and Microsoft 365 Government G3/G5 plans: - You can host online meetings and video calls for up to 1,000 people using Microsoft Teams. - Participants up to 1,000 have fully interactive equal meeting capabilities. - Participants over 1,000 up to 20,000 have View-only capabilities.	Yes
Webinars	Up to 1,000	- Participants up to 1,000 have fully interactive capabilities - Audience interaction configurable. - Can specify presenters.	Yes
Live events	10,000, increased to 20,000 through December 30, 2023	- Broadcast to large audiences - Moderated Q&A for audience interaction. - Can specify producers and presenters, including external presenters. - Supports more advanced production capabilities.	No

CHAPTER 2   TEAMS MEETINGS

2.1.1 Meetings

Teams offers two kinds of meetings: Channel Meetings and Private Meetings

Channel Meetings

If a team has a dedicated channel in Microsoft Teams, it can schedule a channel meeting. Channel meetings have multiple benefits:

- All members can see and join a meeting.
- Any meeting-related discussion before, during, or after a meeting is part of the channel discussion.
- Nonprivate meetings and discussions are visible to any member of the team.
- Meetings can also be started ad hoc from the existing channel conversation

To start a channel meeting, click the camera icon in the Channel Tabs bar (as shown in Figure 2-1).

Figure 2-1. *Starting a channel meeting*

Private Meetings

When meetings involve nonteam members, users can schedule a private meeting. Private meetings provide the following benefits:

- They're visible to invited people only.
- They can be started ad-hoc from existing chat conversations.
- They can be scheduled from the Teams client or Outlook add-in.
- Meeting-related discussions before, during, or after the meeting are accessible through chat.

CHAPTER 2 TEAMS MEETINGS

Meeting Scheduling and Starting

Teams offers different ways to schedule and launch a meeting:

- **Scheduled Meetings:** It is possible to schedule a meeting from the calendar in Teams or from the calendar in Outlook. Teams is connected to your Exchange calendar so that when you schedule a meeting in Outlook, it'll show up in Teams, and vice versa (see the example in Figure 2-2).

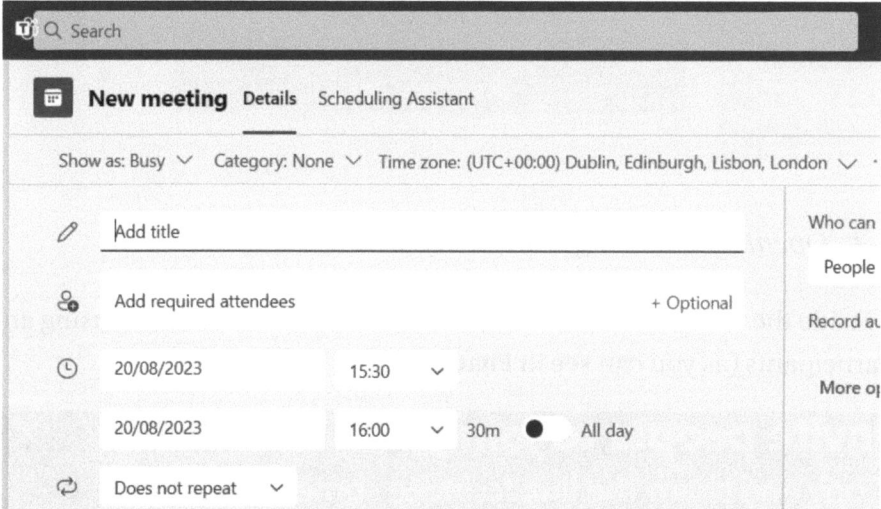

Figure 2-2. Scheduling a meeting from the Teams calendar app

- **Ad-hoc Meetings**: In any Teams chat, you can initiate a meeting instantly by clicking the Meet Now button with the participants in the conversation.

- **Meet now**: From the Teams calendar app you can click "Meet now" to start an empty meeting (see Figure 2-3).

17

CHAPTER 2 TEAMS MEETINGS

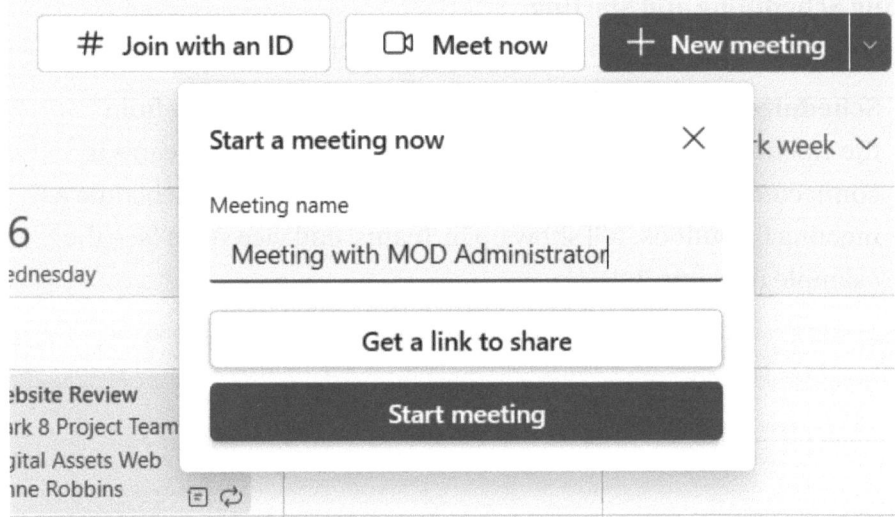

Figure 2-3. Opening a meeting with "Meet now"

From inside the meeting, you can share the link to join the meeting using an invite or add the participants (as you can see in Figure 2-4).

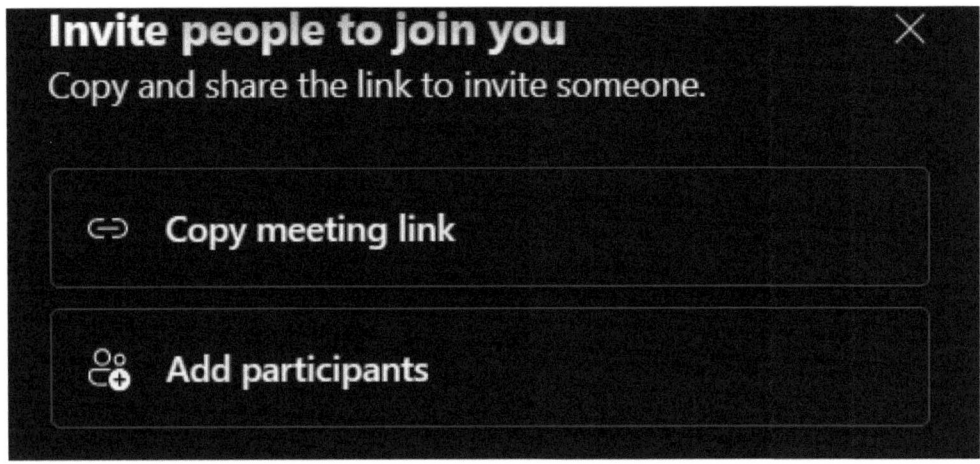

Figure 2-4. Adding participants to a "Meet now" meeting

Additional features available for meetings include:

- **Meeting Registration**: Users can set up meetings that require attendees to register. This helps manage attendance and participation.

- **View-Only Meeting Experience**: Teams offers the capability to host meetings with a capacity of up to 10,000 participants. When the main meeting reaches its maximum capacity, which is set at 1,000 users, additional attendees are accommodated in a view-only mode. Organizers are alerted to this transition when approximately 500 users have already joined. Participants who enter the meeting early and fall within the main capacity limit can enjoy the full spectrum of Teams meeting features, including audio and video sharing, access to shared content, and engagement in meeting chat. On the other hand, attendees who join after the main meeting capacity has been reached will experience the meeting in a view-only mode (see Figure 2-5).

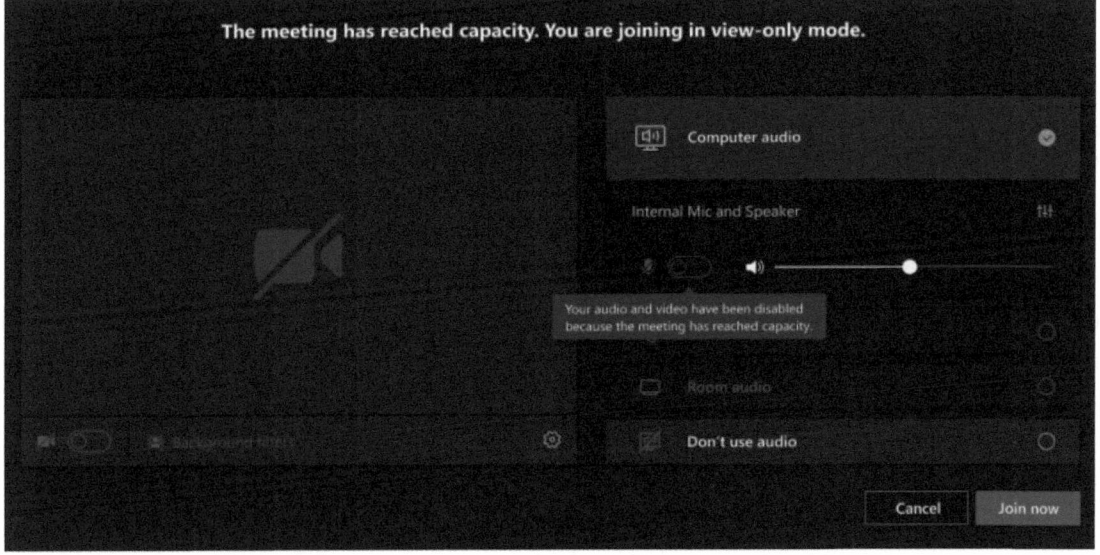

Figure 2-5. Joining a meeting in view-only mode (from support.Microsoft.com)

This view-only mode is accessible through various platforms, including desktop, web, and Teams mobile applications for both Android and iOS.

2.1.2 Webinars

Webinars are structured meetings that involve clear roles for presenters and participants. They differ from Teams meetings in that they provide robust registration management, customizable event and registration sites, and event-specific default meeting options. Section 1.4 will provide an in-depth examination of webinars.

2.1.3 Live Events

Microsoft Live Events (live events) is an extension of Teams designed for one-way communication, with the event host taking the lead, and the primary role of the audience is to consume the content presented by the host. Attendees have the option to watch the event live or view a recording later through Viva Engage or Teams. They can engage with the presenters by participating in moderated Q&A sessions or initiating conversations through Viva Engage.

Live events enable you to schedule and produce events for an audience up to 20,000 people.

A live event enhances engagement by connecting with attendees before, during, and after the event, and it can be used in Teams or Viva Engage.

Chapter 3 provides an in-depth explanation of live events.

2.2 Deploying Teams Meetings and Meeting Policies

Teams uses meeting policies to control available features in meetings, enhancing the experience during the meeting and improving security. Meeting policies are managed in the Teams admin center or via PowerShell and can be customized in two ways.

- Changing the settings in the Global policy (this default policy applies organization-wide). All users are automatically assigned to it.
- Creating a custom policy and assigning it to specific users.

A set of five default policies (AllOn, RestrictedAnonymousAccess, AllOff, RestrictedAnonymousNoRecording, Kiosk) will be already available by default in the tenant, and usually those policies are enough to manage the more common scenarios.

Note You can edit only the Global meeting policy and the custom policies you add. The five default policies listed are usable only as they are.

Policies are deployed in three different ways:

- **Per-organizer Policy**: This policy type affects all participants of a meeting. Whatever policy the organizer has, it is automatically applied to all participants.

- **Per-user Policy**: These policies apply to individual users, regardless of their role as an organizer or participant in a meeting.

- **Per-organizer and Per-user Policy**: This involves a combination of both per-organizer and per-user settings. The availability of certain features in a meeting depends on both the policy settings of the organizer and the individual participants.

To manage the Meeting policies, go to Microsoft Teams admin center, select Meetings and then Meeting Policies.

Teams meeting policies are divided into the following areas:

- Meeting scheduling
- Meeting join & lobby
- Meeting engagement
- Content sharing
- Recording & transcription
- Audio & video
- Watermark

2.2.1 Meeting Scheduling

This part of the policy includes the settings shown in Figure 2-6.

CHAPTER 2 TEAMS MEETINGS

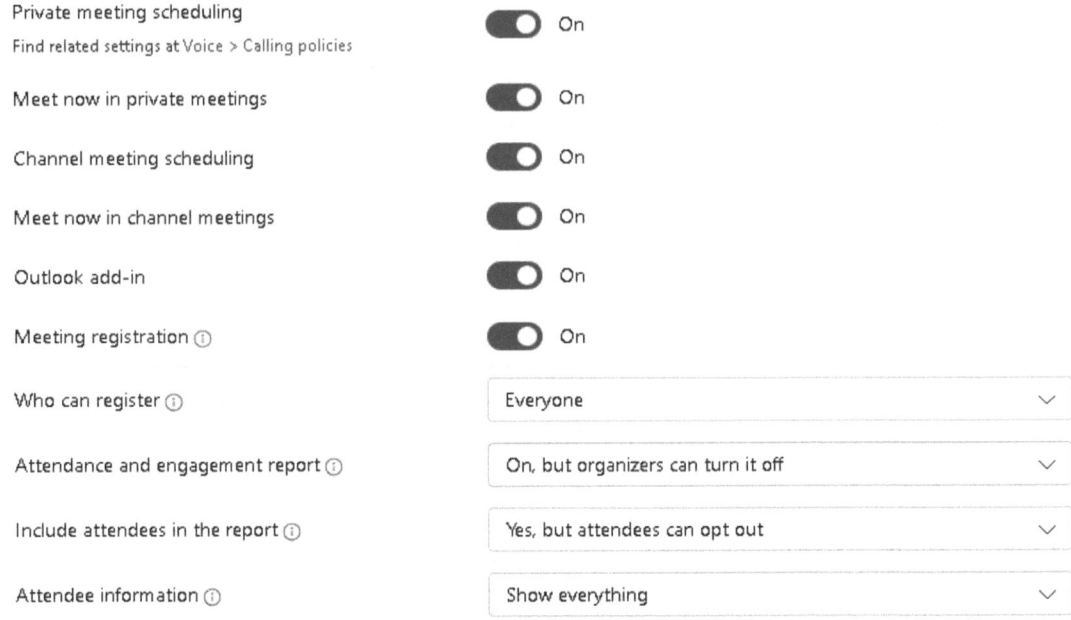

Figure 2-6. *Meeting Policies: Meeting scheduling*

The effects of the policy settings are explained in Table 2-2.

Table 2-2. *Meeting Options. Meeting Scheduling*

Setting	Default	Description
Private meeting scheduling	On	Organizers can schedule private meetings.
Meet now in private meetings	On	Users can start an instant private meeting.
Channel meeting scheduling	On	Organizers can schedule meetings in channels they belong to.
Meet now in channel meetings	On	Organizers can start instant meetings in their channels.
Outlook add-in	On	Organizers can schedule private meetings from Outlook.
Meeting registration	On	Organizers can require registration to join a meeting.

(*continued*)

Table 2-2. (*continued*)

Setting	Default	Description
Who can register	Everyone	Determines who can register if registration is on.
Attendance report	Everyone, unless organizers opt-out	Organizers can toggle attendance reports on or off.
Who is in the report	Everyone, but participants can opt-out	Participants can choose to be included in the Attendance Report.
Attendance summary	Show everything	Displays attendance times and duration for each participant.

2.2.2 Meeting Join & Lobby

This part of the policy includes the settings shown in Figure 2-7.

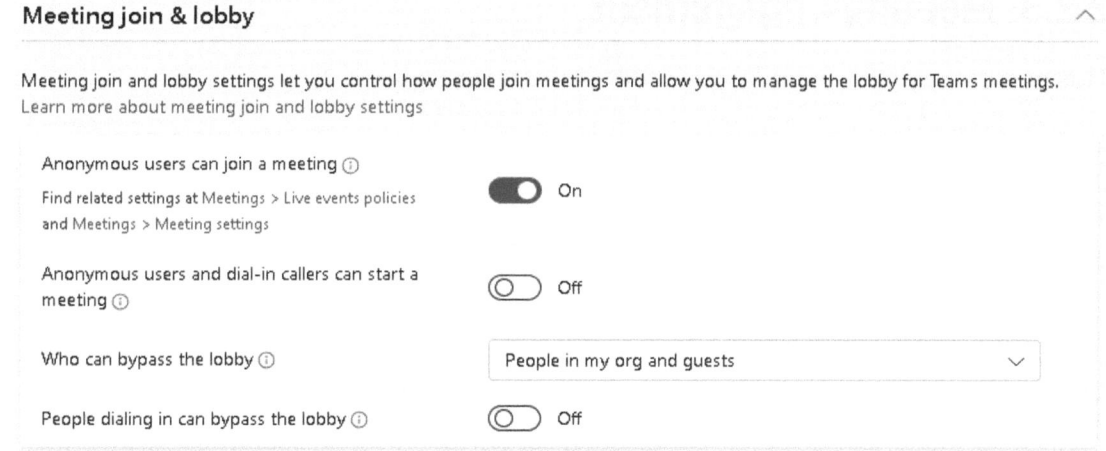

Figure 2-7. *Meeting Policies: Meeting join & lobby*

CHAPTER 2 TEAMS MEETINGS

The effects of the policy settings are explained in Table 2-3.

Table 2-3. Meeting Options. Meeting Join & Lobby

Setting	Default	Description
Anonymous users can join a meeting	On	Allows anyone to join Teams meetings, unless anonymous join is disabled organization-wide.
Anonymous users and dial-in callers can start a meeting	Off	Anonymous users and dial-in callers can start a meeting without a host if the setting is on; otherwise, they wait in the lobby.
Who can bypass the lobby	People in my organization and guests	Defines who can join a meeting directly and who waits in the lobby.
People dialing in can bypass the lobby	Off	Dial-in participants wait in the lobby by default unless the setting is changed by organizers.

2.2.3 Meeting Engagement

This part of the policy includes the settings shown in Figure 2-8.

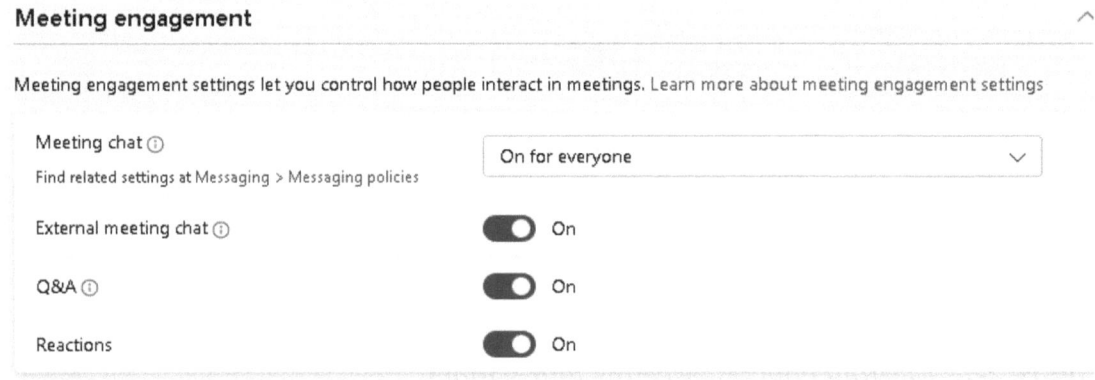

Figure 2-8. Meeting Policies: Meeting engagement

The effects of the policy settings are explained in Table 2-4.

Table 2-4. Meeting Options: Meeting Engagement

Setting	Default	Description
Meeting chat	On for everyone	Allows meeting attendees to participate in chat; anonymous participants have restricted access when this is off.
External meeting chat	On	Enables reading or writing messages in external meeting chats from untrusted organizations.
Q&A	On	Organizers can activate a Q&A for meetings.
Reactions	On	Users can use live reactions during meetings.

2.2.4 Content Sharing

This part of the policy includes the settings shown in Figure 2-9.

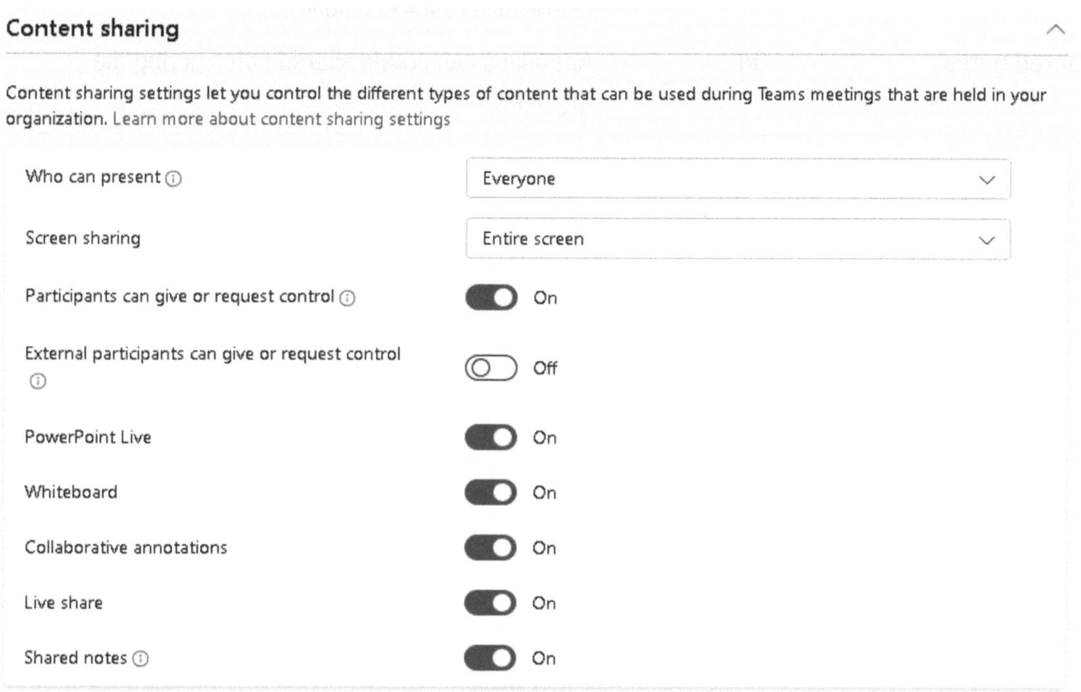

Content sharing

Content sharing settings let you control the different types of content that can be used during Teams meetings that are held in your organization. Learn more about content sharing settings

Who can present	Everyone
Screen sharing	Entire screen
Participants can give or request control	On
External participants can give or request control	Off
PowerPoint Live	On
Whiteboard	On
Collaborative annotations	On
Live share	On
Shared notes	On

Figure 2-9. Meeting Policies: Content sharing

The effects of the policy settings are explained in Table 2-5.

Table 2-5. *Meeting Options. Content Sharing*

Setting	Default	Description
Who can present	Everyone	Presenting rights in Teams meetings can be altered by organizers.
Screen sharing mode	Entire screen	Users can share their desktop/window; configuration details are provided by Microsoft Teams.
Participants can give or request control	On	Participants can control shared screens unless using Teams in a browser.
External participants can give or request control	Off	External users need this enabled by both organizations to control shared screens.
PowerPoint Live	On	Users can share PowerPoint slides; external users inherit the organizer's settings.
Whiteboard	On	Sharing the Whiteboard is allowed; external users follow the organizer's policy.
Shared notes	On	Attendees can create shared notes during the meeting.

CHAPTER 2　TEAMS MEETINGS

2.2.5 Recording & Transcription

This part of the policy includes the settings shown in Figure 2-10.

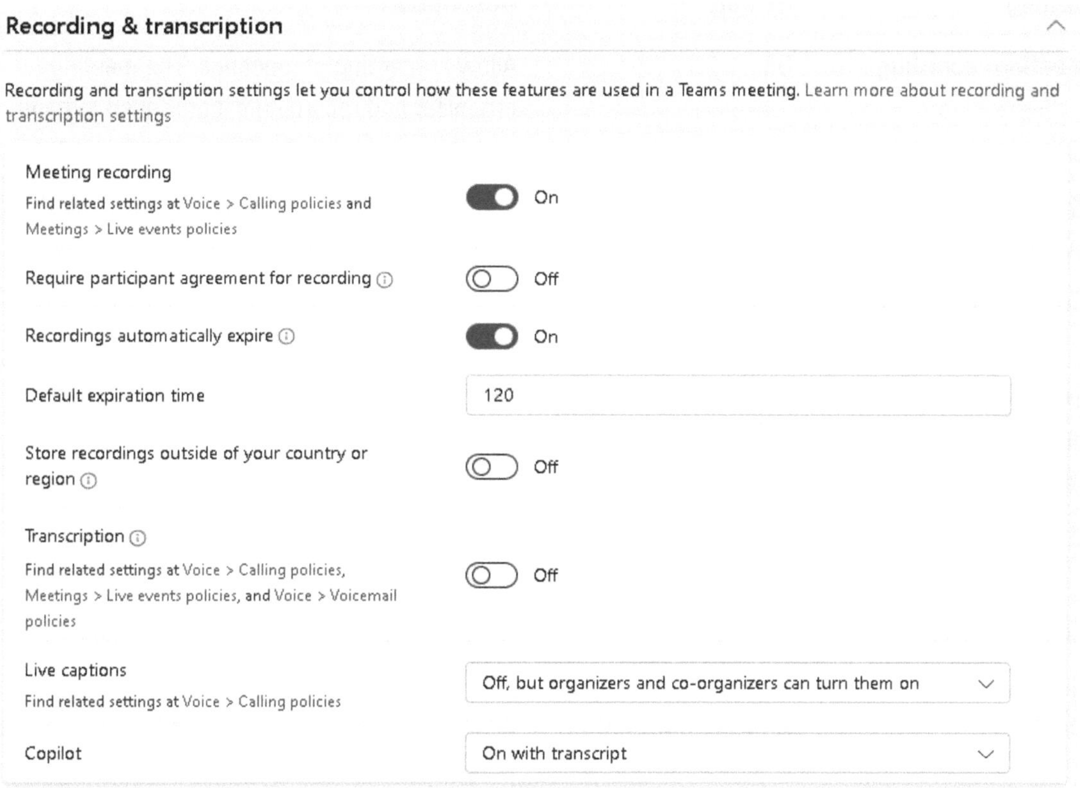

Recording & transcription

Recording and transcription settings let you control how these features are used in a Teams meeting. Learn more about recording and transcription settings

Meeting recording Find related settings at Voice > Calling policies and Meetings > Live events policies	On
Require participant agreement for recording	Off
Recordings automatically expire	On
Default expiration time	120
Store recordings outside of your country or region	Off
Transcription Find related settings at Voice > Calling policies, Meetings > Live events policies, and Voice > Voicemail policies	Off
Live captions Find related settings at Voice > Calling policies	Off, but organizers and co-organizers can turn them on
Copilot	On with transcript

Figure 2-10. *Meeting Policies: Recording & transcription*

The effects of the policy settings are explained in Table 2-6.

Table 2-6. *Meeting Options. Recording & Transcription*

Setting	Default	Description
Meeting recording	On	Allows recording of meetings. The meeting organizer and recording initiator need to have recording permissions to record the meeting.
Recordings automatically expire	On	Recordings expire as per the default expiration time set.
Default expiration time	120	Sets expiration time for recordings between 1 to 99999 days.
Store recordings outside your country or region	Off	Option to store meeting recordings outside of your country or region.
Transcription	On	Enables transcription and captions during playback of recordings.
Live captions	Off, organizers/co-organizers can enable	Organizers and co-organizers can toggle live captions during meetings.
Copilot	On with transcript	Enables Copilot with a transcript that is either persisted or not.

2.2.6 Audio & Video

This part of the policy includes the settings shown in Figure 2-11.

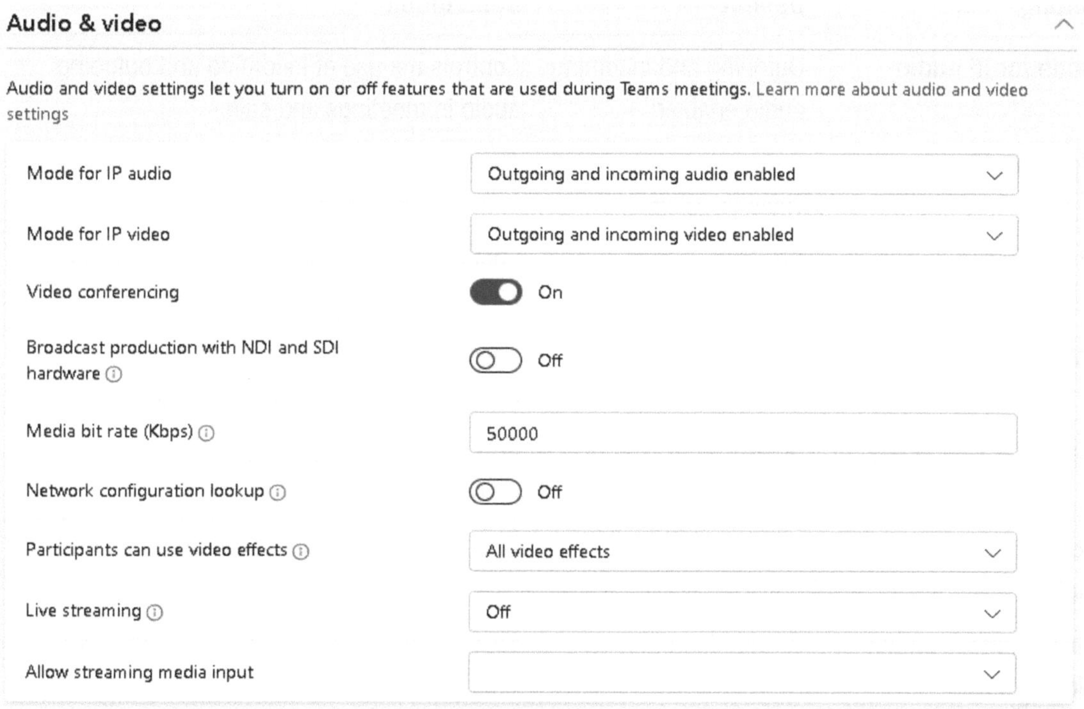

Figure 2-11. Meeting Policies: Audio & video

CHAPTER 2 TEAMS MEETINGS

The effects of the policy settings are explained in Table 2-7.

Table 2-7. *Meeting Options: Recording & transcription*

Setting	Default	Description
Mode for IP audio	Outgoing and incoming audio enabled	Controls the use of incoming and outgoing audio in meetings and calls.
Mode for IP video	Outgoing and incoming video enabled	Allows the use of incoming and outgoing video in meetings and calls.
IP video	On	Enables video in user-hosted meetings and photo/video sharing in Teams mobile.
Local broadcasting	Off	Uses advanced technology for high-quality audio and video over the network.
Media bit rate (Kbs)	50000	Sets media bit rate for calls and meetings, managing bandwidth.
Network configuration lookup	Off	Checks roaming policies when turned on.
Participants can use video effects	All video effects	Participants can customize their video with effects and backgrounds.
Live streaming	Off	Supports streaming Teams meetings to large audiences using RTMP.

CHAPTER 2 TEAMS MEETINGS

2.2.7 Watermark

This part of the policy includes the settings shown in Figure 2-12.

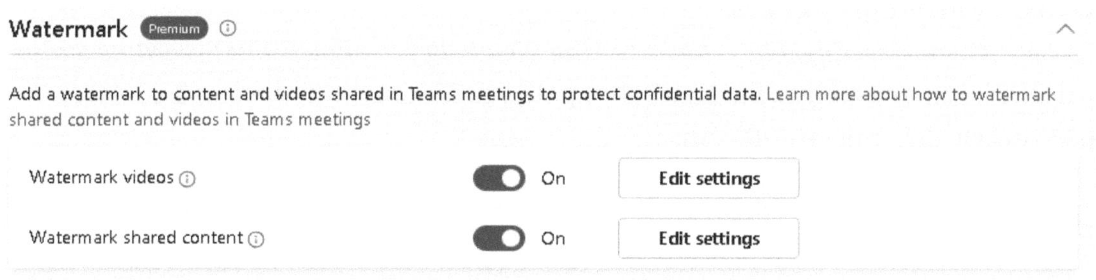

Figure 2-12. Meeting Policies: Watermark

The effects of the policy settings are explained in Table 2-8.

Table 2-8. Meeting Options: Watermark

Setting	Default	Description
Watermark videos	Off	Controls the application of watermarks on attendee videos
Watermark shared content	Off	Manages watermarks on content shared on the screen during a meeting

2.2.8 Manage with PowerShell

Meeting policies can be managed in a consistant way using PowerShell.

- *New-CsTeamsMeetingPolicy*: This command is used by administrators to create new meeting policies for Microsoft Teams.
- *Set-CsTeamsMeetingPolicy*: This command is used by administrators to modify existing meeting policies in Microsoft Teams.

This example creates a new meeting policy named NewPolicy. The policy allows meeting recording and specifically sets the policy to enable cloud recording and IP video.

New-CsTeamsMeetingPolicy -Identity "Tag:NewPolicy" -Description "Policy to allow meeting recording" -AllowCloudRecording $true -AllowIPVideo $true

The command turns off the ability for users assigned to the previously created NewPolicy to record meetings.

Set-CsTeamsMeetingPolicy -Identity "Tag: NewPolicy " -AllowCloudRecording $false

This command assigns the NewPolicy policy to the user with the email adelev@m365x07896792.onmicrosoft.com:

Grant-CsTeamsMeetingPolicy -Identity "adelev@m365x07896792.onmicrosoft.com" -PolicyName "Tag:AllowRecording"

2.3 Assigning Policies in Microsoft Teams

Teams allows you to customize the availability of features for users within an organization by applying various policies, such as those for calling, meetings, and messaging. Recognizing that user requirements differ, you can create and apply custom policies to cater to the specific needs of different user groups.

Teams enables policy management through several methods. You can assign policies directly to individual users or in bulk or to groups that users belong to. Policy packages are also available, providing a predefined set of policies suitable for users with similar roles. The approach you select will depend on the scale of policy management and the number of users needing policy assignments. While global policies set the standard for most users by default, specialized policies can be assigned to users with specific needs.

2.3.1 Users' Effective Policy

In Microsoft Teams, a user can be controlled by only one active policy per policy type.

When you apply policies to groups, it is required to also assign a rank to the different groups, as you can see in Figure 2-13.

CHAPTER 2   TEAMS MEETINGS

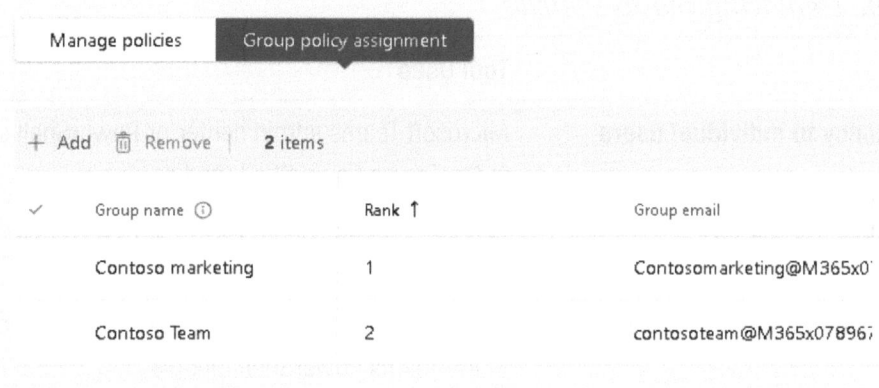

Figure 2-13. *Group policy assignment*

The determining factor for which policy applies to a user is based on the rules of precedence:

- **Direct assignment**: If a policy is directly assigned to a user, either individually or via batch assignment, this policy will have the highest precedence and be the one that is effective for the user.

- **Group assignment**: When there is no direct policy assignment to a user, the policy assigned to a group that the user is a member of will take effect. If the user belongs to multiple groups with different policies of the same type, the policy from the group with the highest ranking (based on group assignment ranking) will apply.

- **Global policy**: If a user has not been directly assigned a policy and is not part of any groups with an assigned policy, then the global (organization-wide default) policy for that policy type will apply to the user.

2.3.2 Ways to Assign Teams Policies

The suggested approach for the policy assignment process is by starting to configure global (organization-wide default) policies, ensuring they cover the broadest user base within your organization. After establishing these default settings, you can then focus on allocating specialized policies to specific users as needed, using one of the solutions in Table 2-9.

Table 2-9. *Deploying Teams Policies*

Action	Tool Used
Assign a policy to individual users	Microsoft Teams admin center or PowerShell cmdlets in the Teams PowerShell module
Assign a policy to a group	Microsoft Teams admin center or PowerShell cmdlets in the Teams PowerShell module
Assign a policy to a batch of users	Microsoft Teams admin center or PowerShell cmdlets in the Teams PowerShell module
Assign a policy package to users	Microsoft Teams admin center or PowerShell cmdlets in the Teams PowerShell module
Assign a policy package to a group	Microsoft Teams admin center or PowerShell cmdlets in the Teams PowerShell module
Assign a policy package to a batch of users	PowerShell cmdlets in the Teams PowerShell module

2.3.3 Check Your Policy Assignments

In the Microsoft Teams admin center, when you allocate policies to users, the assignment status is trackable via the Activity log. This log provides details on network record uploads, policy actions carried out through the Teams admin center and PowerShell, and mass policy assignments (involving more than 20 users) from the admin center, with data retained for the most recent 30-day period. To open the Activity log open the Microsoft Teams admin center and go to the dashboard. Then select Activity Log and View details (as shown in Figure 2-14).

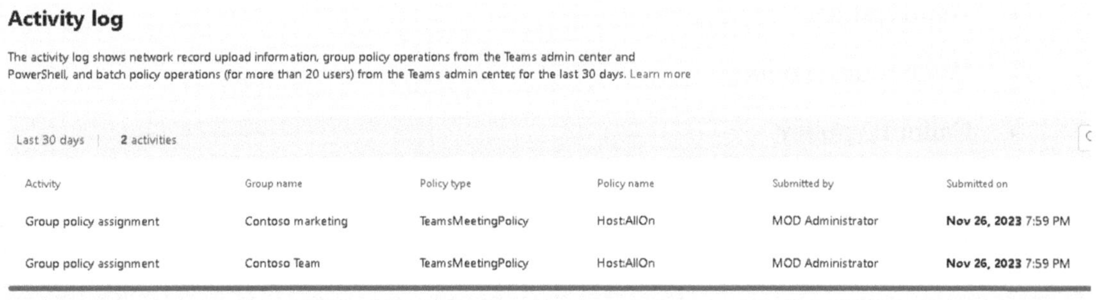

Figure 2-14. Activity log

2.4 Policy Packages in Microsoft Teams

In Microsoft Teams, policy packages consist of preset groups of policies and settings designed for specific roles in the organization. These packages facilitate the allocation of permissions and capabilities to users, reflecting their specific job responsibilities or their consumption of Teams. Rather than individually adjusting policies for different functions within Teams, such as meetings, messaging, or calls, these policy packages aggregate relevant settings, streamlining their implementation.

Tailored for various professional roles—including educators, medical staff, frontline employees, or sales personnel—each policy package incorporates features essential to those roles. For instance, a policy package aimed at educators may activate functionalities such as the ability to record meetings and share educational materials via OneNote, enhancing the teaching experience. Conversely, a package crafted for frontline staff may focus on communication efficiencies like push-to-talk and tools to manage work shifts.

The following policies are usable inside a policy package:

- Messaging policy
- Meeting policy
- App setup policy
- Calling policy
- Live events policy
- Call park policy

CHAPTER 2 TEAMS MEETINGS

- Teams policy
- Voice routing policy
- Caller ID policy
- Update policy
- Events policy

To assign a policy package, admins can use the Microsoft Teams admin center or PowerShell commands, depending on their preferences and the number of users they are managing.

2.4.1 Custom Policy Packages

You can create custom policy packages to group policies for users who share similar roles within your organization. To create a new custom policy package, go to Microsoft Teams admin center, select "Policy packages and then click Add (as shown in Figure 2-15).

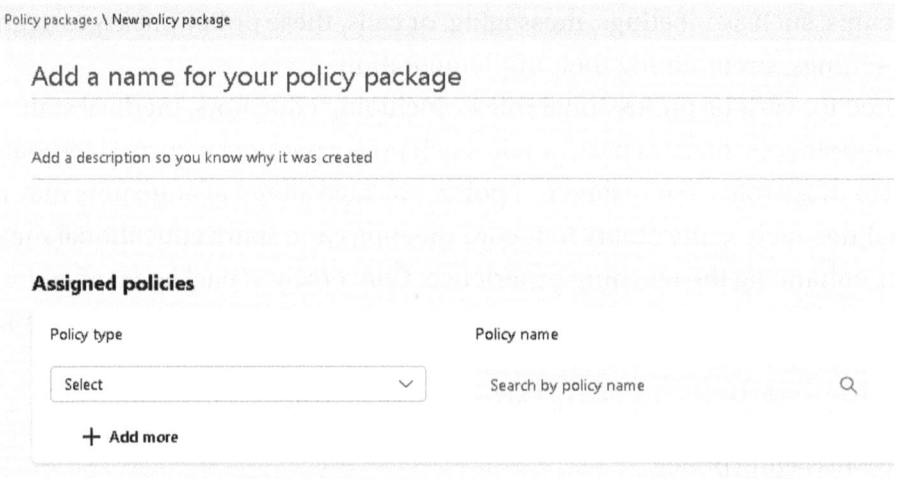

Figure 2-15. *Adding a custom policy package*

2.4.2 Assigning Policy Packages

It is possible to assign policy packages to users and groups in Microsoft Teams.

- **Assigning a policy package to users**: Open the Microsoft Teams admin center, go to Users, and select the user. In the user page, select Policies, and then next to "Policy package," select Edit, as shown in Figure 2-16.

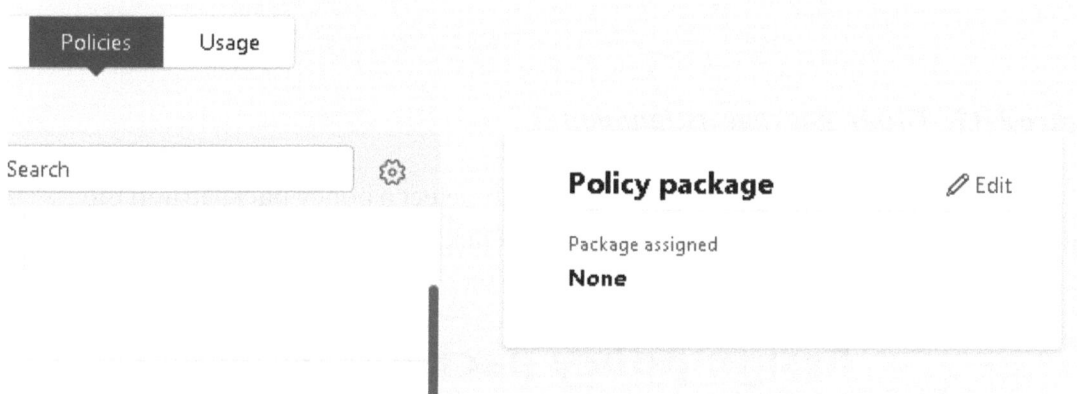

Figure 2-16. Assigning a policy package to a user

- **Assigning a policy to multiple users**: In the Microsoft Teams admin center, go to "Policy packages" and then select the policy package you want to assign. Select "Manage users" and add the users that will have the policy assigned. Click Apply.

- **Assign a policy package to a group**: In the Teams admin center, select "Policy packages" and go to the Group package assignment tab. Click Add (see Figure 2-17).

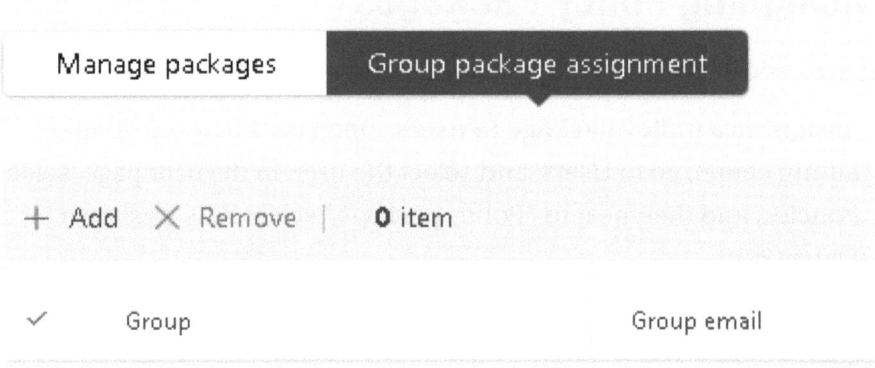

Figure 2-17. Group package assignment

Add the group you want to assign the policy to, select a policy package and the ranking for each policy in the package, and then click Apply (as shown in Figure 2-18).

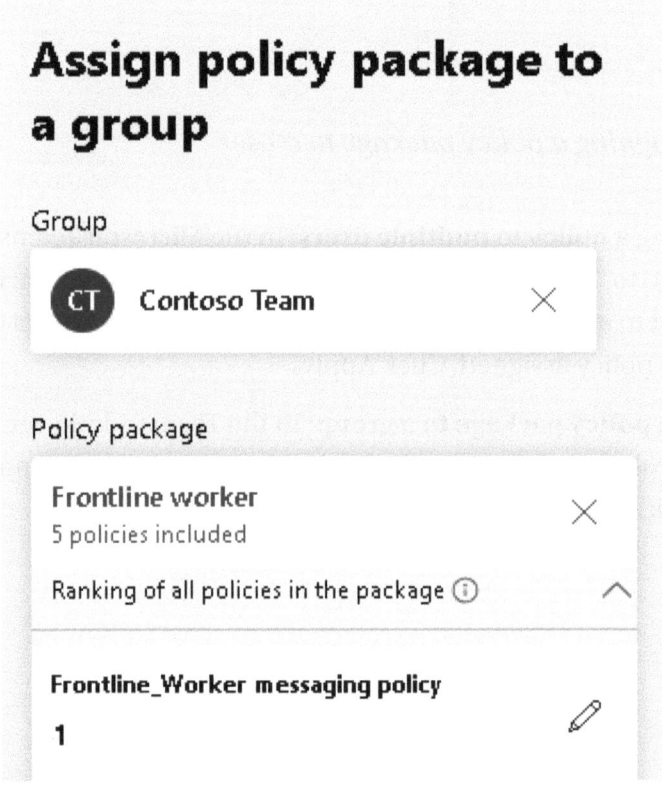

Figure 2-18. Assigning a policy package to a group

2.4.3 Manage with PowerShell

Assigning policies to a group (like a Microsoft 365 group) can be managed via PowerShell.

- `New-CsGroupPolicyAssignment`: This cmdlet is utilized to assign a policy to a Microsoft 365 group, a security group, or a distribution list.
- `Grant-CsGroupPolicyPackageAssignment`: This cmdlet assigns a policy package to a group.

Assign the TestPolicy meeting policy to the security group with the specified ID, as shown here:

```
New-CsGroupPolicyAssignment -GroupId "security-group-id"
-PolicyType "TeamsMeetingPolicy" -PolicyName "
TestPolicy "
```

This assigns the Education_Teacher policy package to the group of teachers:

```
Grant-CsGroupPolicyPackageAssignment -GroupId "teachers-
group-id" -PackageName "Education_Teacher"
```

2.5 Teams Webinars

Microsoft Teams webinars are specialized meeting formats designed for more formal and structured presentations compared to regular Teams meetings. While typical meetings are interactive, with participants freely conversing, sharing content, and collaborating, webinars are meant for situations where there are defined roles—typically, a set of presenters (or experts) who deliver information or training to a larger audience.

Here are key features that differentiate webinars from ordinary Teams meetings:

- Registration Management:
  - Webinars offer advanced registration capabilities. Organizers can set participant capacity limits, opt for manual approval of registrations, and maintain event waitlists to manage attendance effectively. Additionally, custom registration forms can be created to gather information from attendees, providing insights into the audience profile.

- Branding Customization:
  - Teams webinars allow for a customized experience that aligns with your organization's branding. Organizers can add specific images, banners, and color schemes to the event's visual theme, enhancing the professional look and feel.
- Presenter Profiles:
  - To familiarize the audience with the presenters, bios and photos can be included, offering context and background on the experts leading the session.
- Reporting:
  - Webinar organizers have access to reports that deliver valuable data. Before the event, they can track engagement with the registration page, the number of registrants, and any cancellations. Post-event reports include attendance metrics, individual attendee engagement, and more detailed analytics.
- For Teams Premium users, additional features such as manual registration approval and waitlists are available, further enhancing the control over the event's organization.

2.5.1 Creating a Webinar

Open the calendar from a Teams client, select "New meeting," and from the drop-down menu select Webinar.

By default, the webinar will be Public. You can change it from Public to Your organization, which will make the event page and registration available only to people within your organization.

In the Details section you can add co-organizers that are allowed to edit the registration forms, customize the event theme, and so on. In the same section you can also add the presenters.

To add external presenters, select "Add external presenters" and enter the email addresses of the external presenters you want to add. Click Save and send invites, as shown in Figure 2-19.

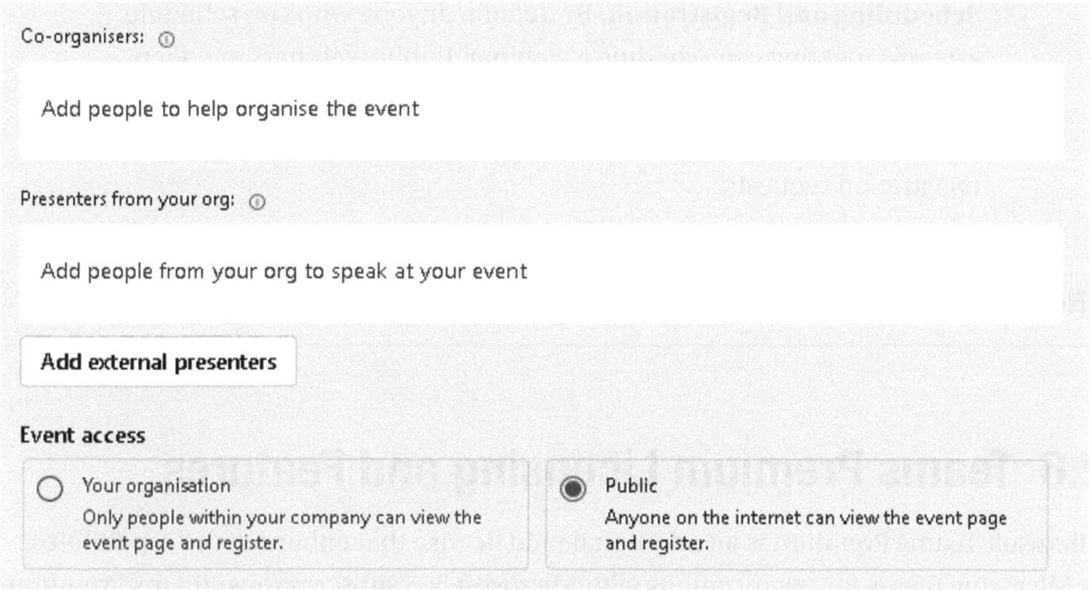

Figure 2-19. Adding co-organizers and presenters

- **Webinar Preparation**: Organizers need to create and publish a registration form to collect attendee information, which is helpful for post-event follow-up and effectiveness measurement. Once the details are finalized and published, automated invitations are sent out, and the registration link can be shared.

- **Attendee Pre-Webinar Steps**: Attendees view the event details, register through the provided form, and receive an email with the webinar link. They can join from up to three devices using their unique URL.

- **During the Webinar**: External attendees will wait in a lobby before being admitted by the organizers. In public webinars, attendee audio and video are disabled by default. The presenter can use polls to engage the audience and can also upgrade an attendee to presenter status if needed. New registrants during the webinar might face a short delay before joining.

- **Post-Webinar Actions**: Organizers can access and download reports on the webinar.

- **Scheduling and Registration**: By default, anyone who can schedule a Teams meeting can schedule a webinar. Public webinars are open to all registrants, while private webinars are for internal users only. When manual registration approval is enabled, organizers can vet registration requests.

Note Manual registration approval is available to Teams Premium users.

2.6 Teams Premium Licensing and Features

Microsoft Teams Premium is an additional paid license that enhances the capabilities of Microsoft Teams for organizations with Microsoft 365 subscriptions. Teams Premium licenses don't replace users' standard Teams licenses, but it provides more customized and intelligent features for meetings, webinars, and large gatherings like town halls, with stronger meeting protection, and superior management and reporting tools. It also offers advanced virtual appointments. Table 2-10 groups the exclusive features of Teams Premium under various categories like Meetings, Webinars, Town halls, Meetings protection, etc.

Table 2-10. Exclusive Features of Teams Premium

Category	Feature
Meetings	Customize meeting templates for your organization
Meetings	Add organization branding to meeting lobbies
Meetings	Customize meeting backgrounds for your organization
Meetings	Customize Together mode scenes for your organization
Meetings	Read live translated captions during meetings
Meetings	Manage what attendees see
Meetings	Use RTMP-In for meetings
Meetings	Hide attendee names

(continued)

Table 2-10. (*continued*)

Category	Feature
Meetings	View engagement reports
Meetings	Translate post-meeting transcriptions (coming soon)
Meetings	Turn on eCDN Meetings*
Webinars	Manage what attendees see
Webinars	Send custom and reminder emails to registrants
Webinars	Create a webinar wait list
Webinars	Webinar organizers can view engagement reports
Webinars	Manually approve registrants
Webinars	View engagement reports
Webinars	Limit the day and time when people can register
Webinars	Use RTMP-In for webinars
Town halls	Broadcast town halls to 20k attendees
Town halls	Host up to 50 town halls simultaneously
Town halls	Town hall Q&A capacity of 20k attendees
Town halls	Automatic Microsoft eCDN for town halls*
Town halls	View Microsoft Town hall insights
Town halls	Town hall organizers can view engagement reports
Town halls	Edit town hall emails
Town halls	View live translated captions in 10 languages
Meetings protection	Add watermarks to meetings
Meetings protection	End-to-end encryption for meetings with up to 50 attendees
Meetings protection	Control who can record
Meetings protection	Prevent copy/paste in meeting chats
Meetings protection	Assign Microsoft Purview Information Protection sensitivity labels for meetings*

(*continued*)

Table 2-10. (*continued*)

Category	Feature
Meetings protection	Custom user policy packages
Meeting recap and intelligent recap	Navigate meeting recordings with autogenerated chapters (coming soon)
Meeting recap and intelligent recap	View when a screen was shared in the meeting transcript
Meeting recap and intelligent recap	View time markers in meeting recordings when you joined or left a meeting
Meeting recap and intelligent recap	Jump to different speakers with speaker timeline markers
Meeting recap and intelligent recap	View AI-generated notes and tasks from meetings
Meeting recap and intelligent recap	View when you were mentioned in a meeting*
Virtual Appointments	Customize the lobby waiting room with themes and logos
Virtual Appointments	Send SMS notifications*
Virtual Appointments	Organizational and departmental analytics
Virtual Appointments	View and manage scheduled appointments in the queue
Virtual Appointments	View and manage on-demand appointments in the queue
Virtual Appointments	Send post-appointment follow-ups (coming soon)
Meet app	View and recap meetings that you missed
Meet app	View and recap meetings that mention you*
Meet app	View when you were mentioned in a meeting*
Meet app	View AI-generated tasks from meetings

2.7 Knowledge Check

Question 1:

What are the different types of meetings available in Microsoft Teams, and what are their participant limits?

1. Meetings can host up to 20,000 participants.
2. Webinars support up to 1,000 interactive participants.
3. Live events are designed for up to 10,000 attendees.
4. Channel meetings are visible to all team members.
5. Private meetings are visible only to invited people.

Question 2:

What features are available for scheduling and starting meetings in Teams?

1. Meetings can be scheduled from the Teams calendar or Outlook.
2. Ad hoc meetings can be started in Teams chats with the "Meet now" button.
3. "Meet now" can start an empty meeting from the Teams calendar app.
4. Meetings have a view-only mode for participants more than 1,000.
5. Private meetings cannot be started ad hoc from existing chat conversations.

Question 3:

Which statements are true regarding configuring and managing Teams meetings?

1. Teams uses meeting policies to control available features in meetings.
2. The Global policy applies to all users by default.
3. Meeting policies can be customized per organizer and per user.
4. All users can edit the Global meeting policy.
5. Meeting policies are managed only via the Teams admin center.

CHAPTER 2   TEAMS MEETINGS

Question 4:

What are the key aspects of Microsoft Teams webinars?

1. Webinars offer advanced registration management.
2. Webinars can accommodate up to 20,000 participants.
3. Webinar organizers can set participant capacity limits.
4. Webinars allow for audience interaction with Q&A sessions.
5. Webinars do not support external presenters.

Question 5:

What are the exclusive features of Microsoft Teams Premium?

1. Customizing meeting templates for an organization.
2. Adding organization branding to meeting lobbies.
3. Automatic translation of post-meeting transcriptions.
4. End-to-end encryption for meetings with up to 50 attendees.
5. Broadcast town halls to 20,000 attendees.

Answers:

Question 1: 1, 2, 3, 4, 5
Question 2: 1, 2, 3, 4
Question 3: 1, 2, 3
Question 4: 1, 3, 4
Question 5: 1, 2, 3, 4, 5

CHAPTER 3

Configure and Manage Audio Conferencing and Live Events

Microsoft Teams meetings can accommodate many different scenarios looking both at the way participants are able to join and at the number of participants. A Teams meeting can host a maximum of 20,000 attendees, with the initial 1,000 participants having fully interactive features such as chat and reactions. Once this threshold is reached, additional attendees will enter in view-only mode. Teams meetings enable both internal and external members of your organization to join.

Every participant in a Teams meeting typically has equal interaction privileges, which include the use of audio and video, chat functionalities, reactions, and the option to share their screen. Nonetheless, these settings are adjustable through the meeting options. When setting up a meeting via the Teams calendar application, these options become accessible after creating the meeting invite. Conversely, when scheduling through Outlook, these options can be adjusted during the invitation process. The meeting options provide the organizer with the authority to manage permissions such as entry without waiting in the lobby, screen sharing rights, and the use of audio and video features, among others.

In this chapter, the following required skills and exam topics are described:

Plan and design Teams meetings

- Plan for PSTN audio conferencing.
- Plan for Teams webinars, live events, and town halls.

- Recommend meeting types based on business requirements (virtual appointments, webinars, live events, town halls and Teams meetings).

Configure and manage audio conferencing

- Configure audio conferencing for Teams.
- Configure a default audio conferencing bridge.
- Configure an audio conference bridge number.
- Configure a toll-free conference bridge number.
- Assign a specific audio conferencing number to a user.
- Configure toll-free audio conferencing.
- Configure the audio conferencing numbers included in meeting invitations.

Configure and manage calling features for Teams Phone

- Enable and configure audio conferencing for a user.

3.1 Meetings Types and Features in Microsoft Teams

Microsoft Teams categorizes its meetings into three distinct types, each serving different purposes:

- **Teams meetings**: These include audio, video, and screen sharing, which are essential for collaboration within Teams.
- **Teams webinars**: These offer tools for scheduling, registering attendees, running interactive presentations, and analyzing attendee data.
- **Teams Live Events (town halls)**: This feature allows broadcasting to large audiences, suitable for events like company town halls.

A comparison of the different kind of meetings is shown in Table 3-1.

Table 3-1. Comparing the Different Types of Meetings

Feature	Meetings	Webinars	Live Event/Town Halls
Lobby	✔	✔	•
Attendee mic and camera	✔	✔	•
End-to-end encryption	Premium	•	•
Watermarks	Premium	•	•
Theme	Premium	Premium	Premium
Streaming	Above 1,000 participants	•	Automatic
Registration	Optional	✔	•
Interactive participants	1,000 (Enterprise plans)		
	300 (Business plans)	1,000	•
Streaming participants	10,000 (Enterprise plans only)	•	Town halls: 10,000
			Premium town halls: 20,000
Maximum total participants	11,000 (Enterprise plans only)	1,000	Town halls: 10,000
			Premium town halls: 20,000
Breakout rooms	✔	•	•

✔ Feature available
• Feature not available

Some of the features require a Teams Premium license (indicated with Premium in Table 3-1).

Teams Premium introduces an enhanced version of the existing Teams functionality, adding features that allow for more customization, smarter interactions, and increased security in meetings. Furthermore, it expands its advanced features to cover more meeting scenarios, such as virtual appointments and webinars.

3.2 Introducing Teams PSTN Audio Conferencing

Dial-in options for meetings provide a valuable alternative for people who are traveling or otherwise unable to access the Microsoft Teams application on their laptops or mobile devices.

Other scenarios for dial-in could include times when Internet connectivity is unstable, when app functionality is limited due to older hardware, or when users need to be discreet in their participation, such as when attending from a public or shared space.

PSTN audio conferencing in Microsoft Teams enables users (up to 1,000 phone attendees) to call in to Teams meetings from their phones.

Audio conferencing licenses are available as part of a Microsoft 365 or Office 365 E3 and E5 subscriptions or as an add-on service for a Microsoft 365 Business Standard and E1 subscription. The Audio Conferencing licenses are required only for individuals who will schedule or manage the meetings. Participants who join meetings by dialing in do not require licenses or any additional configuration. A meeting organizer can also dial out using the Teams app to have other people join the same meeting using their phones. See Figure 3-1.

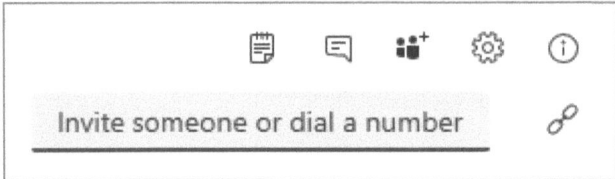

Figure 3-1. *Calling out from a Teams meeting*

In addition to getting phone numbers for individual users, it's also possible to search and acquire toll or toll-free phone numbers for services such as audio conferencing (for conference bridges). These numbers are called *service numbers*. To add service numbers, go to the Teams admin center, select Voice and then Phone Numbers, click Add, and then click New Service Numbers, as shown in Figure 3-2.

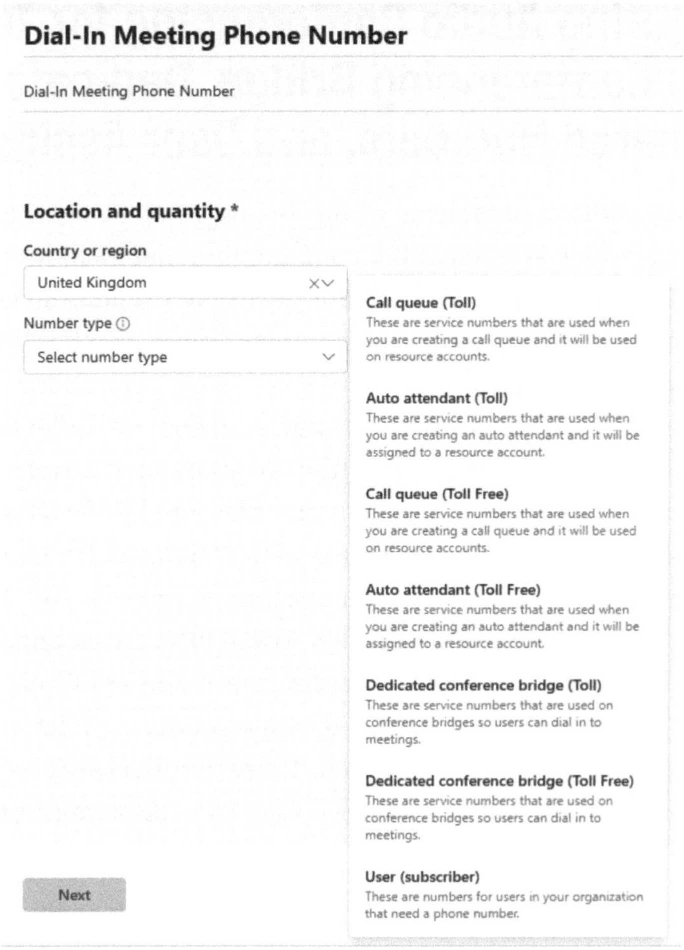

CHAPTER 3   CONFIGURE AND MANAGE AUDIO CONFERENCING AND LIVE EVENTS

Figure 3-2. Buying service numbers

To enable a toll-free service number and the ability to dial out from meetings, you should set up communications credits. Teams communications credits act as a prepaid balance that organizations can use to manage and pay for additional calling services in Microsoft Teams.

3.3 Configuring Audio Conferencing for Teams (Audio Conferencing Bridge, Dedicated and Shared Numbers, and User Assignment)

As part of deploying audio conferencing within Teams, you'll be provided with an audio conferencing bridge, which is essentially a configuration that includes one or several phone numbers. These numbers are automatically listed in Teams meeting invitations. You have the option to modify these phone numbers as well as other settings related to your audio conferencing bridge.

The function of the audio conferencing bridge is to connect callers dialing into a meeting by phone. It utilizes voice prompts from an automated system to guide the caller, and depending on the configuration, it may play join notifications and ask callers to state their names. The configuration settings of the Microsoft bridge also enable customization of notification alerts, the attendee joining process, and the creation of PINs that meeting organizers will use in Teams. These PINs are essential for organizers to initiate meetings in case they are unable to access the Teams application.

Regarding the dial-in numbers associated with an audio conferencing bridge, they fall into two categories: Shared and Dedicated. These numbers are accessible to any individual attempting to join audio meetings hosted by your organization.

- Dedicated numbers are exclusive to your organization's users and offer the flexibility to modify the language prompts for callers. Acquiring a service phone number is necessary for these dedicated numbers.

- Shared numbers are available also to other Microsoft 365 tenants, with no option to alter the language prompts for incoming calls.

A default audio conferencing number can be designated by an organizer in meeting invites, but any phone number linked to your conferencing bridge can be utilized by a caller to join a meeting.

To deploy a Dedicated number, it is required to follow the steps already explained to buy a service number. As soon as the service number procurement process is completed, it will be available in the Teams admin center. Go to Voice and then Phone Numbers. You can assign the phone number to a conference bridge by selecting it and clicking Edit. From the drop-down menu, select "Assigned to" and then select "conference bridge," as shown in Figure 3-3.

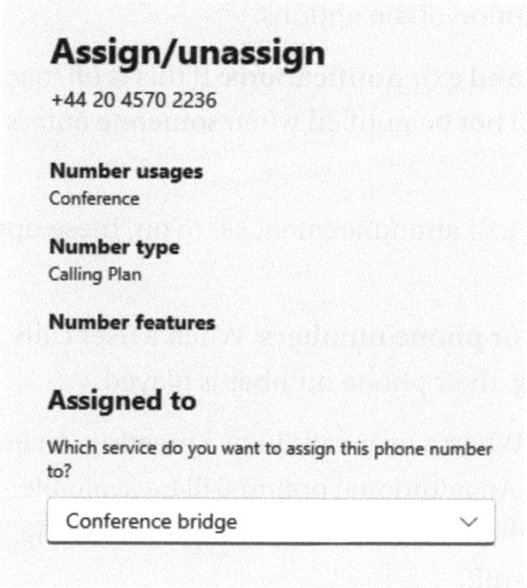

CHAPTER 3 CONFIGURE AND MANAGE AUDIO CONFERENCING AND LIVE EVENTS

Figure 3-3. Assigning a service number to a conference bridge

To manage the conference bridge settings, open the Teams admin center, select Meetings and then select "Conference bridges. Some parameters, which will be applied to all the bridges, are available in "Bridge settings" (as for Figure 3-4).

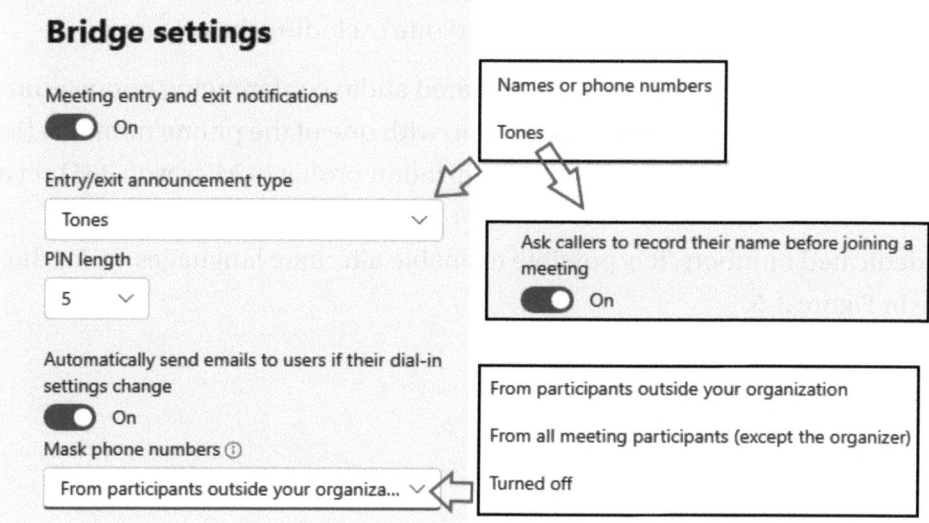

Figure 3-4. Bridge settings options

Here is a quick description of the options:

- **Meeting entry and exit notifications**: If this is off, users already in the meeting will not be notified when someone enters or leaves the meeting.
    - With entry/Exit announcement set to on, these options are available:
        - **Names or phone numbers**: When a user calls into the meeting, their phone number is played.
        - **Tones**: When a user calls in to a meeting, an audio tone is played. An additional option will be available: "Ask callers to record their name before joining the meeting." This can be set to on or off.
- **PIN length**: Select the number of digits you want for the PIN.
- **Automatically send emails to users if their audio dial-in settings change**: This can be set to on or off
- **Mask phone numbers**: if on, the phone numbers of participants to the meeting are hidden. It is possible to enable it only for participants outside the organization or for everyone excluding the organizer.

When audio conferencing is enabled, shared audio conferencing phone numbers are automatically assigned to the organization with one of the phone numbers (located in the same region as the one set in the organization profile in Microsoft 365) set as the default.

For dedicated numbers, it is possible to enable alternate languages, as for the example in Figure 3-5.

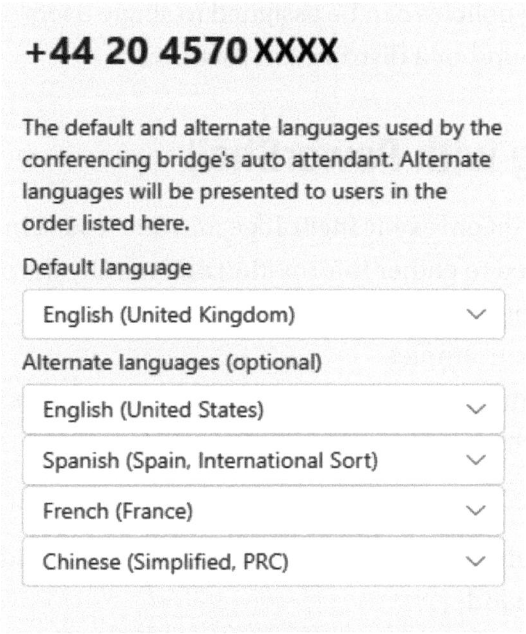

CHAPTER 3   CONFIGURE AND MANAGE AUDIO CONFERENCING AND LIVE EVENTS

Figure 3-5.   Dedicated phone number language settings

To manage the audio conferencing policies, go to the Teams admin center, select Meetings and then select Audio Conferencing. A Global (Org-wide default) policy will be already deployed, but it is possible to create additional policies. The settings are "Include toll-free numbers in meeting invites created by users of this policy" and the option to add one or more toll numbers (see Figure 3-6).

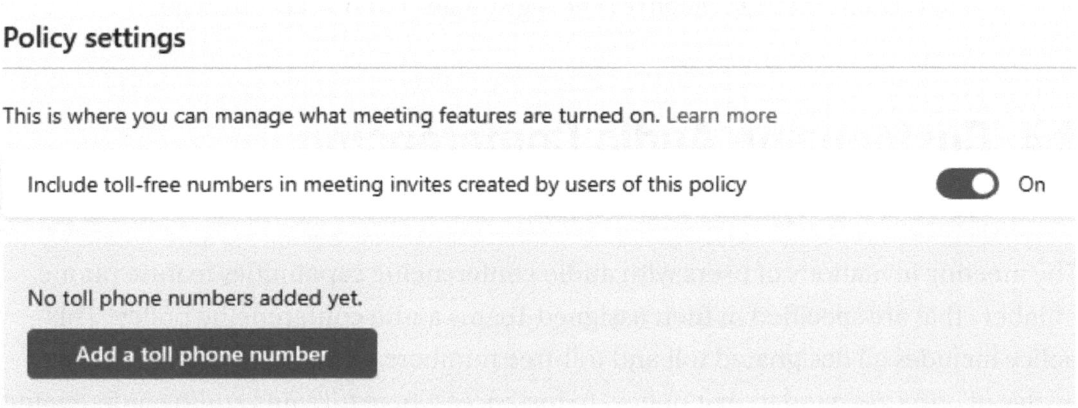

Figure 3-6.   Audio conferencing policies

Audio conferencing policies can be assigned to single users or to groups (Microsoft 365 groups, security groups, or a distribution lists).

3.3.1 Managing with PowerShell

The `Get-CsOnlineDialInConferencingBridge` and `Set-CsOnlineDialInConferencingBridge` cmdlets are used to gather information and modify the settings of a Microsoft audio conferencing bridge.

Here are a few usage examples.

To get information regarding the existing conference bridges (in our example the name of the bridge will be Conference Bridge), use this:

```
Get-CsOnlineDialInConferencingBridge
```

To change the default service number for the conference bridge to *+44204570xxxx*, use the following command:

```
Set-CsOnlineDialInConferencingBridge -Name "Conference Bridge" -DefaultServiceNumber +44204570xxxx
```

To rename a conference bridge to Test Bridge, use the following commands:

```
$bridge = Get-CsOnlineDialInConferencingBridge -Name "Conference Bridge"

$Bridge.Name = "Test Bridge"

Set-CsOnlineDialInConferencingBridge -Instance $bridge
```

3.4 Customizing Audio Conferencing in Meeting Invitations

The meeting invitations of users with audio conferencing capabilities feature phone numbers that are specified in their assigned Teams audio conferencing policy. This policy includes all designated toll and toll-free numbers, which then appear in the invites of users assigned to that policy. In instances where a Teams audio conferencing policy is applied to a user but lacks any specific toll or toll-free numbers, the system defaults to using the individual user's preset default conferencing toll and toll-free numbers in their meeting invitations.

CHAPTER 3   CONFIGURE AND MANAGE AUDIO CONFERENCING AND LIVE EVENTS

To manage the Audio Conferencing settings for a Teams user, go to the Teams admin center, select Users, select "Manage users," and select the user you want to modify. In the Account page, click Edit in the Audio Conferencing column (as shown in Figure 3-7).

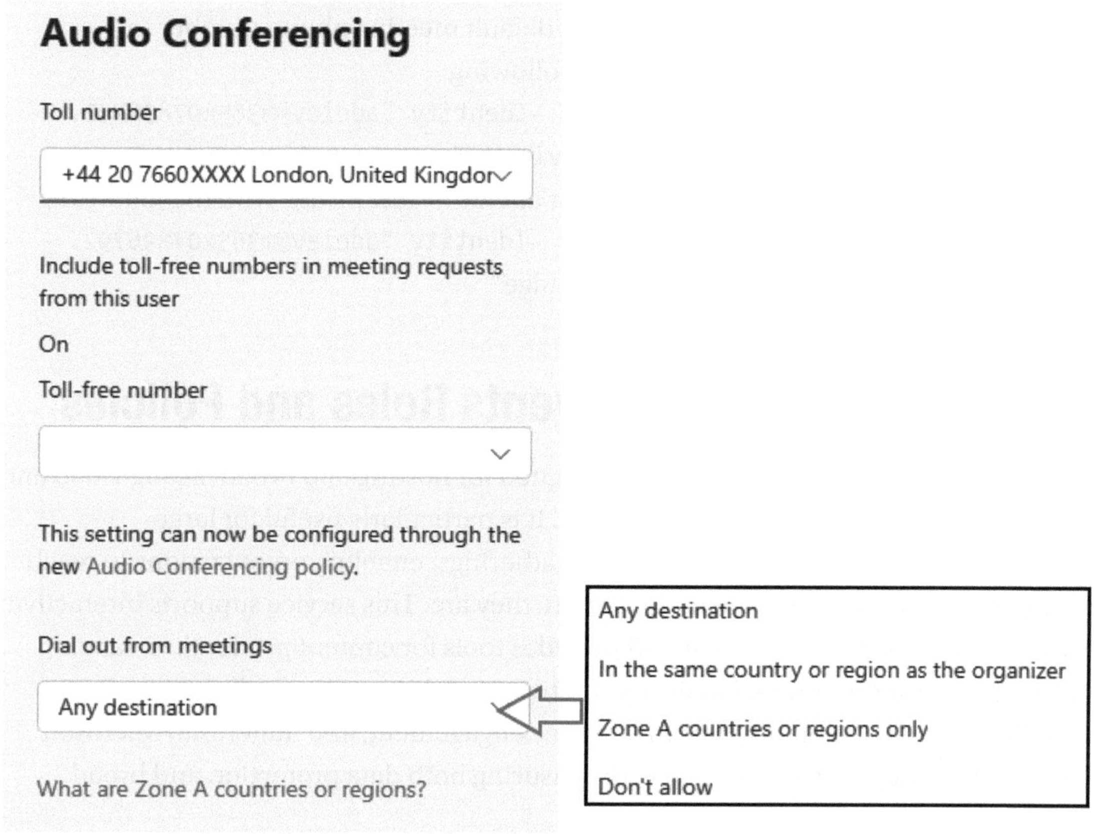

Figure 3-7. Teams user audio conferencing options

Dial-out calls to countries and regions not included in the Zone A countries and regions list are charged per minute using communications credits.

3.4.1 Managing with PowerShell

The `Get-CsOnlineDialInConferencingUser` and `Set-CsOnlineDialInConferencingUser` cmdlets are used to gather information and modify the settings of Teams audio conferencing for a user.

Here are some examples.

Retrieve the audio conferencing information for the user adelev with the following:

```
Get-CsOnlineDialInConferencingUser -Identity adelev@
m365x07896792.onmicrosoft.com
```

Reset the meeting leader's PIN and set a default meeting phone number to +44207660xxxx for the user adelev with the following:

```
Set-CsOnlineDialInConferencingUser -Identity "adelev@m365x07896792.onmicrosoft.com" -ResetLeaderPin -ServiceNumber +44207660xxxx
```

Set the conference bridge assignment for adelev to Test Bridge with the following:

```
Set-CsOnlineDialInConferencingUser -Identity "adelev@m365x07896792.onmicrosoft.com" -BridgeName "Test Bridge"
```

3.5 Setting Teams Live Events Roles and Policies

Microsoft Teams live events is a feature designed for hosting and broadcasting video and meeting content to a broad online audience. It is particularly useful for large-scale meetings such as company town hall gatherings, enabling organizations to reach employees and stakeholders no matter where they are. This service supports interactive features for audience engagement and provides tools for content production, ranging from simple setups to professional-quality streams. Additionally, it offers recording capabilities, analytics for insight into attendee engagement, and adheres to Microsoft 365's security and compliance standards, ensuring both data protection and broad accessibility.

3.5.1 Teams Live Events Roles

Large live streaming events, such as those conducted through Microsoft Teams live events, require a coordinated effort from a dedicated team known as the *event group*. This group works behind the scenes to ensure the event runs smoothly and successfully. The event group typically consists of various roles with distinct responsibilities, as described in Table 3-2.

CHAPTER 3 CONFIGURE AND MANAGE AUDIO CONFERENCING AND LIVE EVENTS

Table 3-2. *Teams Live Event Roles*

Role	Responsibilities
Organizer	• Schedules a live event • Sets up event with correct permissions • Creates the live event • Sets attendee permissions • Selects production method • Configures event options (e.g., moderated Q&A) • Invites attendees • Selects event group members • Manages post-event reports
Producer	• Hosts the event to ensure great viewing experience • Starts and stops the live event • Shares own video • Shares participant video • Shares active desktop or window • Selects layouts
Presenter	• Presents audio, video, or screen • Moderates Q&A

Here is an organizer checklist for live events:

- **Equipment Setup**: Ensure you have the right equipment if you're using non-webcam cameras.

- **Event Information**: Compile basic event details such as title, date, location, and a description. Invite your event group (producers, presenters, Q&A moderators) before attendees and provide them with the attendee link once the event is created.

- **Event Settings**: Configure important settings, such as:

  - Access control, especially for sensitive information.

  - Q&A feature activation and moderator.

59

- Support links for attendee assistance.

- Recording options for on-demand viewing and MP4 file access post-event.

- **Invite Attendees**: Distribute the event link through various channels such as Teams, email, websites, or collaboration groups.

- **Test Run**: Perform a comprehensive check to ensure that all the devices and settings are working as expected.

3.5.2 Teams Live Events Policies

Within your organization, the global policy, or org-wide default policy, applies to all users unless you specify a custom policy. Under the default settings of this global policy, the ability to schedule live events in Teams is activated for all users, facilitating the organization of webinars and large meetings. However, live captions and subtitles, which also include transcription services, are not automatically enabled; they must be turned on if required. The default accessibility setting allows every member of the organization to participate in live events, ensuring inclusive access. Additionally, the recording of live events is configured to automatically occur, ensuring that every session is captured for future reference, compliance, or archival purposes. This default configuration can be tailored to meet specific organizational needs by creating and assigning a custom policy that modifies these settings.

If you want to check or edit the existing default policy, choose Global (Org-wide default) by going to the Microsoft Teams admin center, selecting Meetings, then selecting "Live events policies," and finally selecting "Manage policies" (see Figure 3-8).

Global (Org-wide default)

Default policy for users who aren't assigned to a policy.

Live events scheduling	On	
Transcription for attendees Find related settings at Meetings > Meeting policies, Voice > Calling policies, and Voice > Voicemail policies	Off	
Who can join scheduled live events Find related settings at Meetings > Meeting policies and Meetings > Meeting settings	Everyone	⇐ Everyone Everyone in the organization Specific users or groups
Record an event Find related settings at Meetings > Meeting policies and Voice > Calling policies	Organizer can record	⇐ Always record Never record Organizer can record

Figure 3-8. *Global Live Event policy*

The available options are listed in Table 3-3.

Table 3-3. *Live Event Policies Available Settings*

Setting	Summary
Title	Title of the policy displayed on the live events policy page, limited to 64 characters without special characters
Description	A friendly description added to the policy for clarity
Live events scheduling	Enables users in the organization to create and schedule live events in Teams
Transcription for attendees	Applies to Teams-produced events; enables live captions and subtitles for attendees
Who can join scheduled Live events	Option to set who can join: Everyone, People in my organization, or Specific users/groups
Recording setting	Determines if Live events will always record, never record, or give the organizer the option to record

From the "Manage policies" screen, it is also possible to define additional policies by selecting Add.

A policy may be allocated to users individually or via batch assignment. Alternatively, policies can be applied to a group to which the users belong.

CHAPTER 3 CONFIGURE AND MANAGE AUDIO CONFERENCING AND LIVE EVENTS

It is possible to configure settings for live events that are held in your organization like setting up a support URL and configuring a third-party video distribution provider. These settings apply to all live events that are created in your organization. These settings are available in the Microsoft Teams admin center by selecting Meetings and then "Live events settings" (see Figure 3-9).

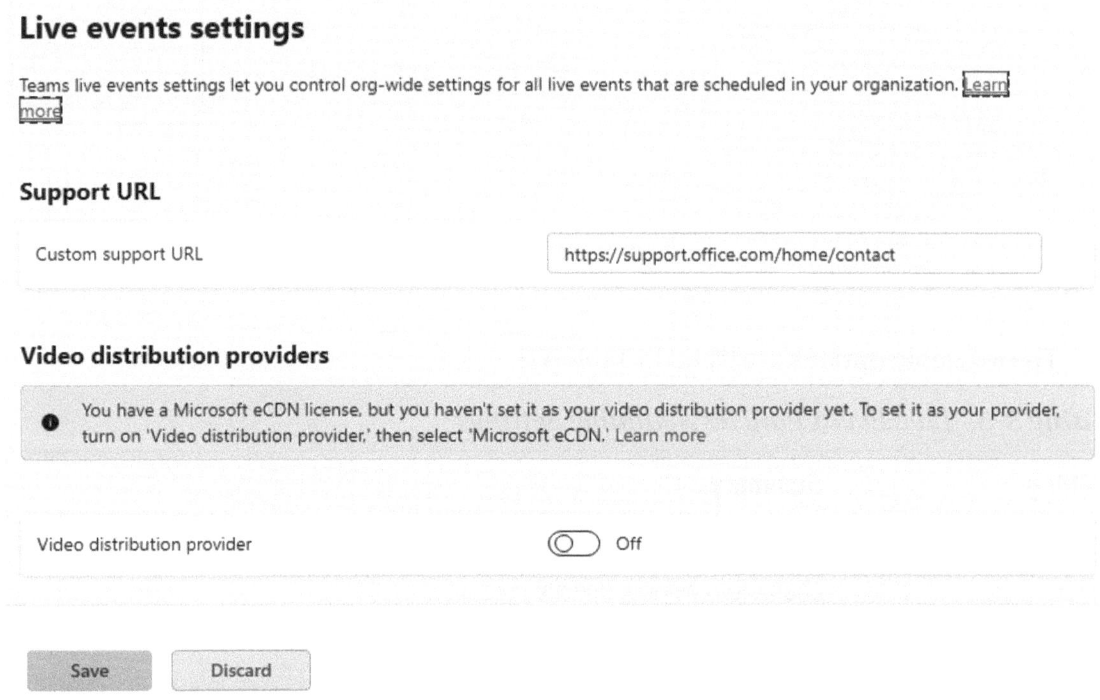

Live events settings

Teams live events settings let you control org-wide settings for all live events that are scheduled in your organization. Learn more

Support URL

Custom support URL   https://support.office.com/home/contact

Video distribution providers

ⓘ You have a Microsoft eCDN license, but you haven't set it as your video distribution provider yet. To set it as your provider, turn on 'Video distribution provider,' then select 'Microsoft eCDN.' Learn more

Video distribution provider   ⊙ Off

[Save] [Discard]

Figure 3-9. *Live events settings*

3.5.3 Live Events Video Distribution Providers

Live event videos use adaptive bitrate streaming (ABR), with each viewer receiving their own unicast stream, which can consume significant Internet bandwidth. To reduce this, Microsoft offers its enterprise content delivery network (eCDN) for optimizing bandwidth without compromising viewing experiences. Microsoft eCDN, integrated with Teams, Stream, and Viva Engage, employs peer-to-peer technology within a corporate network to reduce WAN bandwidth usage.

For scaling video delivery, Microsoft suggests leveraging its trusted video delivery partners. Several pre-integrated SDN/eCDN solutions are available for Teams streaming.

- **Hive Streaming**: This is a software-based solution for live and on-demand enterprise video distribution, requiring no additional hardware. It also offers browser-based analytics to assess network impact.

- **Kollective**: This is a cloud-based, smart-peering platform that uses existing network infrastructure to deliver various content forms efficiently and securely.

- **Ramp OmniCache**: This provides network distribution for seamless video content delivery across WANs. It will soon support live events in Teams.

- **Riverbed**: Known for network optimization, Riverbed extends its solutions to accelerate Microsoft Teams and other enterprise SaaS services, enhancing workforce productivity from anywhere.

3.5.4 Managing with PowerShell

The following PowerShell commands are used to manage Teams broadcast policies

- `Get-CsTeamsMeetingBroadcastPolicy`: This retrieves the current Teams meeting broadcast policies in your organization. It allows you to view settings and configurations of these policies.

- `Set-CsTeamsMeetingBroadcastPolicy`: This modifies existing Teams meeting broadcast policies. You can use this to change settings or configurations within a specific policy.

- `New-CsTeamsMeetingBroadcastPolicy`: This creates a new Teams meeting broadcast policy. This is used when you need to implement a new set of rules or configurations for broadcasting meetings in Teams.

- `Grant-CsTeamsMeetingBroadcastPolicy`: This assigns a specific Teams meeting broadcast policy to users or groups. This cmdlet enables you to enforce certain broadcast settings for different users or groups within your organization.

- `New-CsGroupPolicyAssignment`: This creates a new group policy assignment in Teams. This is used to apply policy settings to a specific group of users, often for managing permissions or features available to that group.

Here are a few usage examples.

To retrieve all the Teams meeting broadcast policies currently in place in your organization, use this:

```
Get-CsTeamsMeetingBroadcastPolicy
```

To create a new broadcast policy named NewPolicyName with a custom description, use this:

```
New-CsTeamsMeetingBroadcastPolicy -Identity "NewPolicyName" -Description "Policy for specific broadcast requirements"
```

The following command modifies an existing policy named NewPolicyName, enabling the scheduling of broadcast meetings under this policy:

```
Set-CsTeamsMeetingBroadcastPolicy -Identity "NewPolicyName" -AllowBroadcastScheduling $True
```

The following command assigns the broadcast policy NewPolicyName to the user adelev@m365x07896792.onmicrosoft.com:

```
Grant-CsTeamsMeetingBroadcastPolicy -Identity "adelev@m365x07896792.onmicrosoft.com" -PolicyName "NewPolicyName"
```

To assign the NewPolicyName Teams meeting broadcast policy to a group identified by GroupObjectID (you need to replace GroupObjectID with the actual object ID of the group you're targeting), use this

```
New-CsGroupPolicyAssignment -PolicyType TeamsMeetingBroadcastPolicy -PolicyName "NewPolicyName" -GroupObjectId "GroupObjectID"
```

Organizations have the option to set up their third-party video provider through PowerShell. To proceed, they need to secure the license ID or API token and API template from their provider. With these details in hand, they can execute the following command (here, the example uses Hive Streaming as the provider):

```
Set-CsTeamsMeetingBroadcastConfiguration
-AllowSdnProviderForBroadcastMeeting $True
-SdnProviderName hive -SdnLicenseId {license ID GUID
provided by Hive} -SdnApiTemplateUrl "{API template URL
provided by Hive}"
```

3.6 Create a Custom Meeting Template in Microsoft Teams

Custom meeting templates in Microsoft Teams require Teams Premium. Custom templates allow meeting organizers to configure various meeting options. These templates can be configured to either allow organizers to modify certain options or to lock certain settings, preventing any changes. Up to 50 custom templates can be created.

Each template option includes:

- **Default Value:** The preset value applied when a template is selected for a meeting.

- **Visibility**: Determines whether the meeting organizer can view this option.

- **Lock Status**: Controls whether the meeting organizer can alter the preset option. If an option is locked, it cannot be modified by the organizer.

To add a custom meeting template, go to the Teams admin center, select Meetings, and click "Meeting templates." Click Add.

Enter a name and description for your template. Remember, both the name and the description will be shortened to 40 characters in Teams, but hovering over them reveals their full length.

Select the desired settings for the template.

- If you want to disable the meeting organizer's ability to modify a setting, choose the setting and then click Lock.

- To hide a setting from the meeting organizer, choose the setting and click Hide.

Click Save to finalize the template.

The meeting template has five different parts.

- Security
- Audio & video
- Recording & transcription
- Roles
- Meeting engagement

Table 3-4 summarizes the available options.

Table 3-4. Options for Teams Meeting Templates

Category	Option	Description
Security	Sensitivity label	Determines the meeting's sensitivity label. Cannot be altered in the template after saving, but organizers can change it if unlocked. May override other template options.
	Who can bypass the lobby?	Defines who can join the meeting directly without waiting in the lobby.
	People dialing in can bypass the lobby	Indicates if phone participants can directly join the meeting.
	End-to-end encryption	Decides whether to use end-to-end encryption for the meeting. Disables recording and transcription when enabled.
	Enable watermark for screenshare	Adds a watermark to shared screen content.
	Enable watermark for video	Adds a watermark to attendees' video feeds.
Audio & Video	Allow mic for attendees	Allows attendees to unmute themselves when enabled.
	Allow camera for attendees	Permits attendees to turn on their cameras when enabled.

(*continued*)

Table 3-4. (*continued*)

Category	Option	Description
Recording & Transcription	Record meetings automatically	Automatically records meetings when enabled.
	Who can record	Defines who can record the meeting, either organizers only or both organizers and presenters.
Roles	Announce when people dialing in join/leave	Plays a sound when phone participants join or leave the meeting.
Meeting Engagement	Meeting chat	Controls the availability of meeting chat, including restrictions before and after the meeting.
	Allow reactions	Enables the use of reactions in the meeting, necessary for the raise hand feature.
	Q&A	Allows attendees to use the Q&A feature during the meeting.
	Manage what attendees see	Enables organizers to preview and approve shared content before it's visible to others.

3.7 Meeting Themes

As part of Teams Premium, an add-on license enhancing Teams meetings with more personalization, intelligence, and security, and meeting themes is available.

Meeting themes are designed to create a branded meeting environment by integrating visual elements like an organization's logo, brand imagery, and color scheme into various meeting interfaces. However, branded meetings are not yet supported in Microsoft Teams Rooms.

You can see a list of the features available for Teams meeting themes in Table 3-5.

CHAPTER 3   CONFIGURE AND MANAGE AUDIO CONFERENCING AND LIVE EVENTS

Table 3-5. *Features in Teams Meeting Themes*

Feature Category	Description	Additional Notes
Branded Meeting Interfaces	Incorporates organizational colors and imagery into pre-join and lobby screens, meeting controls, etc.	Users with high-contrast display settings in Teams meetings will not see branded content.
Organizational Custom Backgrounds	Allows the use of organization-specific backgrounds to display logos or brand imagery during meetings.	Exclusive to Teams Premium licensed participants. Not available to guests and anonymous participants.

Meeting themes will be automatically applied as the default setting for meetings. It is possible to switch back to the standard Microsoft Teams theme by disabling this feature prior the start of the meeting. To disable this setting while a meeting is ongoing, you will need to restart the meeting.

To turn off meeting themes for a meeting, go to the Teams Calendar and open your meeting. Select Options and click "More options. Then turn off the Meeting Theme toggle.

3.8 Meeting Options in Microsoft Teams

Meeting options consist of settings that can be managed inside the Teams client to allow, restrict, or disable specific features within a meeting (see Table 3-5). Organizers can modify these options to influence participant engagement and interaction throughout the session.

While an organization's IT admin sets the default meeting options, organizers retain the flexibility to tailor them for individual meetings Table 3-5 Meeting options in Teams.

Meeting Option	Function
Sensitivity	Adds security to confidential meetings by controlling available options. Certain features in the meeting may be unavailable depending on which label you choose.
Who can bypass the lobby?	Determines who can directly enter meetings and who must wait in the lobby.
People dialing in can bypass the lobby	Allows phone participants to join the meeting directly.
Announce when people dialing in join or leave	Sends alerts when phone participants enter or exit the meeting.
Choose co-organizers	Assigns some attendees with most of the organizer's capabilities.
Who can present	Directs to Teams meeting roles for assigning and changing presenter roles.
Manage what attendees see	Limits visibility to shared content and participant screens during the meeting.
Allow mic for attendees	Controls whether attendees can use their microphones.
Allow camera for attendees	Regulates attendee camera usage to keep focus on presenters or content.
Record automatically	Sets meetings to be recorded from the start automatically.
Meeting chat	Adjusts when attendees can participate in the chat.
Turn off copying or forwarding of meeting chat	Prevents copying and forwarding of chat content in Teams Premium.
Allow reactions	Manages the setting for live reactions during the meeting.
Provide CART Captions	Offers real-time speech-to-text translation with CART captions.
Enable Green room	Allows organizers and presenters to prepare separately before the meeting.
Enable language interpretation	Adds real-time translation services to meetings.
Q&A	Allows attendees to ask and reply to questions during the meeting.

(*continued*)

Meeting Option	Function
Who can record	Decides if presenters can record the meeting in Teams Premium.
End-to-end encryption	Provides encryption for meeting data in Teams Premium.
Apply a watermark to shared content	Watermarks shared content with participant details in Teams Premium.
Allow participants to rename themselves	Permits participants to change their display name during a meeting.
Allow attendance report	Enables the generation of attendance reports for meetings.
Meeting Theme	Applies organizational branding to the meeting interface in Teams Premium.

3.9 Live Events in Microsoft 365

Microsoft 365 live events can be organized on platforms like Microsoft Stream, Teams, or Yammer, enabling attendees to join in from any location and on various devices. Live events feature high-definition video and interactive elements, ensuring participants, even those in different time zones, can stay connected. Post-event, recordings are easily accessible, complete with AI-driven transcriptions and speaker detection, allowing viewers to revisit and search the content conveniently.

The steps for creating and delivering a live event are as follows:

- **Schedule**: An organizer sets up the live event. This involves organizing and planning the event, which can be done using Microsoft Teams. The organizer uses tools to schedule and prepare the event details.

- **Produce using Teams**: Presenters are prepared to present the content. They use Microsoft Teams, where they can share their webcams and screen content. This step is crucial for creating interactive and engaging live events.

CHAPTER 3 CONFIGURE AND MANAGE AUDIO CONFERENCING AND LIVE EVENTS

- **Produce using app/device:** The producer uses an RTMP device, which is a software or hardware encoder, to produce the event with a professional broadcast quality. This step is more technical and may involve multiple production tools and external devices to enhance the live event's quality.

- **Going Live:** The producer goes live with the event, streaming high-definition video content, which can include interactive discussions and presentations.

- **Cloud delivery:** This involves using Azure Media Services to process and store the video content in the cloud, ensuring high-quality delivery of the live stream.

- **Network delivery:** This step involves a third-party electronic content delivery network (eCDN) to efficiently distribute the live event's content across different geographical locations, helping to overcome bandwidth limitations and providing a good viewing experience.

- **View:** The audience participates by watching the live event on various devices, including desktops, mobile phones, and web browsers. They can interact in real time, participate in Q&A sessions, and feel connected with the event's presenters or leaders.

Figure 3-10 shows a diagram of these steps.

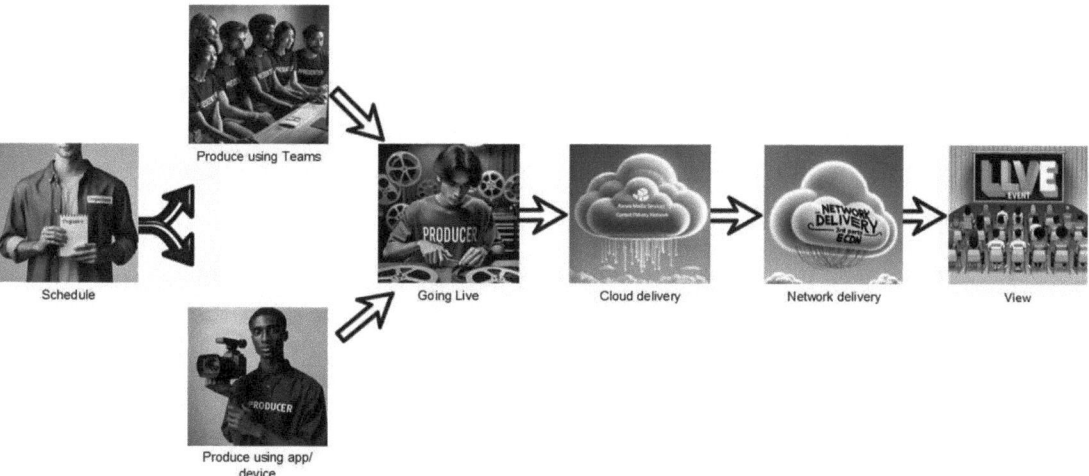

Figure 3-10. *The steps from creating to delivering a live event*

71

Microsoft 365's live events feature are enabled via various platforms.

- **Teams**: This platform is ideal for structuring comprehensive events accessible to employees, customers, and partners. It offers the ability for presenters to broadcast via a webcam and share their screens seamlessly. Attendees can join from any device with browser access, benefiting from features such as moderated Q&A and live captions to enrich their experience. For high-end events, organizers can integrate professional video production tools for a more polished broadcast.

- **Yammer**: This is best suited for engaging with a widespread internal audience or addressing the entire employee base on ongoing matters. It facilitates interactive sessions like CEO town halls and AMAs. Yammer supports webcams, screen-sharing, and higher-quality production tools for enhanced broadcasting.

- **Stream**: Use this service for streaming live or on-demand videos targeting education, training, or niche subjects within the organization. Stream allows for embedding broadcasts on intranet pages, making them accessible for later viewing. It also supports high-quality production for professional-grade broadcasts.

The features available for live events vary based on the service used and the chosen event type. As a producer or presenter, and as a viewer or participant, one will have access to a different set of tools.

Live events support two main production modes:

- **Teams Production**: Previously known as Quick Start, this mode lets you use Microsoft Teams for a straightforward sharing of webcams, screens, and the addition of other presenters, mirroring regular meetings.

- **External App or Device Production**: Formerly called External Encoder, this method involves connecting a software or hardware encoder through RTMP(S) for a more advanced production setup.

3.10 Knowledge Check

Question 1:
What features are available for participants in a Teams Meeting?

1. Audio and video capabilities.
2. Chat functionalities.
3. Screen sharing options.
4. Ability to enter in view-only mode after 1,000 participants.
5. End-to-end encryption.

Question 2:
What settings can be adjusted in Microsoft Teams Meeting options?

1. Automatic entry for participants without waiting in the lobby.
2. Screen sharing rights for all attendees.
3. Use of audio and video features by participants.
4. Maximum number of interactive participants.
5. Option to share meeting recordings post-event.

Question 3:
What are the requirements and features of PSTN audio conferencing in Microsoft Teams?

1. Available as part of Microsoft 365 E3 and E5 subscriptions.
2. Enables up to 1,000 phone attendees to dial in.
3. Licenses required for all meeting participants.
4. Dedicated and shared numbers for audio conferencing bridge.
5. Automated system with voice prompts for callers.

Question 4:
What are the key aspects of configuring audio conferencing for Teams?

1. An audio conferencing bridge is provided with phone numbers.
2. Dedicated numbers are exclusive to the organization.

3. Shared numbers are modifiable for incoming call language prompts.
4. PINs are necessary for organizers to initiate meetings.
5. Toll-free numbers require communications credits setup.

Question 5:
What are the primary roles in Teams Live Events and their responsibilities?

1. Organizer schedules the event and sets permissions.
2. Producer starts and stops the live event.
3. Presenter shares their screen and moderates Q&A.
4. Producer invites attendees to the event.
5. Organizer manages post-event reports.

Answers:
Question 1: 1, 2, 3
Question 2: 1, 2, 3
Question 3: 1, 2, 4, 5
Question 4: 1, 2, 4, 5
Question 5: 1, 2, 3, 5

CHAPTER 4

Introducing Teams Phone

The integration of Teams Phone within an organization's infrastructure enhances collaboration and removes the gap between traditional telephony and the modern workplace. Connecting Microsoft Teams to the Public Switched Telephone Network (PSTN) enables users to make and receive external calls using the Teams client.

Teams, as other modern communication services, uses Session Initiation Protocol (SIP) trunks to connect to the PSTN. A SIP trunk is a virtual version of a traditional phone line that uses the SIP standard to facilitate voice over IP (VoIP) communications. SIP trunks carry voice data over the Internet rather than through traditional telephone lines. In addition to voice, SIP trunks can handle video calls, conferencing, and instant messaging. They allow for the addition or removal of channels to adjust capacity as needed, without the physical limitations of traditional phone lines.

In this chapter, the following required skills and exam topics are described:

Plan and design Teams Phone and PSTN connectivity

- Identify licensing requirements to enable Teams Phone for users, shared devices, and Teams resource accounts.
- Identify PSTN connectivity requirements.
- Plan for Teams Phone Mobile.
- Plan for Operator Connect.
- Plan for Communication Credits or pay-as-you-go calling subscriptions.
- Plan usage scenarios for service and user phone numbers.
- Choose between porting and acquiring phone numbers.
- Plan a solution to acquire or port phone numbers based on PSTN connectivity method (DR, OC, TPM, Teams Calling Plans).

CHAPTER 4   INTRODUCING TEAMS PHONE

- Recommend Teams Phone devices.

- Plan for and recommend analog devices, Session Initiation Protocol (SIP) handsets, and SIP devices.

- Identify an appropriate compliance recording solution.

- Identify an appropriate certified contact center solution.

4.1 Licensing for Teams Voice

The following are the minimum requirements for PSTN connectivity in Teams:

- A Teams Phone add-on license (that requires for the user to already have a Microsoft Teams license). Note: this license was previously called Teams Phone System.

- A PSTN provider to give the incoming and outgoing connectivity to the PSTN network (Microsoft with Calling Plans or a telco of your choice).

Table 4-1 lists the voice features included in the Teams Phone add-on license.

Table 4-1. Teams Phone Features

Category	Feature
Call Management	Cloud Auto Attendants
	Cloud Call Queues
	Music on Hold
	Call Answer/Initiate
	Call Forwarding & Simultaneous Ring
	Group Call Pickup & Forward to Group
	Transfer a Call & Consultative Transfer
	Transfer to Voicemail Mid Call
	Call Park and Retrieve

(continued)

Table 4-1. (*continued*)

Category	Feature
	Call Phone Number from Search
	Caller ID
	Device Switching
	Presence-Based Call Routing
	Integrated Dial Pad
Collaboration & Communication	Federated Calling
	Make and Receive Video Calls
Voicemail Features	Cloud Voicemail
	Cloud Voicemail User Settings
Advanced Call Features	Secondary Ringer
	Distinctive Ring Alerts (Teams only)
	Shared Line Appearance
	Busy on Busy (Teams only)
	Call Blocking
	Common Area Phones
	Media Bypass Support (Direct Routing only)
	Unassigned Number Routing

There are three ways to meet the requirements for PSTN connectivity, depending on the Microsoft 365/Office 365 license you already have and on the kind of PSTN connectivity you plan to use for the specific user. Table 4-2 summarizes the options.

Table 4-2. *Licensing Options for Teams Phone*

Base Plan	PSTN via Microsoft Calling Plans	PSTN via Direct Routing or Operator Connect

Teams Essentials (Microsoft Entra ID)	• Teams Phone with Calling Plan bundle licenses
	Or
	• Teams Phone Standard licenses plus one of the following
	  ◦ Domestic Calling Plan
	  ◦ International Calling Plan
	  ◦ Pay-As-You-Go Calling Plan
		Teams Phone Standard licenses

Microsoft 365 Business, E1/E3, A1/A3, F1/F3, or G1/G3 plan (plus Microsoft Teams Enterprise or Microsoft Teams EEA for customers subscribing after 1st of April 2024)	• Teams Phone with Calling Plan bundle licenses
	Or
	• Teams Phone Standard licenses plus one of the following
	  ◦ Domestic Calling Plan
	  ◦ International Calling Plan
	  ◦ Pay-As-You-Go Calling Plan
		Teams Phone Standard licenses

Microsoft 365 E5/A5/G5 plans (plus Microsoft Teams Enterprise or Microsoft Teams EEA for customers subscribing after 1st of April 2024)	Domestic Calling Plan, International Calling Plan, or Pay-As-You-Go Calling Plan licenses	

Here are more details about the various options:

- **Teams Essentials (or Microsoft 365 Business, E1/E3, A1/A3, F1/F3, or G1/G3 plans) with Teams Phone and a Microsoft Calling Plan**: Microsoft will handle all the phone number management and billing. It's important to check the availability of the Calling Plans license in your region. Calling Plans could be bought in a bundle with the Teams Phone license or as stand-alone plans.

CHAPTER 4 INTRODUCING TEAMS PHONE

- **Teams Essentials (or Microsoft 365 Business, E1/E3, A1/A3, F1/F3, or G1/G3 plans) with Teams Phone Standard Licenses**: You purchase Teams Phone Standard licenses and DDIs from a third-party PSTN carrier.

- **Microsoft 365 E5/A5/G5 Plans**: For those with Microsoft 365 E5, A5, or G5 plans, the Teams Phone is typically included, but there's still a need to choose a PSTN connectivity option (which could be Microsoft Calling Plans or a third-party provider). This option is suitable for organizations that already have an E5/A5/G5 plan and are looking to add voice and calling capabilities.

Note Starting April 1, 2024, all new Enterprise customers who wish to provide workers with both Microsoft Teams and the value in existing Microsoft 365 or Office 365 Enterprise suites (E1/E3/E5) will need to purchase two SKUs: one E1/E3/E5 (no Teams) suite and one Teams standalone (Microsoft Teams Enterprise or Microsoft Teams EEA). See the details at `https://learn.microsoft.com/en-us/microsoftteams/teams-add-onlicensing/microsoft-teams-add-on-licensing`.

Microsoft Teams Rooms and Microsoft Teams Shared Devices (common area phones, Teams displays for hot-desking, and Teams panels for meeting spaces) use dedicated licenses.

For Microsoft Teams Rooms, there are two different licenses available:

- **Teams Rooms Basic**: This is a free license that supports up to 25 rooms and provides core meeting and device management functionality for all Teams Rooms devices. It's meant to be used for smaller organizations.

- **Teams Rooms Pro**: This is designed for larger or more complex environments. This license offers enhanced meeting experiences and advanced management and security features. It supports scaling operations and enables inclusive hybrid meetings. Teams Rooms Pro is suitable for organizations looking to operate a larger number of devices across various locations.

79

- **Microsoft Teams Shared Devices**: This allows for the designation of certain devices as shared within the office environment. It's a good solution in environments where employees do not have fixed workstations or where resources are shared among multiple users.

The Microsoft Teams Shared Devices license includes the following service plans:

- Microsoft Teams
- Microsoft Teams Phone
- Microsoft Intune (Microsoft Intune Plan 1 and Plan 2)
- Microsoft Entra ID P1
- Exchange Online Plan (Cloud-based voicemail capabilities only)

Note The license is also supported for the Teams Android mobile application. This enables Android phones to be set up as shared devices. With this license, all the calling features supported on devices like common area phones (for example, call queues) are available through the Teams Android app.

4.1.1 Teams Usage Scenarios

These are some usage scenarios for Teams Phone with user phone numbers:

- **Remote Work**: Employees working remotely can use Teams Phone to make and receive calls as if they were in the office.
- **Global Collaboration**: Teams with members spread across different countries can use Teams Phone to communicate internally and externally.
- **Business Continuity**: In case of emergency, Teams Phone allows business communications to continue without interruption.

These are some usage scenarios for Teams Phone with service phone numbers:

- **Customer Support**: Teams Phone can be used to set up a customer support line.

- **Integration with customer relationship management (CRM)**: Teams Phone numbers can be integrated with CRM systems to log calls automatically.

- **Event Hotline Management**: For organizations hosting conferences, trade shows, or large corporate events, a Teams Phone service number can be set up as an event hotline.

4.2 PSTN Connectivity Options

There are several options available to deliver PSTN connectivity in Teams:

- **Operator Connect**: In this option, Microsoft collaborates with certified telecom operators to provide PSTN connectivity to Teams. The phone numbers, also known as direct dial-ins (DDIs), are allocated and manageable within the Teams admin center. This approach provides flexibility in provider selection, akin to Direct Routing.

- **Microsoft Teams Phone Mobile**: Mobile telephony integrates with Teams, allowing users to have a single number across mobile and Teams.

- **Microsoft Calling Plans**: Users are given a direct phone number from Microsoft, and PSTN services are delivered through Microsoft's cloud.

- **Direct Routing**: Direct Routing allows organizations to connect their own SBC to Microsoft Teams. This enables the use of existing PSTN connectivity or a third-party telephony provider.

It is common for organizations to deploy a combination of these solutions to meet the needs of their various offices, branches, and international locations.

CHAPTER 4   INTRODUCING TEAMS PHONE

For example, a multinational company could use Microsoft Calling Plans for smaller branches or remote offices where the main driver is the simplicity and ease of deployment. At the same time, larger offices might opt for Direct Routing, leveraging existing telephony infrastructure and customizing call flows. In regions where specific telecom partnerships are cheaper or required due to local regulations, Operator Connect could be the preferred choice.

By combining different connectivity options, organizations can create a flexible and robust communication ecosystem that is efficient and cost-effective.

4.2.1 Porting Existing Phone Numbers or Obtaining New Ones

Choosing between porting existing phone numbers and acquiring new ones for use with Microsoft Teams depends on several factors related to your organization's needs, existing infrastructure, and plans.

Porting existing phone numbers gives the following advantages:

- **Familiarity**: Keeps existing phone numbers, which can be important for maintaining client relationships and brand recognition

- **Continuity**: Ensures business operations continue without the need for updating contacts with a new number

- **Saves time**: Avoids distributing new numbers to clients and updating marketing materials

Acquiring new phone numbers gives the following advantages:

- **Speed**: Acquiring new numbers is typically quicker (it doesn't require porting process).

- **Clean slate**: It is ideal for organizations undergoing rebranding or those looking to establish a separate identity for different departments.

- **Scalability**: It allows to add numbers as your organization grows.

When considering the option of porting phone numbers, it's essential to evaluate several factors. First, check the availability of porting services in your region and confirm whether your current service provider permits it. The porting process itself can be time-

CHAPTER 4   INTRODUCING TEAMS PHONE

consuming and requires effective coordination between your existing provider and the new telco. Additionally, it's crucial to be aware of any specific regulatory compliance requirements that govern number porting in your region.

4.2.2 Operator Connect

Operator Connect is an alternative for integrating PSTN connectivity with Microsoft Teams and Phone System. This solution is particularly suitable for organizations in locations where the Microsoft Calling Plan is unavailable or for those preferring to use an operator participating in the Microsoft Operator Connect Program. It's also ideal for organizations looking to switch to a new operator to enable calling functionalities within Teams.

To enable an Operator, follow these steps:

1. In the Teams admin center, select Voice and then Operator Connect.

2. Click All Operators and select the operator you want to enable. You have the option to filter the operators by the country where their service is available and by the type of service you want to enable, as shown in Figure 4-1.

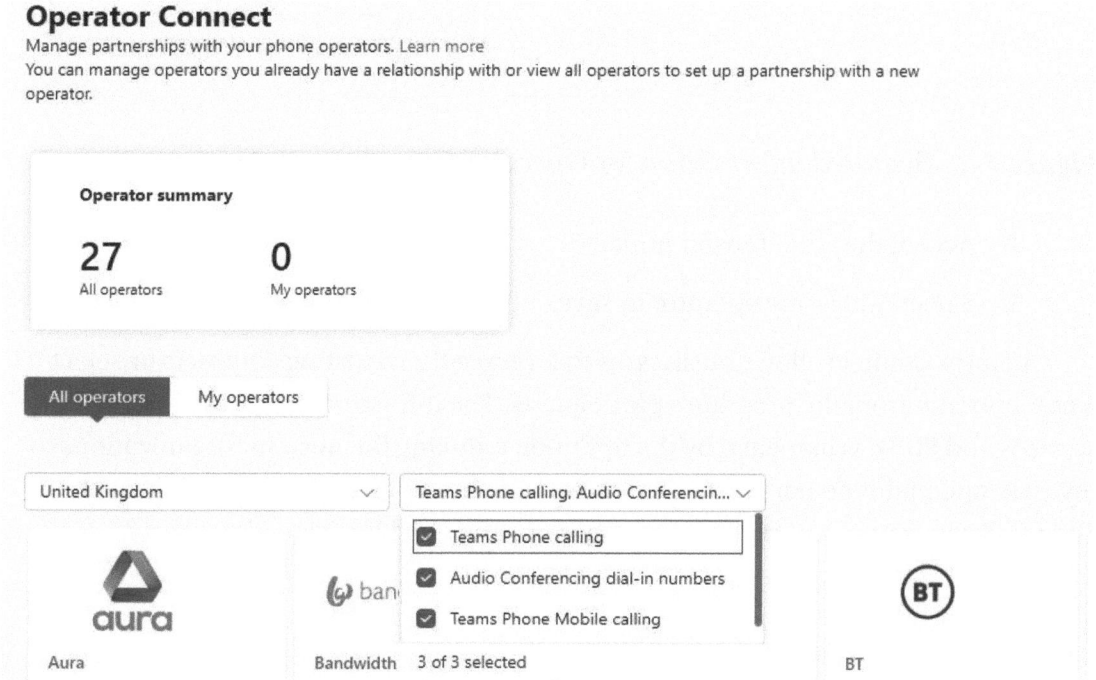

Figure 4-1.   Selecting an operator for Operator Connect

CHAPTER 4   INTRODUCING TEAMS PHONE

3. Confirm the countries where you are planning to deploy the service and complete with your contact information (see Figure 4-2).

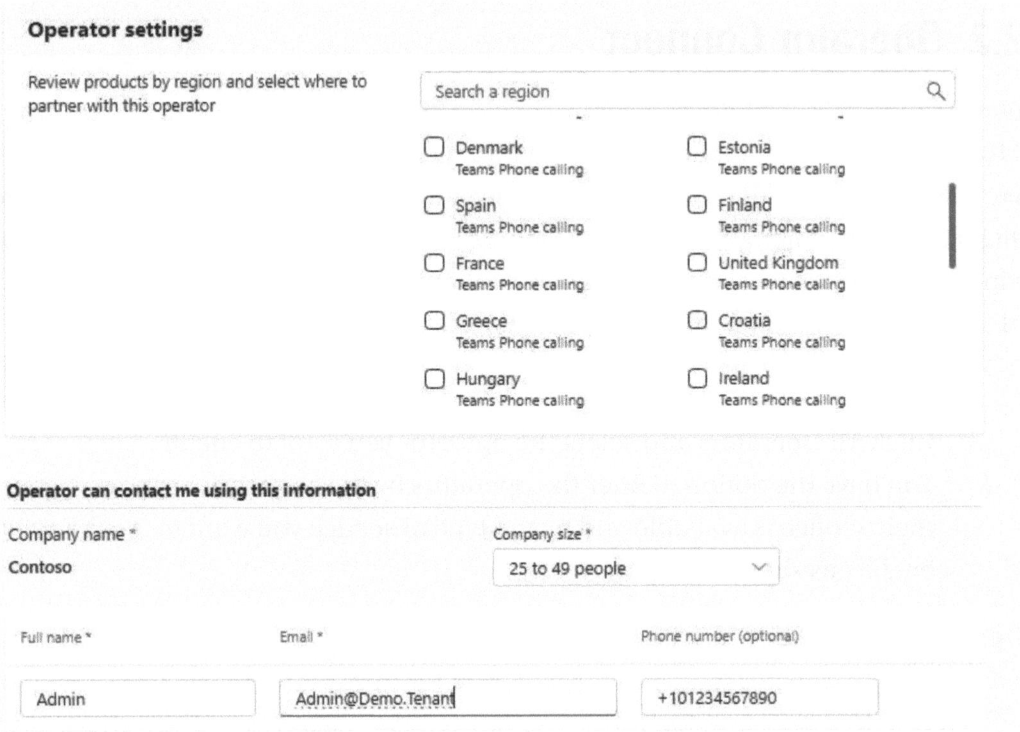

Figure 4-2. Required information for Operator Connect

4. Accept the data transfer notice.

5. Select Add as my operator to save.

Operator Connect allows businesses to leverage their existing contracts or select a new operator from the program's participants. The infrastructure, including PSTN services and SBCs, is managed by the operator, reducing the need for organizations to invest in and maintain hardware. Deployment is simplified and expedited through the Teams admin center, where phone numbers can be quickly assigned to users.

CHAPTER 4 INTRODUCING TEAMS PHONE

4.2.3 Teams Phone Mobile

Teams Phone Mobile enables users to use one phone number, linked to a SIM card, across both their mobile and desk phones within Microsoft Teams. Teams Phone Mobile leverages Azure for Operators to connect operators' mobile networks and the Microsoft Office 365 cloud (as explained in Figure 4-3).

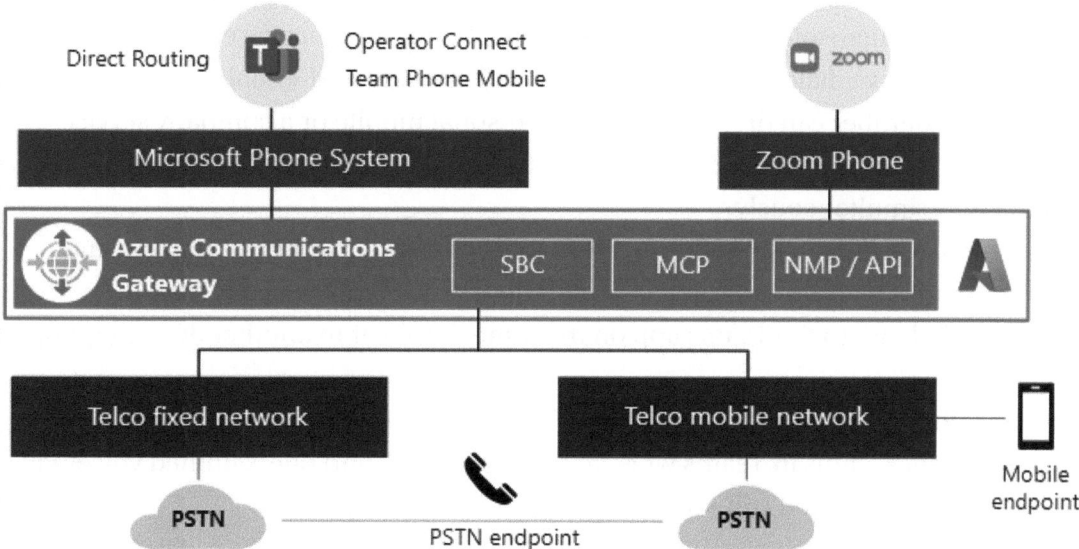

Figure 4-3. *Azure Communications Gateway (https://learn.microsoft.com/ en-us/azure/communications-gateway/overview)*

This program is perfect for organizations with departments that require mobility and that prefer using a primary company-owned mobile number with Teams Phone. The following are the key benefits:

- A unified business number accessible on mobile, desk phones, and Microsoft Teams, improving flexibility and security for users in different locations.

- A reliable communication solution with backup options over cellular and Internet connections.

- Simplified support and reduction of redundant services, enabling organizations to streamline their services and minimize the number of devices they manage.

- Advanced security, privacy, and compliance features, applying enterprise-level policies to voice calls on mobile devices.

- Comprehensive mobile integration, offering combined call history, a unified voicemail system, and synchronized presence information across Teams and mobile devices.

Teams Phone Mobile offers a variety of features that enhance the calling experience for users within Microsoft Teams. It allows users to make and receive calls using their smartphone's native dialer or Teams interface with a single SIM-enabled business number. This number can display as either a personal mobile or a company service number for outbound calls, while inbound calls ring both the smartphone and the active Teams clients simultaneously.

The service facilitates smooth transitions of calls between different devices and Teams endpoints without dropping the call. This includes moving calls from the smartphone's dialer to the Teams app on the same device or to another device equipped with Teams.

Teams Phone Mobile also aggregates call history across Teams and phone dialers, updates presence status in Teams when a user is on a call, and offers unified voicemail and business unanswered call settings across all Teams endpoints.

4.2.4 Calling Plans and Transferring Phone Numbers to Microsoft

Microsoft calling plans for Teams provide full Private Branch Exchange (PBX) capabilities through Teams Phone, enabling outbound calls to the PSTN. Microsoft acts as the carrier (with availability that varies by region).

There are three main calling plan options: Domestic, International, and Pay-As-You-Go.

- For Domestic calling plans, users can call within their assigned country, with several zone-based options reflecting different regions.

- International calling plans include both domestic and international minutes, allowing calls to 196 countries.

- The Pay-As-You-Go plan charges for outgoing calls per minute, suitable for users with varied call needs.

CHAPTER 4 INTRODUCING TEAMS PHONE

Calling plans can be purchased and assigned to users according to organizational needs.

If your organization decides to port your existing numbers to Microsoft (for the usage with calling plans) instead of acquiring new ones, the process includes the following high-level steps:

1. Use the porting guide in the Microsoft Teams admin center to initiate the transfer of your phone numbers from your current provider to Teams, after which Microsoft becomes your service provider.

2. Before starting, review the details in "What's a port order?" If you have service numbers or a large quantity of user phone numbers, refer to the documentation on managing phone numbers for your organization to download the necessary forms.

3. To create a port order, navigate to Voice and then Phone numbers in the Teams admin center, select Numbers, and then select Port to begin the porting wizard (see Figure 4-4).

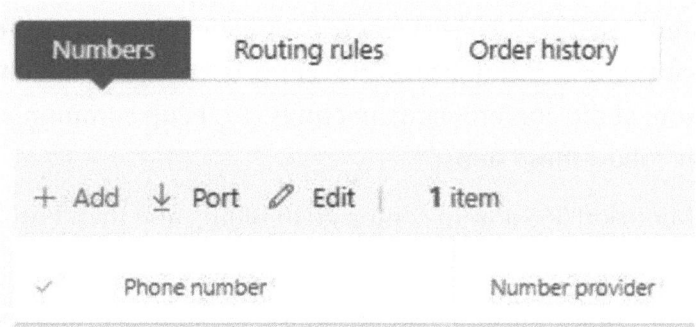

Figure 4-4. Starting the porting process from the Teams admin center

4. Follow the prompts through the wizard, providing details such as country/region, number type, and assignment of numbers. Input account information including order name, notification emails, and requested transfer date.

5. Enter the specifics of the port type (full or partial), requestor's details, and current provider's information like the billing telephone number and account details.

6. Upload a CSV file containing the phone numbers you want to transfer.

7. Complete your order by uploading a signed letter of authorization (LOA). If you haven't downloaded the LOA, do so. Then print it, have it signed by an authorized person, scan it, and upload it.

8. After uploading the LOA, submit your order for it to be processed.

9. If you are porting more than 999 numbers or if issues arise, you may need to manually submit a port order to the TNS Service Desk for your region.

4.2.5 Communications Credits

Communications credits are recommended by Microsoft for users with any type of Microsoft Teams calling plan—be it Domestic, International, or Pay-As-You-Go—and for those using audio conferencing who need to make calls to destinations not covered by their existing plans or subscriptions.

Upon signing up for calling plans and/or audio conferencing, a certain number of minutes are allotted based on the user's country or region. Should the allocated minutes be depleted without communications credits set up, users will be unable to place further calls or dial out from audio conferencing meetings. To set up communications credits for your organization, follow these steps:

1. In the Microsoft 365 admin center, go to Billing and then Purchase Services.

2. Search for Communication Credits in the "Search all product categories" search box. Click Details (as shown in Figure 4-5).

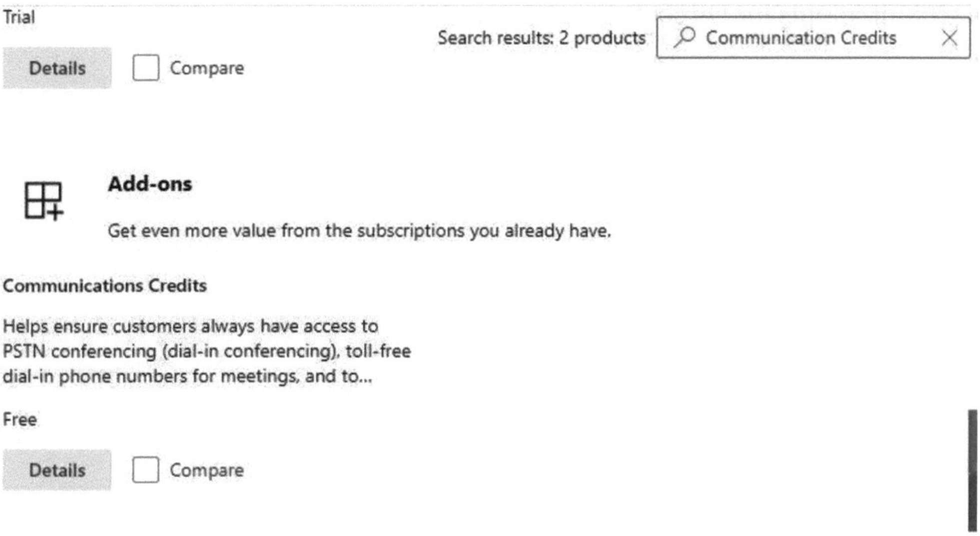

CHAPTER 4 INTRODUCING TEAMS PHONE

Figure 4-5. Adding communications credits

3. Review the information and click Buy.

4. Complete the payment information.

Note If you enable Auto-recharge, your account will be automatically recharged when the balance falls below the threshold that you set.

4.2.6 Direct Routing

Direct Routing allows the connection of a customer-provided SBC to Microsoft Teams Phone, enabling on-premises PSTN connectivity. This service is particularly useful if your organization needs to connect to third-party analog devices or call centers or has an existing PSTN carrier contract.

Direct Routing is compatibility with almost any telephony trunk and provides interoperability between customer-owned telephony equipment (like PBX and analog devices) and Teams.

The requirements for Direct Routing are as follows:

- A supported session border controller
- Telephony trunks connected to the SBC for external connectivity
- A Microsoft 365 tenant
- A domain added to your Microsoft 365 or Office 365 organizations, excluding the default `*.onmicrosoft.com domain`
- A public IP address and DNS entry for the SBC
- A public trusted certificate for the SBC
- Connection points for Direct Routing via specific FQDNs
- Firewall IP addresses and ports for Direct Routing media and Microsoft Teams media, with configurations for SIP Proxy and Media Processor

Chapter 5 (Using Direct Routing with Teams Phone) will expand on the design and requirement of Direct Routing.

4.3 Teams Phone Devices

Microsoft has established the Teams Devices Certification Program alongside its range of peripherals and endpoints. This program is designed to assist customers in choosing devices specifically built for Microsoft Teams. Microsoft Teams certified hardware includes a variety of devices and peripherals that have undergone official testing and approval by Microsoft for compatibility with Teams. This certification process guarantees that the hardware meets Microsoft's stringent standards for quality, reliability, and compatibility, ensuring optimal performance with the Teams platform. The primary aim of this certification is to offer users a smooth and efficient experience when utilizing Microsoft Teams for communication and collaboration.

Key characteristics of Microsoft Teams certified hardware include the following:

- **Compatibility**: These devices are guaranteed to work seamlessly with Microsoft Teams, including integration with Teams features and functionalities.

- **Quality**: Certified hardware typically offers high-quality audio and video capabilities, ensuring clear communication during calls and meetings.

- **Reliability**: These products are tested for durability and reliability, ensuring they can withstand regular use in various environments, from individual workstations to conference rooms.

- **Ease of Use**: Certified devices often feature user-friendly design and controls that are optimized for Microsoft Teams, making them easy to set up and use.

- **Enhanced Features**: Many certified devices come with additional features like noise cancellation, high-definition audio and video, easy access to Teams controls, and more.

Types of Microsoft Teams certified hardware include the following:

- **Headsets**: Both wired and wireless, designed for individual use with clear audio and noise-canceling features

- **Conference Room Equipment**: Such as Microsoft Teams Rooms systems, including cameras, microphones, speakers, and touchscreens for collaborative team meetings

- **Desk Phones**: Traditional telephone devices with dedicated Teams buttons and integration

- **Webcams and Cameras**: For high-quality video conferencing

- **Speakerphones**: Portable audio devices for individuals or small groups

A list of the certified devices is available on the Microsoft website shown in Figure 4-6.

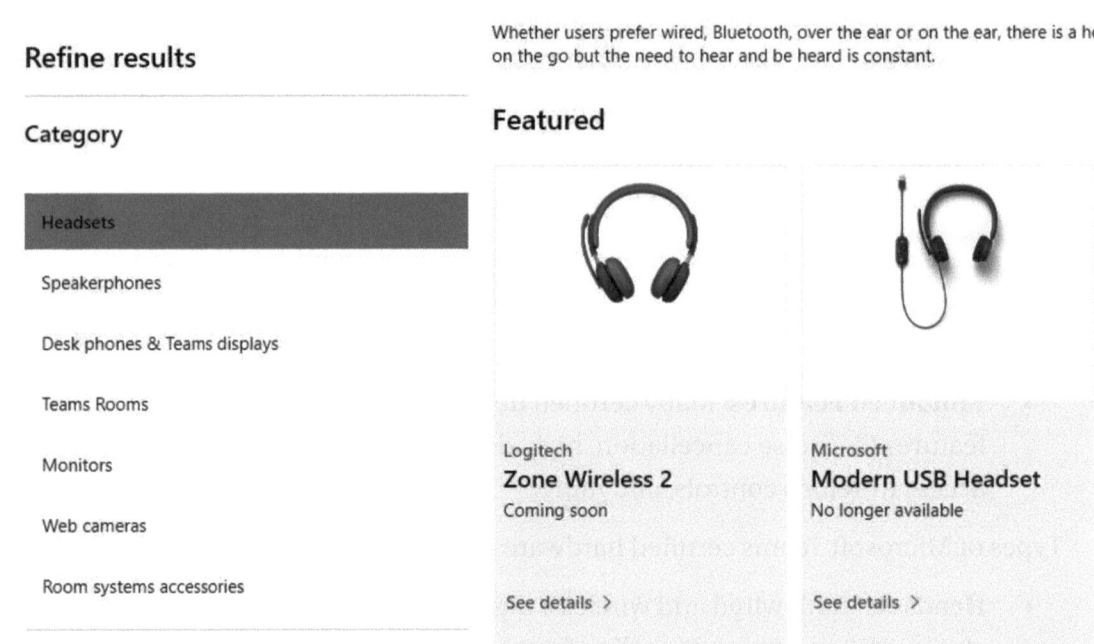

Figure 4-6. *Teams certified devices*

When selecting Microsoft Teams hardware for your business, several key factors should be considered.

- **Organizational Needs**: Assess your organization-specific requirements.

- **User Preferences**: Consider the preferences of the people who will be using the hardware.

- **Compatibility with Existing Systems**: Ensure that the Teams hardware you select is compatible with your current systems and devices.

- **Budget**: Establish a budget for your Teams hardware.

It's critical to determine the usage profiles within your organization, particularly deciding whether a personal devices or a shared space devices are needed.

4.3.1 Personal Devices

Personal devices are typically assigned to individual users, signed in with their account, and require a Teams feature license. They are one-to-one devices (one device per user). They can be paired with the Teams desktop client and may connect to headsets.

Assess how many individuals need personal devices and consider roles and responsibilities to determine eligibility.

4.3.2 Shared Space Devices

Shared space devices are used for specific functions such as common area phones or meeting room devices, requiring a dedicated account and feature license. These have a one-to-many relationship, meaning one device is shared by multiple users.

Evaluate the number of rooms and spaces requiring shared devices and decide if all spaces will have the same type of device.

4.4 Teams Phone SIP Gateway

Microsoft Teams SIP Gateway (SIP Gateway) is a feature within the Microsoft Teams platform designed to enable the integration of Session Initiation Protocol (SIP)-enabled devices with Microsoft Teams. SIP is a widely used protocol for managing multimedia communication sessions, including voice and video calls. The primary function of the SIP Gateway is to act as a bridge, connecting traditional telephony hardware with the modern digital communication capabilities of Microsoft Teams. With the SIP Gateway, users can sign in to Teams using their corporate credentials and make and receive calls using a compatible SIP device. This compatibility extends to a variety of devices, including Skype for Business IP phones that run standard SIP firmware, Cisco IP phones with multiplatform SIP firmware, and devices from other vendors like Poly, Yealink, and AudioCodes. For a complete list of the device compatible with SIP Gateway refer to the Microsoft website at `https://learn.microsoft.com/en-us/microsoftteams/sip-gateway-plan#compatible-devices`.

For companies leveraging existing devices, SIP Gateway offers a range of features including: make calls, receive calls, multiple simultaneous calls, hold/resume, mute/unmute, voicemail, sign-in and sign-out, Teams meetings participation, call transfers, local call forwarding, set do not disturb (DND) from sip devices, call queues, and voice apps support.

4.4.1 Preparing the Microsoft Teams SIP Gateway

The first step to configure SIP Gateway is to verify the network requirements:

- Open your firewall to Microsoft 365 and Teams (for a complete list of the required URLs and IPs check the article at https://learn.microsoft.com/en-us/microsoft-365/enterprise/urls-and-ip-address-ranges).

- Make sure the SIP device's HTTPS traffic bypasses any corporate proxy.

- Open the UDP port in the range 49152 to 53247 for IP ranges 52.112.0.0/14 and 52.122.0.0/15.

- Open the TCP port. Open TCP port 5061 for the IP ranges 52.112.0.0/14 and 52.122.0.0/15.

- Open the following IP addresses for HTTP and HTTPS: 13.75.175.145, 52.189.219.201, 51.124.34.164, 13.74.250.91, 13.83.55.36, 23.96.103.40.

After the previous checks, enable the SIP Device support in your tenant: go to the Teams admin center, select Voice, select "Calling policies", and then select "Manage policies." Select or create the appropriate calling policy assigned to the users. Select Edit. Turn on "SIP devices can be used for calls" and then select Save (see Figure 4-7).

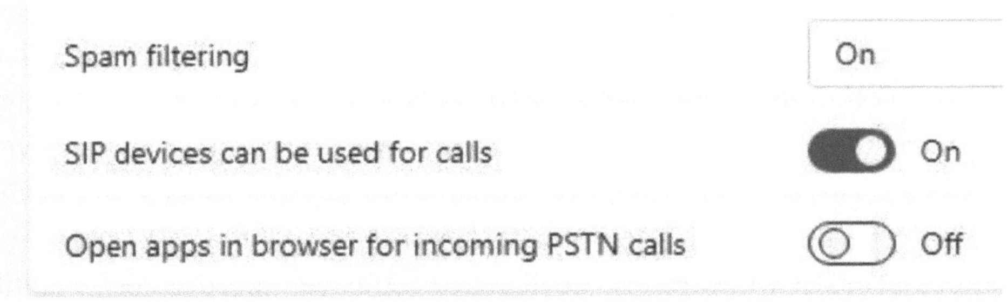

Figure 4-7. Enabling the SIP Device support

Alternatively, you can enable this feature using PowerShell with the command:

```
Set-CsTeamsCallingPolicy -Identity Global
-AllowSIPDevicesCalling $true
```

4.5 Analog Devices with Teams Phone System

Many organizations still depend on analog devices (like door access systems, elevator phones, and desk devices) for specific scenarios. Integrating these into Microsoft Teams is crucial to avoid data gaps and productivity issues.

Solutions for connecting analog devices to Teams include the following:

- **Dedicated technology (Analog Telephone Adapter)**: This integration typically requires technologies like an Analog Telephone Adapter (ATA) and an SBC for direct routing. Calls from an analog device go through the ATA, into the SBC, and then are routed to Microsoft Teams endpoints or PSTN devices based on the chosen strategy.

- **Using Teams Phone SIP Gateway**: Teams Phone SIP Gateway is a feature that is designed to connect analog devices, like regular desk phones and conference phones, to the Teams Phone System. It works by transforming the signals from these devices into a type that Teams can understand and use, acting like a bridge between the old and new technology.

- **Connect using an operator**: Connect the ATA to a SIP trunk or mobile connectivity provider for PSTN access. This method doesn't integrate directly with Teams' phone capabilities but allows for calling between Teams and analog devices.

4.5.1 Integrate Using Analog Telephone Adapter

An organization can connect its existing analog communication tools, such as telephones and fax machines, to the Microsoft Teams Phone System by using ATA devices and an SBC with a PSTN SIP trunk. The objective is to enable the in-house analog devices to engage with the PSTN network. To digitally enable the analog devices, they are hooked up to an ATA. This device translates the analog signals into digital data that can traverse a digital network. The ATA and the analog devices are connected within the organization's local area network (LAN).

In the scenario described, the business utilizes the Direct Routing feature of the Microsoft Teams Phone System. The SBC, which may be located within a wide area network (WAN) or provided as a cloud-based service (such as Microsoft Azure), is tasked with the secure handling and routing of voice data between Teams, the ATAs, and the SIP trunk (PSTN connection), as shown in Figure 4-8.

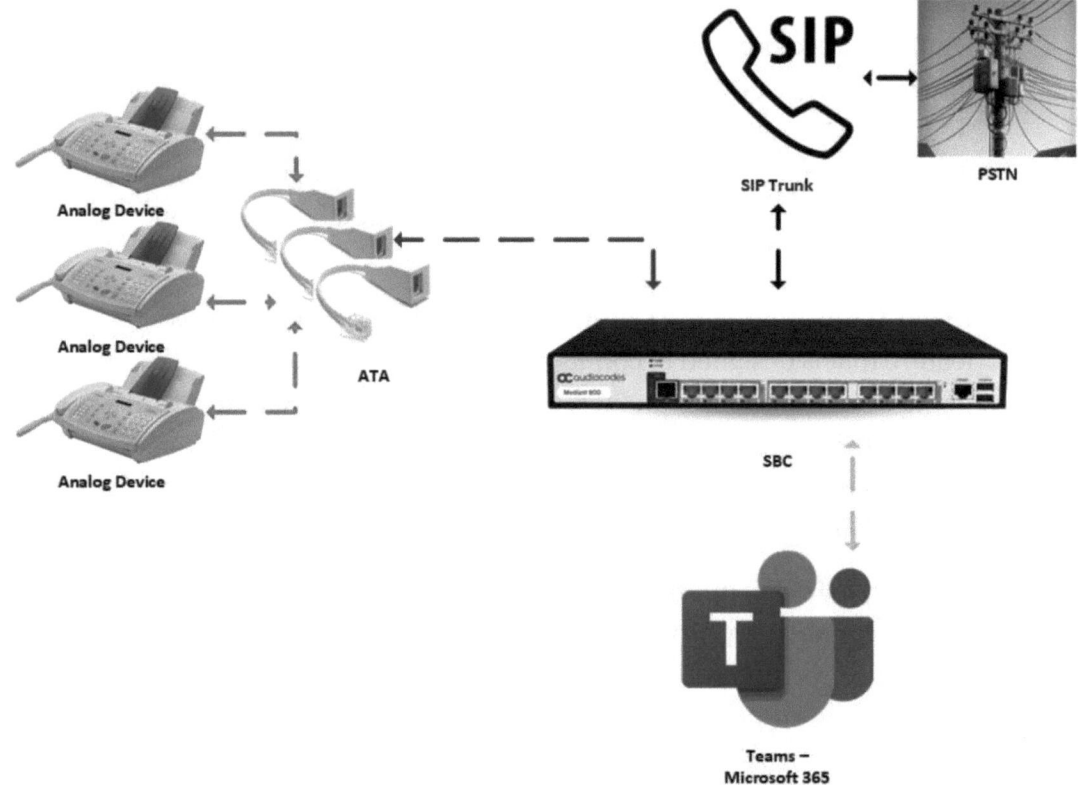

Figure 4-8. *Connecting analog devices via SBC and Direct Routing*

4.5.2 Integrate Using SIP Gateway

Support for analog devices with the SIP Gateway is facilitated through the use of compatible ATAs from vendors as AudioCodes, Cisco, and Poly. Each device requires either a user or a common area phone license, with no extra licensing costs specifically for SIP functionality.

4.5.3 Integrate Using an Operator

Another option is to integrate your ATA or gateway with a SIP trunk or mobile network for PSTN connectivity. In this scenario, the ATAs aren't directly linked to Teams Phone. Instead, they communicate through complete phone numbers. This means Teams Phone users can call analog devices and vice versa using these numbers. Notably, in this setup, there's no requirement for a Microsoft Teams license. However, it's important to note that the phones won't be identified within Teams, meaning they won't be searchable by name. To connect, users must dial the full phone number.

4.6 SIP Handsets and SIP Devices

Connecting SIP devices to Microsoft Teams is a process that allows these devices to function within the Teams ecosystem for making and receiving calls. The supported method is to use the SIP Gateway; this works only for SIP-compatible devices included in the list of supported hardware (see Section 4.4).

The steps for Connecting SIP Devices to Teams are as follows:

1. Check that your network satisfies the requirements for SIP Gateway.

2. Reset your SIP phone to factory settings and update to a supported version of the firmware.

3. Configure SIP Gateway in the tenant.

4. **Provisioning Server URL**: Depending on your geographical location (EMEA, Americas, APAC), you need to set the corresponding SIP Gateway provisioning server URL in your DHCP (Dynamic Host Configuration Protocol) server:

   - EMEA: http://emea.ipp.sdg.teams.microsoft.com
   - Americas: http://noam.ipp.sdg.teams.microsoft.com
   - APAC: http://apac.ipp.sdg.teams.microsoft.com

5. **Device Configuration**: Configure each SIP device with the necessary parameters. This usually involves entering the provisioning server URL and other network details into the device's settings (like DHCP option 42: NTP server).

6. **Sign-In and Authentication**: Users can then sign in to Teams directly on their SIP device using their Teams credentials.

Once provisioned, the SIP devices will display the Teams logo and provide a sign-in option.

4.7 Deploying Compliance Voice Recording in Microsoft Teams

Compliance voice recording refers to the process of systematically recording voice communications within Microsoft Teams to adhere to legal and regulatory requirements. This feature is essential for organizations that need to maintain records of conversations for compliance, monitoring, and auditing purposes. Policy-based recording in Microsoft Teams enables organizations to automatically record calls and meetings for compliance with corporate or regulatory policies. Microsoft Teams doesn't natively support compliance recording. Instead, it integrates with certified third-party solutions to enable this functionality.

Microsoft Teams supports compliance recording on various licenses including Microsoft 365 A3/A5/E3/E5, Business Premium, Teams Rooms, and Microsoft Teams Shared Devices. However, it does not support compliance recording for E911 emergency services.

The compliance recording solutions for Teams incorporates four primary categories of recording functionality: Convenience, Functional, Organizational, and Lawful Intercept. These categories define the initiation, storage, notification, access, and retention of recordings. Users under compliance recording policies are notified when recording is in progress and are informed of any policy or recorder errors affecting calls. Communications admins manage recording policies, monitor recording-related issues, and support internal compliance officers with operational analytics. Compliance officers collect and analyze Teams communications to meet compliance obligations. The compliance recording solution integrates with Teams through Azure-based services (bots) using Microsoft's communications platform and Microsoft Graph. The recorder

CHAPTER 4   INTRODUCING TEAMS PHONE

is the core component, designed for high availability and geographical distribution to reduce latency. Partners developing these solutions must meet specific Microsoft Graph's communications APIs and SDK requirements. When a Teams call is initiated, the third-party recording solution is invited as a hidden additional participant and records the call. This includes direct calls, group calls, and even meetings.

Teams' administrators create and assign compliance recording policies to users or groups determining which recorder is used for each user. Microsoft Teams has a certification program for compliance recording, ensuring that partner solutions meet quality, compatibility, and reliability standards. This list of certified partners provides various solutions for Teams compliance recording.

4.7.1 Managing with PowerShell

Compliance recording policies are managed using Microsoft PowerShell and can be applied at the tenant, per-user, and security group level for each organization. The PowerShell command New-CsOnlineApplicationInstance is used specifically for creating a new instance of an online application (in this case, the recorder) within the Teams environment.

```
New-CsOnlineApplicationInstance -UserPrincipalName recorder.bot
@M365x07896792.OnMicrosoft.com -DisplayName " M365x07896792 Compliance
Recorder" -ApplicationId abc12345-6789-def0-1234-xxxxxxxxx
```

ApplicationId is the parameter that links this instance to an application registered in Entra. The numerical value is a globally unique identifier (GUID) that corresponds to the specific application in Entra and ensures that the correct application with its configured permissions and capabilities is being instantiated in Teams. It is important to write down the ObjectId of the application instance, because it will be required later in the configuration process. In our example, it is 55491f46-41b6-4df3-b08c-cb09c2b9134e (see Figure 4-9).

```
ApplicationId     : abc12345-6789-def0-1234-f2e1f609d511
DisplayName       : M365x07896792 Compliance Recorder
ObjectId          : 55491f46-41b6-4df3-b08c-cb09c2b9134e
PhoneNumber       :
TenantId          : 55d1c745-1aa4-44de-8ae8-34f040840471
UserPrincipalName : recorder.bot@M365x07896792.OnMicrosoft.com
```

Figure 4-9. Information about the application instance

The PowerShell command New-CsTeamsComplianceRecordingPolicy is used to create a new Teams compliance recording policy. Compliance recording policies in Teams are used to define and manage how and when calls and meetings are recorded, particularly for compliance with regulatory or organizational requirements. For example, to create a compliance recording policy, we could use the following PowerShell:

```
New-CsTeamsComplianceRecordingPolicy -Identity
RecordedUsersPolicy -Enabled $true -Description
"Compliance Recording Policy for Recorded Users"
```

The Teams client supports notifications for recordings through visual and audio notices.

It is now required to modify the compliance recording policy, to associate the compliance recording application with the RecordedUsersPolicy policy, as in the following example:

```
Set-CsTeamsComplianceRecordingPolicy -Identity
RecordedUsersPolicy -ComplianceRecordingApplications
@(New-CsTeamsComplianceRecordingApplication -Id
55491f46-41b6-4df3-b08c-cb09c2b9134e -Parent
RecordedUsersPolicy)
```

Finally, the compliance policy can be assigned to a user (AllanD@M365x07896792.OnMicrosoft.com) with the Grant-CsTeamsComplianceRecordingPolicy command, as in the following example:

```
Grant-CsTeamsComplianceRecordingPolicy -Identity
AllanD@M365x07896792.OnMicrosoft.com -PolicyName
RecordedUsersPolicy
```

4.8 Integrating Third-Party Call Centers with Teams

There are three primary ways to integrate third-party call centers with Teams: Connect, Extend, and Power models. Each offers unique features and integration methods.

- **Connect Model**: This model operates with an SBC and Direct Routing. The contact center solution connects to Teams via SIP trunks. The calls are routed back and forth between the call center platform and the Teams users via the SBC.

- **Advantages**: This enables seamless integration with existing PSTN services.
- **Challenges**: This may require more complex network configurations and compatibility checks with existing telephony systems.

- **Extend Model**: This model uses cloud communications Graph APIs. A specific application instance is installed to manage call flow within Teams.
  - **Advantages**: It maintains call data within the Teams ecosystem, enhancing security and compliance.
  - **Challenges**: It requires specific application development and deployment within the Teams framework.

- **Power Model**: This method integrates deeply with Teams using the Teams SDK, allowing direct control over call routing and management.
  - **Advantages**: It offers the most integrated experience with advanced features.
  - **Challenges**: Development necessitates a higher level of expertise in both Teams and Azure platforms.

When integrating third-party call centers with Microsoft Teams, you should consider elements like ensuring compatibility with Teams, meeting security and compliance standards, providing a seamless user experience for agents and customers, providing the ability to scale the solution with organizational growth, and evaluating the cost-effectiveness of different integration models.

Another important aspect are advanced features that a third-party call center integration with Teams could include like skill-based routing to direct calls to qualified agents, and the use of AI, automation, and tools like Power BI for real-time analytics and enhanced customer interactions.

CHAPTER 4   INTRODUCING TEAMS PHONE

4.9 Knowledge Check

Question 1:

Which of the following are necessary for PSTN connectivity in Teams?

1. Teams Phone add-on license.
2. PSTN provider for incoming and outgoing connectivity.
3. Microsoft 365 E5/A5/G5 plans.
4. Direct Routing or Operator Connect.
5. Teams Essentials with Microsoft Calling Plan.

Question 2:

What features are included in the Teams Phone add-on?

1. Cloud auto attendants.
2. Federated calling.
3. Distinctive ring alerts (Teams only).
4. Shared line appearance.
5. Cloud voicemail user settings.

Question 3:

Which statements are true regarding Teams Rooms licensing?

1. Teams Rooms Basic supports up to 25 rooms and is free.
2. Teams Rooms Pro is designed for larger environments with advanced features.
3. Teams Rooms Basic is suitable for international use.
4. Teams Rooms Pro supports hybrid meetings and device management.
5. Both Teams Rooms Basic and Pro licenses include Microsoft Intune.

Question 4:
Select the correct statements about Operator Connect in Teams Phone.

1. It is suitable where Microsoft Calling Plan is unavailable.
2. Operators are managed through the Teams admin center.
3. It requires separate contracts with telecom operators.
4. It offers flexibility in provider selection.
5. It is managed by Microsoft without third-party involvement.

Question 5:
Identify the correct steps for managing compliance voice recording in Teams.

1. Use `New-CsOnlineApplicationInstance` to create a recorder instance.
2. Assign RecordedUsersPolicy using `Grant-CsTeamsComplianceRecordingPolicy`.
3. Modify policy with `Set-CsTeamsComplianceRecordingPolicy`.
4. Integration requires native Teams recording services.
5. Notification for recordings is supported through the Teams client.

Answers:
Question 1: 1, 2, 4
Question 2: 1, 2, 3, 4, 5
Question 3: 1, 2, 4
Question 4: 1, 2, 4
Question 5: 1, 2, 3, 5

CHAPTER 5

Using Direct Routing with Teams Phone

Direct Routing, introduced in Chapter 4, is one of the available methods to integrate Microsoft Teams with the Public Switched Telephone Network (PSTN). It enables users to make and receive calls by connecting Teams with a PSTN carrier, and it is particularly useful when the carrier doesn't offer Operator Connect. Direct Routing is also a solution for interoperability with third-party PBXs and to enable legacy analog devices with Teams. As you can see in Figure 5-1, the SBC will route calls between Teams, on-prem, and the PSTN.

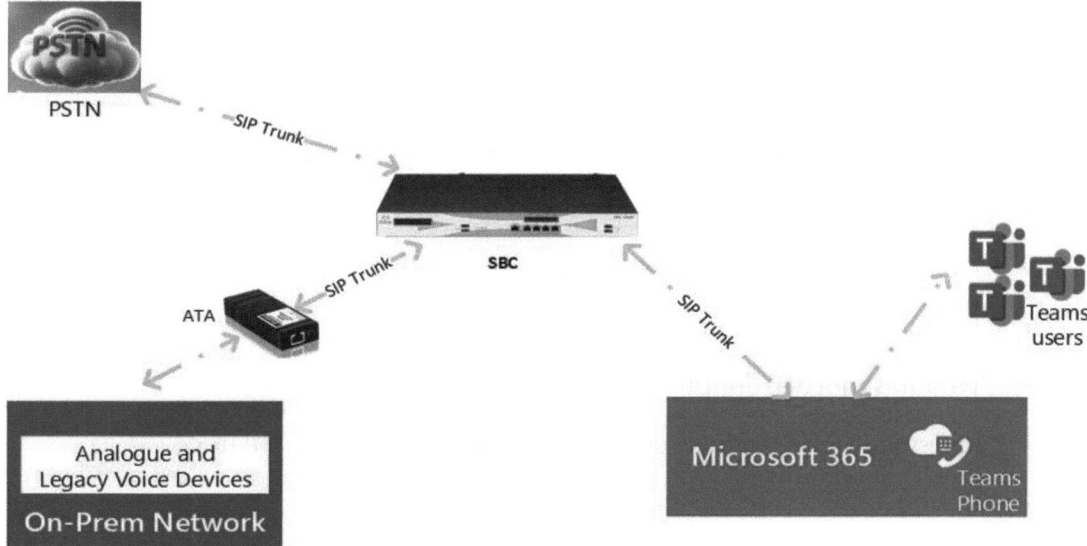

Figure 5-1. PSTN calling flow in Direct Routing

CHAPTER 5   USING DIRECT ROUTING WITH TEAMS PHONE

The process requires connecting a supported SBC (which may be managed by a carrier or partner) to Teams. Direct Routing supports connecting different SIP trunks from different providers to the same SBC, which enables organizations to provide Teams Phone to users in different geographical areas (or with agreements with different telcos) on the same device.

Note   *Telco* is short for a telecommunications company, a type of business entity that provides services in the field of telecommunication. With Direct Routing, telcos are responsible for enabling communication over their PSTN infrastructure using a SIP trunk as a connector to the SBC.

In this chapter, the following required skills and exam topics are described:
Configure and manage Direct Routing for Teams Phone

- Configure connectivity for Teams Phone to an SBC.
- Create and configure an online PSTN gateway.
- Create PSTN usage records.
- Create and configure a voice route.
- Create and configure voice routing policies.
- Validate Direct Routing SBC connectivity.
- Troubleshoot firewall issues for Direct Routing.
- Troubleshoot certificate issues for Direct Routing.
- Troubleshoot Direct Routing SBC connectivity.
- Troubleshoot SIP option issues for Direct Routing.
- Investigate and diagnose calling issues by using an SBC SIP trace.
- Design and configure Location-Based Routing (LBR).
- Design and configure Local Media Optimization (LMO).
- Configure trunk translation rules.
- Configure on-network conferencing for Direct Routing.
- Configure an SBA.

Manage emergency call routing policies for Direct Routing is a topic that will be explained in Chapter 6.

5.1 Teams and the SBCs

SBCs are essential for Teams Direct Routing as they provide integration of Microsoft Teams with traditional telephony systems. They provide crucial functions such as security, protocol conversion, call quality management, and policy enforcement, while also supporting high availability and redundancy.

5.1.1 Supported SBCs

The first step to deploy Direct Routing is to select a supported SBC. The list of certified vendors and solutions is available on the Microsoft Learn website (`https://learn.microsoft.com/en-us/microsoftteams/direct-routing-border-controllers`). The SBCs in the list are both based on physical hardware or on software-based virtual devices. Virtual SBCs can be deployed in public clouds such as Amazon Web Services (AWS) and Microsoft Azure, as well as on on-prem virtualization platforms like Hyper-V and VMware. For example, if you search for "SBC" in the Azure marketplace, you will find a list of available solutions from various vendors (as shown in Figure 5-2).

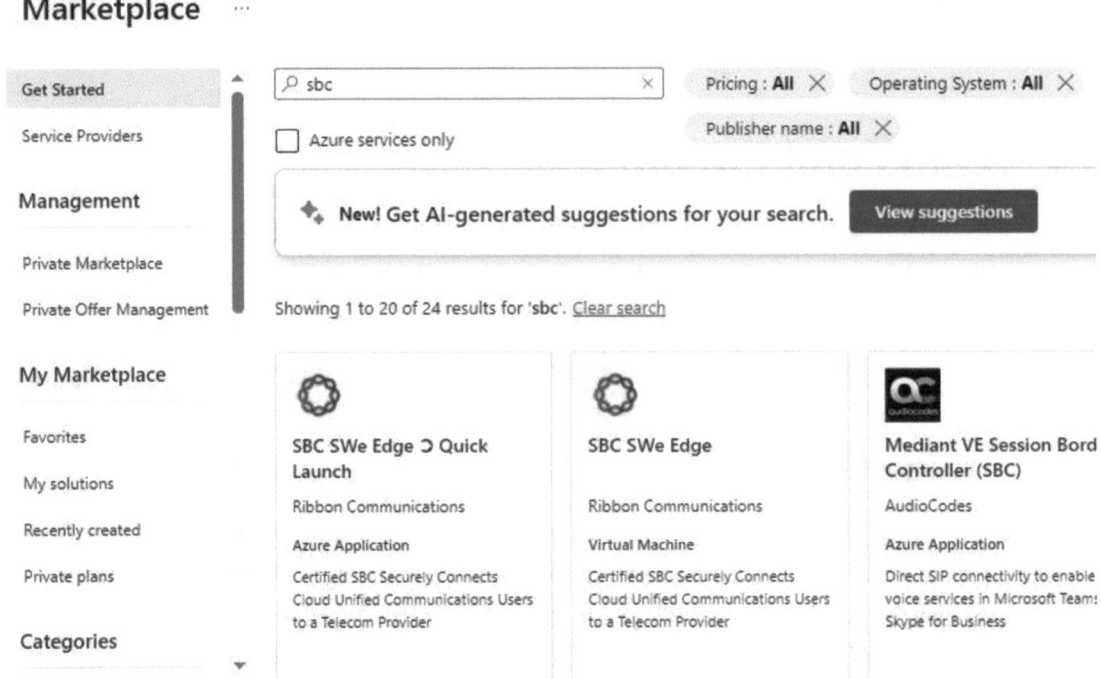

Figure 5-2. SBCs available in the Azure Marketplace

5.1.2 Choosing Between a Cloud-Based SBC and an On-Prem SBC

When choosing between a cloud-based SBC and an on-premises SBC, it is important to weigh the benefits and drawbacks of each option. A key factor to consider is the availability of SIP trunks from local telcos. If the only option for PSTN connectivity is a physical connection, an on-premises SBC is the only solution to bridge communication between the service provider, the users, and Teams Phone.

On-prem SBCs also provide the following benefits:

- **Complete control**: On-premises deployment offers total control over the hardware and network.

- **Performance reliability**: An on-prem SBC could provide a more stable and consistent call quality with reduced latency, as the data doesn't travel over the Internet.

Cloud SBCs have the following benefits:

- **Scalability and flexibility**: It is easy to adapt to call volume changes without the need for physical hardware expansion.

- **Cost-effectiveness**: They reduce the need for hardware investments and ongoing maintenance costs associated with physical infrastructure.

- **Global reach**: Public clouds have a global network that enhances connectivity and service quality across different geographical locations.

- **High availability**: Cloud platforms typically offer better uptime and redundancy, ensuring continuous service availability. It is possible to deploy multiple SBCs in different locations to grant high availability.

- **Rapid recovery**: Cloud environments enable quicker restoration of services in the event of a disaster.

5.1.3 Survivable Branch Appliance for Direct Routing

So far, we have assumed that a reliable Internet connection is always available to enable PSTN calling, connecting users, Teams Phone, SBC, and telco. However, for some companies or some branches, maintaining PSTN calling through Direct Routing during an Internet outage is a crucial requirement. The scenario considered here happens when a customer branch loses the connection to the Internet (and Microsoft 365) but maintains an operational intranet, allowing users to access an on-prem SBC with a local PSTN connectivity. To grant that the PSTN calling is available in Teams during a similar situation, a Survivable Branch Appliance (SBA) is required (see Figure 5-3).

CHAPTER 5   USING DIRECT ROUTING WITH TEAMS PHONE

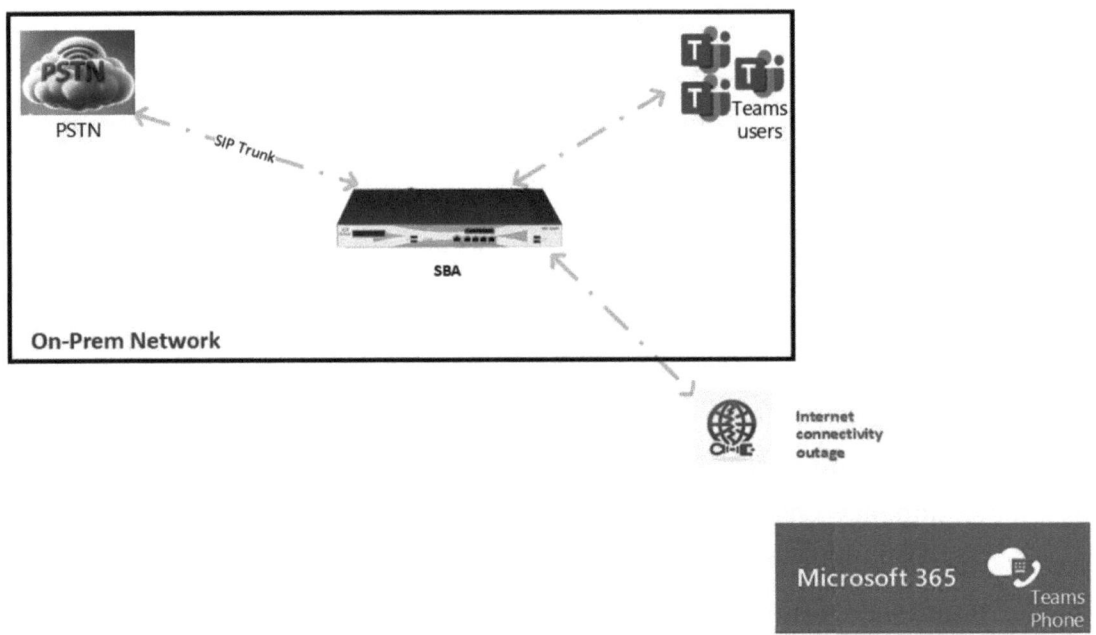

Figure 5-3. *Logical schema with location of an SBA*

SBA is a feature supported with the following clients: Microsoft Teams desktop (Windows and macOS), Teams app (on Android and iOS), and Teams Phones. When there's an Internet outage, the Teams client automatically switches to the SBA. This switch is automatic, and users do not need to take any action. Ongoing calls continue without interruption, ensuring a consistent call experience even during connectivity issues.

During the outage, the Teams client that is using the SBA has a reduced list of available features but can make and receive PSTN calls via the local SBA. Holding/resuming PSTN calls is supported too. Once the Internet connection is restored, the Teams client automatically switches back to its normal operation mode (reconnecting to other Teams services).

The call history (Call Data Records) is uploaded from the SBA to the cloud as soon as the connectivity is restored.

5.2 Configuring the SBC for Direct Routing

Deploying an SBC for Direct Routing has some prerequisites that are critical for a successful integration with Microsoft Teams. Meeting the prerequisites in the following list is essential for enabling PSTN connectivity, facilitating voice communication, and ensuring a reliable calling experience for users within the organization:

- **A supported SBC**: We explained this in Section 5.1.1.

- **Telephony (SIP) trunks connected to the SBC**: The trunks are the communication path between the SBC and various telephony entities, such as telcos, PBX systems, analog telephony adapters, and others.

- **Enterprise Office 365 Tenant**: An instance of Microsoft 365, known as a Microsoft 365 tenant, is uniquely dedicated to a particular organization, with its data residing in a predefined geographic region.

- **Domains**: When a Microsoft 365 tenant is created, a default domain in the form of `<organization_name>.onmicrosoft.com` is automatically provisioned by Microsoft. It is possible to add domains to the tenant, known as *custom domains*. To deploy Direct Routing, at least one custom domain is required.

- **Public IP address for the SBC**: This is required to communicate with the Microsoft 365 and Teams infrastructure in the cloud.

- **Fully qualified domain name (FQDN) for the SBC**: Direct Routing SBCs require a FQDN, in the format of `<SBC_name>."customdomain"`. The FQDN could be part of the custom domain, like `sbc.customdomain.net` or part of a subdomain like `sbc.voice.customdomain.net`.

Note If you register a custom domain dedicated for your Direct Routing SBC, you need to add at least one user to the previous domain and assign it a license. This step is required to activate this newly registered domain. The license and the user can be removed as soon as the domain is active.

- **Public DNS entry for the SBC**: This is a public DNS record that associates the SBC's FQDN with its public IP Address.

- **Public trusted certificate for the SBC**: All the SBCs used for Direct Routing must have a public certificate from a supported public CA. The certificate can be single name, can have a list of subject alternative names (SANs), or can use a wildcard.

- **Firewall ports for Direct Routing**: Both on-prem and cloud-deployed SBCs usually have a firewall protecting them from Internet threats. The list of the required ports for Direct Routing is available at https://learn.microsoft.com/en-us/microsoft-365/enterprise/urls-and-ip-address-ranges?view=o365-worldwide (in the section "Skype for Business Online and Microsoft Teams").

5.2.1 Deploying the SBC

To connect your SBC to Direct Routing, execute the following steps:

In the Teams admin center (TAC), go to Voice and then Direct Routing. Then click the SBCs tab and click Add (as in Figure 5-4).

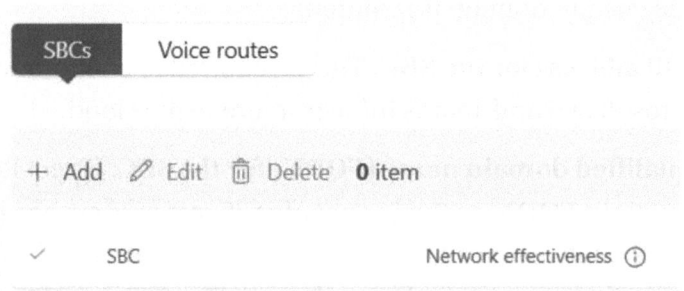

Figure 5-4. *Adding an SBC in the tenant*

Enter the FQDN for the SBC. Configure the settings for the SBC, based on your organization's needs (the default settings are shown in Figure 5-5). When you're done, click Save.

CHAPTER 5   USING DIRECT ROUTING WITH TEAMS PHONE

SBC settings

When you are adding this SBC, you can turn on or off the SBC and change settings that are specific to the SBC.

Enabled	Off
SIP signaling port	5067
Send SIP options	On
Forward call history	Off
Forward P-Asserted-Identity (PAI) header	Off
Concurrent call capacity	24
Failover response codes	408, 503, 504
Failover time (seconds)	10
SBC supports PIDF/LO for emergency calls	Off

Figure 5-5. *Basic settings for a Direct Routing SBC*

The SIP signaling port is the listening port that will be used by your SBC to connect to Teams for Direct Routing.

5.3 Calls Flow in Direct Routing

When a Team user (with a Teams Phone license) dials a phone number to make an outgoing call, some controls and policies are applied.

- **Calling policies**: Calling policies are configurations determine the calling features and permissions available to users within an organization. These policies govern various aspects of voice communication, such as making and receiving calls, call forwarding, voicemail, and more. Calling Policies will be discussed in Chapter 6.

- **Voice routes**: In a voice route, you have a dialed number pattern that will be matched with the phone number the user is trying to call. The pattern is written using Regular Expression Language. If the number dialed matches the pattern, the configured SBCs will be used to route the call, and a list of PSTN usages will be linked to this voice route.

    (PSTN Usages: PSTN usages are logic containers used to connect different voice routes.)

- **Voice routing policies**: In a voice routing policy, you list PSTN usage records that create a link to voice routes. Voice routing policies are applied to Teams users to decide how their PSTN calls are managed. The order in which the PSTN usage records are used is established in the voice routing policy (as shown in Figure 5-6).

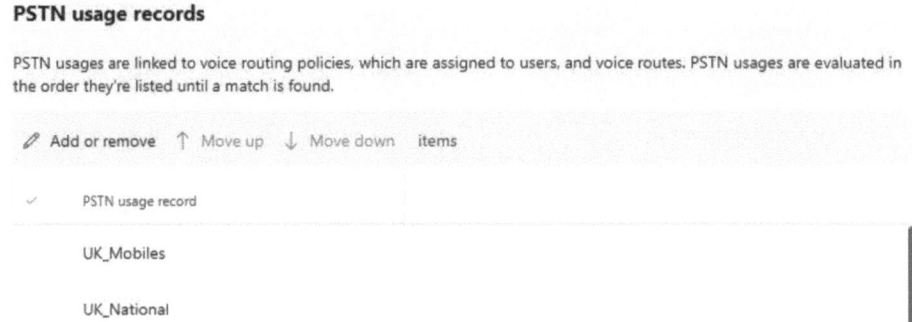

Figure 5-6. PSTN usages in a voice routing policy

5.3.1 Configuring the Call Flow for Direct Routing

To configure the call flow using Direct Routing in a tenant, the following steps should happen:

1. Create voice routes that match UK phone numbers using regular expressions.

2. Link PSTN usages to these voice routes to manage routing.

3. Apply a voice routing policy to users that includes these PSTN usage records.

4. Based on the voice routing policy, the system evaluates the PSTN usage records in the specified order.

5. The appropriate voice route is selected, and the call is routed through the configured SBCs to the PSTN.

Let's take as an example the configuration steps for a UK tenant (we are assuming that the user has both a Phone System license and an assigned phone number). The following actions are required:

1. **Create voice routes:**

    - Define voice routes with dialed number patterns for UK phone numbers.

    - Use Regular Expression Language to specify patterns (e.g., ^\+44 for UK numbers).

2. **Link PSTN usages:**

    - Create PSTN usage records and link them to the voice routes.
        - Example: Create a PSTN usage record named UKPSTNUsage linked to a voice route matching UK numbers.

3. **Define voice routing policies:**

    - Create a voice routing policy that includes the PSTN usage records.
        - Example: Create a policy named UKVoiceRoutingPolicy that lists UKPSTNUsage as a priority.

4. **Assign policies to users:**

    - Assign the AllowCalling calling policy to users to ensure they have the necessary permissions.

    - Apply the UKVoiceRoutingPolicy to users to manage their PSTN calls.

5.4 Troubleshooting Direct Routing

This chapter is designed to equip you with the troubleshooting techniques required to ensure the reliability and performance of your Direct Routing telephony infrastructure integrated with Microsoft Teams.

CHAPTER 5   USING DIRECT ROUTING WITH TEAMS PHONE

5.4.1 Validate Direct Routing SBC Connectivity

The first check required to validate your SBC connectivity is executed in the TAC. Go to Voice and then Direct Routing and click the SBCs tab. Your SBC should be listed there. As an alternative, you can use the PowerShell command `Get-CsOnlinePSTNGateway`. For example, use `Get-CsOnlinePSTNGateway -Identity SBC_name.customdomain.custom`.

The results of the previous command should have the Enabled parameter set to True (see the following example):

- **Identity**: SBC_name.customdomain.custom
- **Fqdn**: _name.customdomain.custom
- **Enabled**: True
- **SendSipOptions**: True

The SendSipOptions parameter set to True is important for the second validation step.

To ensure the successful pairing through outgoing SIP options, access the SBC management interface. Verify that the SBC receives 200 OK responses to its outgoing OPTIONS messages. This confirmation indicates that the SIP communication path is functioning correctly, and the SBC is successfully reaching the Direct Routing service.

Ideally, in the TAC, the SBC should have no alarms in the TAC (as in Figure 5-7).

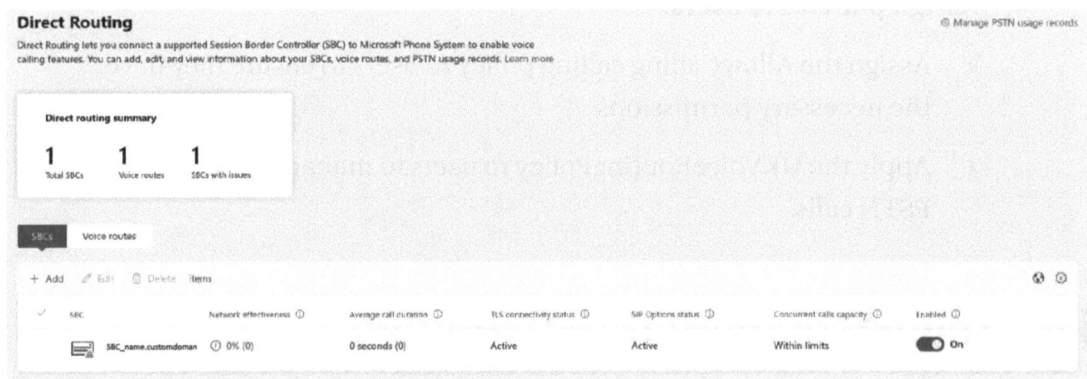

Figure 5-7. *Correctly paired SBC in the TAC*

However, if you are using a hosted SBC that is shared by multiple companies, the TAC will show errors related to TLS (Inactive) and "SIP options status" (Warning). This is an expected behavior.

5.4.2 Troubleshoot Firewall Issues for Direct Routing

In Section 5.2, we mentioned that all the firewall ports in the Microsoft 365 URLs and IP address ranges must be open. Specifically, for Direct Routing, make sure that the following firewall ports are open:

- **SIP signaling (TCP/UDP)**: Port 5061 (this is the value you configured when setting up the SBC)
- **Media ports (UDP)**: Typically, within the range of 49152–53247

5.4.3 Troubleshoot Certificate Issues for Direct Routing

Certificates are critical for establishing secure connections between the Session Border Controller (SBC) and Microsoft Teams. To validate the certificate, follow these steps:

1. Ensure that the certificates used by the SBC are still valid. This involves checking the expiration date and the certificate chain.
2. Ensure that the SBC is configured to use the correct certificate for its communications with Microsoft Teams.
3. The common name (CN) or subject alternative name (SAN) in the certificate must match the fully qualified domain name (FQDN) of the SBC (unless you are using a wildcard certificate).
4. The SBC must trust the root and intermediate certificates in the chain.
5. Ensure the certificate has not been revoked.
6. Ensure that the SBC is using an updated list of trusted certificate authorities (CAs).

5.4.4 Troubleshoot Direct Routing SBC Connectivity

When setting up Direct Routing for Microsoft Teams, you might encounter various Session Border Controller (SBC) connectivity issues, such as:

- SIP OPTIONS not received.
- TLS connection problems.

- The SBC does not respond.
- The SBC is marked as inactive in the Azure portal.

These issues are often caused by problems with TLS certificates or incorrect SBC configurations.

This is an overview of the SIP options process:

- The SBC sends a TLS connection request with a certificate to the SIP proxy server's FQDN.
- If valid, a TLS connection is established, and the SBC sends SIP OPTIONS to the SIP proxy.
- The SIP proxy checks the SBC FQDN in the Record-Route or Contact header.
- If recognized, the SIP proxy sends a 200 OK response and marks the SBC as online in the Azure portal.

Here are some of the SIP options issues:

- SBC Doesn't Receive 200 OK Response.
    - Ensure TLS 1.2 is enabled.
    - Use a certificate from a trusted CA, not self-signed.
    - Verify that the FQDN in the SBC configuration matches the one in the Azure Communication resource.
- SBC Receives 200 OK but Not SIP OPTIONS
    - Check that the FQDN in the Record-Route or Contact header resolves correctly.
    - Ensure firewall rules allow incoming connections from all SIP proxy signaling IP addresses.

Here are some of the TLS connection issues:

- Invalid TLS Version
    - Configure TLS version to 1.2 on the SBC.

- Self-signed or Untrusted CA Certificate

    ◦ Use a certificate from a trusted CA. Refer to the list of supported CAs in the Microsoft documentation.

- Untrusted SIP Proxy Certificate

    ◦ Install the Baltimore CyberTrust Root and DigiCert Global Root G2 certificates on the SBC.

- Expired or Invalid Certificate

    ◦ Renew and install the SBC certificate from a trusted CA.

    ◦ Remove old TLS connections and re-establish them with the new certificate.

- Missing Certificates in TLS Hello Message

    ◦ Ensure all required certificates, including intermediate ones, are correctly installed.

5.4.5 Investigate and Diagnose Calling Issues by Using an SBC SIP Trace

To effectively investigate and diagnose calling issues using an SBC SIP trace, follow these steps:

1. Enable SIP tracing on the SBC.
2. Reproduce the issue.
    - Conduct a test call to reproduce the issue.
3. Capture SIP trace data.
    - Start the SIP trace before initiating the test call.
    - Stop the SIP trace once the call is completed.
4. Analyze the SIP trace.
    - Identify key SIP messages: Look for key SIP messages such as INVITE, TRYING, RINGING, OK, and BYE.

- Check for errors: Identify any SIP error responses like 404 (Not Found), 486 (Busy Here), 503 (Service Unavailable), etc.
- Follow the call flow: Verify the sequence of SIP messages to ensure they follow the correct call flow.

5. Diagnose common issues.
    - No Response to INVITE: If the INVITE message does not receive a response, check for connectivity issues or misconfigured routing.
    - Error Responses: Analyze the error code to determine the specific problem like these:
        - **404 Not Found**: The destination number is not recognized. Verify the dial plan and routing configuration.
        - **486 Busy Here**: The called party is busy. Confirm the availability of the called party.
        - **503 Service Unavailable**: There is a service issue. Check the SBC's capacity and network conditions.

6. Examine headers and fields.
    - **From and To Headers**: Ensure that the calling and called party information is correct.
    - **Contact Header**: Verify that the contact header contains the correct address information for routing responses.

5.5 Additional Configurations for Direct Routing

In this section, we will see some of the advanced configurations and design principles that can improve Microsoft Teams Direct Routing. Those features are meant to ensure high-quality, location-aware, and resilient voice services.

5.5.1 Design and Configure Location-Based Routing

Location-based routing (LBR) restricts toll bypass (the process of routing PSTN calls over the Internet to leverage the less costly available telco) for Microsoft Teams users based on their geographic location. This is particularly important in regions where bypassing the Public Switched Telephone Network (PSTN) provider to reduce long-distance calling costs is illegal.

The LBR feature uses the configurations made in the network topology (network regions, sites, subnets, and trusted IPs). The topic of network configuration and optimization for Teams is the focus of Chapter 10.

LBR applies only to Direct Routing and not to Calling Plan or Operator Connect. Calls between a Teams user and the PSTN, if LBR is enabled, are evaluated, and toll bypass is allowed or restricted.

The flow for a call when LBR is enabled is as follows:

- Check if the Teams user is enabled for Location-Based Routing (Teams Calling policy).

- Determine the Teams user's endpoint network site location and its enablement status for LBR.

- Verify the network site location of the PSTN gateway being used by the call.

- Confirm if the PSTN gateway used by the call is enabled for LBR.

- In transfer scenarios, the routing of the PSTN call is based on the routing settings of the person transferring the call and the LBR settings of the recipient.

- In conferencing and group call scenarios, checking if a Teams user with restricted toll bypass is or has been part of the call.

In any scenario where the user or the location is not enabled to LBR, the PSTN call will happen as described previously in the call flow in Direct Routing.

5.5.2 Design and Configure Local Media Optimization (LMO)

Local media optimization (LMO) for Direct Routing in Microsoft Teams enhances voice quality by managing media traffic flows between Teams clients and session border controllers (SBCs).

In Microsoft Teams we have two different kinds of traffic:

- **Media traffic:** Refers to the actual content data being transmitted during real-time communications such as voice calls, video calls, and screen sharing. This data is time-sensitive and requires consistent bandwidth to ensure high-quality interactions.

- **Signaling traffic:** Involves the control messages used to establish, manage, and terminate connections between users. This includes setting up calls, managing call states (e.g., hold, transfer), and tearing down sessions when they end. Signaling traffic is less bandwidth-intensive than media traffic but is crucial for coordinating communication sessions.

Audio traffic is the one relevant for Direct Routing. In audio-only calls, media traffic is the primary data mover. Signaling data is minimal compared to the continuous stream of audio data. Media traffic has a direct impact on voice quality and the user experience.

In a typical setup without media optimization, audio packets are sent from the SBC to the Microsoft Teams platform and then routed to the Teams endpoint. If the user is within the company's network, the media stream must cross the firewall twice: once from the SBC to Office 365 and again from Office 365 to the user. This process consumes additional bandwidth and increases the packet transmission time.

When the Microsoft Teams endpoint can directly connect to the SBC's external IP address, the call can utilize Media Bypass. With Media Bypass, audio data flows directly between the Teams endpoint and the SBC, avoiding the firewall and optimizing routing. Furthermore, you can enhance network performance by prioritizing Microsoft Teams audio data through Quality of Service (QoS) settings.

You can also configure the SBC to provide an internal network adapter to use for Media Bypass. In that case, the media traffic between the SBC and the Teams client stays in the internal network.

Note In all Media Bypass scenarios, signaling traffic is still sent to the Microsoft Teams platform in the cloud (as shown in Figure 5-8).

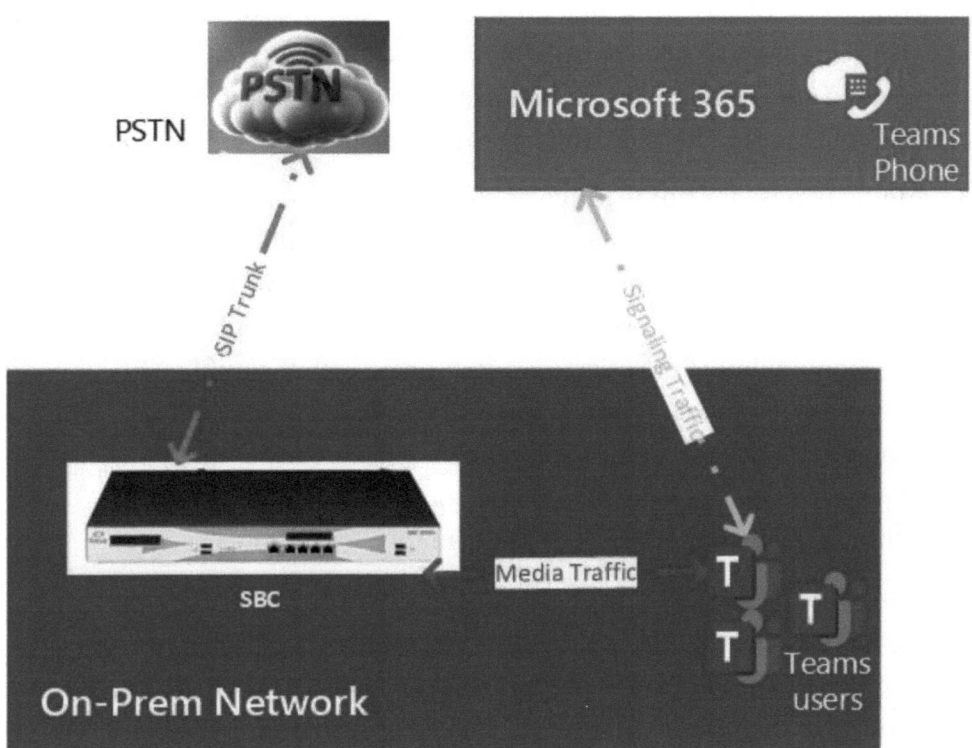

Figure 5-8. Media traffic and signaling traffic split in Media Bypass

LMO supports various network topologies and local telephony setups, keeping media local within corporate network subnets and allowing media streams even behind firewalls.

- **Local media optimization with centralized SBC for branch offices**: In this setup, branch offices use Media Bypass with a centralized SBC located in the datacenter. Different phone number ranges for the offices terminate at this single SBC. The SBC handles routing between branch office users and the Microsoft Teams platform, optimizing media flow and reducing firewall traversal.

- **Local media optimization with proxy SBC**: This scenario involves implementing a Proxy SBC in the main datacenter alongside local SBCs at branch sites. The Proxy SBC manages central communication with the Microsoft Teams platform, while local SBCs handle PSTN connections. Calls are routed through the Proxy SBC to Teams and vice versa. This setup is beneficial when a centralized SBC isn't feasible due to regulatory or technical constraints, requiring only one SBC instance to interface with Microsoft Teams.

- **Media bypass for home office and mobile users**: Media Bypass and Local Media Optimization can also benefit home office and mobile users. Microsoft Transport Relay servers, located in worldwide datacenters, facilitate optimized audio data transmission. By allowing the Teams subnet networks to communicate with the public SBC IP address, audio data from home users is routed to the nearest Transport Relay server, which then connects directly to the SBC. This approach minimizes the path length, optimizing audio packet runtime and enhancing media performance for remote users.

Teams clients require a matching network site for trusted IPs.

To set up Media Bypass and Local Media Optimization, you first need to verify whether your SBC's current firmware supports these features. Next, configure your network topology in the TAC to ensure the Teams platform understands your network setup. You can enable or disable Media Bypass using two modes: Always Bypass or Local Only.

- **Always Bypass**: Media flows through the local downstream SBC's internal IP regardless of the user's exact location.

- **Only for Local Users**: Media flows directly to the local downstream SBC's internal IP only when the user is in the same branch office.

You can enable the Media Bypass modes using PowerShell, for example, to enable the previously configured SBC to the Always Bypass mode:

```
Set-CsOnlinePSTNGateway -Identity SBC_name.customdomain.custom -BypassMode Always
```

5.5.3 Configure Trunk Translation Rules

Microsoft Teams Direct Routing trunk translations rules enable you to adjust caller and called numbers at the trunk level. Some possible scenarios include the following:

- Using localized numbers without the country code.
- Converting all caller line IDs to the office number

Number Translation Rules support the following:

- **Inbound calls**: Calls from a PSTN endpoint (caller) to a Teams client (callee)
- **Outbound calls**: Calls from a Teams client (caller) to a PSTN endpoint (callee)

The policy is implemented at the SBC level. Multiple translation rules can be assigned to an SBC, and these rules are applied sequentially based on their order as listed in PowerShell. Additionally, you have the flexibility to reorder the rules within the policy.

These are the PowerShell commands to use:

- New-CsTeamsTranslationRule
- Set-CsTeamsTranslationRule
- Get-CsTeamsTranslationRule
- Remove-CsTeamsTranslationRule

For example, let's create a translation rule that converts a dialed number starting with 020 (London area code) to the E.164 format.

```
New-CsTeamsTranslationRule -Identity "LondonRule"
-Pattern "^\+44(20)(\d{8})$" -Translation "+4420$2"
-Description "Translate London numbers to the E.164"
```

You can update the translation rule (for example, change the description) using the Set-CsTeamsTranslationRule command.

```
Set-CsTeamsTranslationRule -Identity "LondonRule"
-Description "Updated rule for translating London
numbers"
```

To apply the translation rules to an SBC, use the `Set-CsOnlinePSTNGateway` command, as in the following example:

```
Set-CsOnlinePSTNGateway -Identity SBC_name.customdomain.
custom -InboundTeamsNumberTranslationRules "LondonRule"
-OutboundTeamsNumberTranslationRules "LondonRule"
```

To remove the translation rules, the command used will be the same, with the `$null` value.

```
Set-CsOnlinePSTNGateway -Identity SBC_name.customdomain.
custom -InboundTeamsNumberTranslationRules $null
-OutboundTeamsNumberTranslationRules $null
```

5.5.4 Configure On-Network Conferencing for Direct Routing

On-network conferencing allows organizations to direct inbound and outbound audio conferencing calls to Microsoft dial-in numbers using Direct Routing. This feature is designed exclusively for Microsoft dial-in numbers and does not accommodate third-party dial-in numbers or outbound PSTN calls from the Microsoft Audio Conferencing Bridge.

To enable on-network conferencing, the requirements are as follows:

- Ensure all users enabled for audio conferencing use Teams for all meetings.
- Assign audio conferencing licenses to all users using on-network conferencing.
- Set up the audio conferencing service.
- Set up your session border controller (SBC) for Direct Routing.

Service numbers can be found in the Teams admin center or using the `Get-CsOnline DialInConferencingBridge` PowerShell cmdlet.

Here's how to route dial-out calls:

- Create PSTN usages.
- Configure voice routes.

- Create audio conferencing voice routing policies.

  New-CsOnlineAudioConferencingRoutingPolicy "Policy 1" -OnlinePstnUsages "United Kingdom"

- Assign policies to users.

  Grant-CsOnlineAudioConferencingRoutingPolicy -Identity "<User Identity>" -PolicyName "Policy 1"

5.5.5 Configure an SBA

The concept of survivable branch appliance (SBA) for Direct Routing was introduced in Section 5.1.3.

Microsoft provides the SBA as a distributable code to SBC vendors, which integrate it into their firmware or offer it as a stand-alone package. The SBA can operate either on a separate virtual machine (VM) or on dedicated hardware.

These are the prerequisites for SBA deployment:

- Obtain the latest firmware from the SBC vendor.

- The SBC must be configured for Media Bypass (see Section 5.5.2).

- TLS 1.2 must be enabled in the operating system of the virtual machine hosting the SBA.

- Firewall configuration:

  - **Port 3443, 4444, and 8443**: These ports are used by the Microsoft SBA Server to communicate with the Teams client and should be allowed on the firewall.

  - **Port 5061 (or configured port on the SBC)**: This port is used by the Microsoft SBA Server to communicate with the SBC and should be allowed on the firewall.

  - **UDP port 123**: This port is used by the Microsoft SBA Server to communicate with the NTP server and should be allowed on the firewall.

  - **Port 443**: This port is used by the Microsoft SBA Server to communicate with Microsoft 365 and should be allowed on the firewall.

- Defining Azure IP ranges and service tags:
  - Follow the guidelines described at https://www.microsoft.com/download/details.aspx?id=56519.

SBA is supported on the following Microsoft Teams clients: Microsoft Teams Windows desktop, Microsoft Teams macOS desktop, Teams for Mobile, and Teams Phones.

All configuration for the SBA feature is done using Teams PowerShell cmdlets.

For example, let's assume you want to configure the SBA with the FQDN sba.customdomain.custom using PowerShell.

1. Create the SBA.
   - `New-CsTeamsSurvivableBranchAppliance -Fqdn sba.customdomain.custom -Description "Custom Domain SBA"`

2. Create the Teams branch survivability policy.
   - `New-CsTeamsSurvivableBranchAppliancePolicy -Identity CustomPolicy -BranchApplianceFqdns "sba.customdomain.custom"`

3. Modify the SBA policy.
   - Add an SBA to a policy:
     - `Set-CsTeamsSurvivableBranchAppliancePolicy -Identity CustomPolicy -BranchApplianceFqdns @{add="sba.customdomain.custom"}`

4. Assign the policy to a user.
   - `Grant-CsTeamsSurvivableBranchAppliancePolicy -PolicyName CustomPolicy -Identity adelev@M365x07896792.onmicrosoft.com`

5. Register an application for the SBA with Microsoft Entra ID.
   - To enable different SBAs in your tenant to read the required data from Microsoft 365, you need to register an application with Microsoft Entra ID.

- Register the Application (https://docs.microsoft.com/en-us/azure/active-directory/develop/quickstart-register-app)

- Set the Implicit Grant Tokens: Access tokens and ID tokens should be selected.

- Set the API Permissions: Add Skype and Teams Tenant Admin Access under application permissions with application_access_custom_sba_appliance.

- Create the client secret: Create a client secret and copy it immediately after creation. It should have a description and an expiration period.

5.6 Knowledge Check

Question 1:

What are the key benefits of using a cloud-based SBC for Direct Routing in Microsoft Teams?

1. Complete control over hardware and network.
2. Scalability and flexibility to adapt to call volume changes.
3. Performance reliability with reduced latency.
4. Cost-effectiveness by reducing hardware investments.
5. Global reach with enhanced connectivity.

Question 2:

Which steps are required to configure an SBA for Direct Routing?

1. Obtain the latest firmware from the SBC vendor.
2. Configure the SBC with a Calling Plan.
3. Enable TLS 1.0 in the operating system.
4. Allow specific firewall ports for SBA communication.
5. Set up Azure IP ranges and service tags.

CHAPTER 5   USING DIRECT ROUTING WITH TEAMS PHONE

Question 3:

What configurations are necessary for implementing Location-Based Routing (LBR) in Direct Routing?

1. Enable Teams users for LBR.
2. Define network site locations for users and PSTN gateways.
3. Verify routing settings for PSTN call transfers.
4. Apply LBR settings to conferencing scenarios.
5. Configure toll bypass restrictions based on geography.

Question 4:

Which features are supported by the Survivable Branch Appliance (SBA) for Direct Routing during an Internet outage?

1. Automatic switch to SBA by Teams clients.
2. Making and receiving PSTN calls via SBA.
3. Continuous support for ongoing calls.
4. Uploading call history (CDR) to the cloud post-restoration.
5. Full feature set of Teams services.

Question 5:

What are the primary functions of an SBC in Microsoft Teams Direct Routing?

1. Security and protocol conversion.
2. Call quality management.
3. Policy enforcement.
4. High availability and redundancy support.
5. Integration with traditional telephony systems.

Answers

Question 1: 2, 4, 5
Question 2: 1, 4, 5
Question 3: 1, 2, 3, 4
Question 4: 1, 2, 3, 4
Question 5: 1, 2, 3, 4, 5

CHAPTER 6

Configuring Teams Phone

To enable and manage Teams Phone effectively within your organization, policies are essential. The policies detailed in this chapter influence several key features, including how calls are routed, the presentation of the caller phone numbers during PSTN calls, and the management of incoming calls. Additionally, dynamic emergency calling completes the phone system by routing emergency calls based on the current location of the Teams client and enabling notifications to security personnel. In countries like the United States and Canada, stringent regulations on emergency call routing make configuring these settings particularly crucial.

In this chapter, the following required skills and exam topics are described:

Configure Teams Phone policies:

- Create a dial plan.
- Configure calling policies.
- Configure call park policies.
- Configure caller ID policies.
- Configure call hold policies for users.
- Configure outbound call restrictions.
- Configure inbound call blocking.
- Configure routing of unassigned numbers.
- Assign voice policies through policy packages.
- Configure compliance recording policies.

Configure dynamic emergency calling:

- Design dynamic emergency calling scenarios.
- Configure emergency calling locations.

CHAPTER 6   CONFIGURING TEAMS PHONE

- Configure emergency calling policies.
- Configure networks and locations (Location Information Service (LIS).
- Validate emergency address and emergency calling from Teams clients.
- Enable external location lookup model.

6.1 Configure Teams Phone Policies

Teams phone policies are configurations within Microsoft Teams that control how users interact with the calling features. These policies help manage and control call functionalities in an organization.

6.1.1 Teams Dial Plans

E.164 is an international standard that outlines a numbering plan for the PSTN. This standard specifies the general format for international telephone numbers, which are restricted to a maximum of 15 digits. The digit sequence is divided into a country code, consisting of 1 to 3 digits, and a subscriber number, which can be up to 12 digits long. Teams is engineered to manage only phone numbers that are correctly formatted respecting the E.164 standard. Dial plans are a set of normalization rules that modify the number dialed by a user to make them coherent with the E.164 standard. Normalization rules use Regular Expression Language to adjust the phone number.

Every Teams user can have only one assigned dial plan. There are two types of dial plans: service-scoped and tenant-scoped.

- **Service-scoped dial plans**: These are predefined for each country or region where Teams Phone is available. Users are automatically assigned the appropriate service country/region dial plan based on their usage location. These plans cannot be changed by administrators.
- **Tenant-scoped dial plans**: These are created by organizations to augment the existing service country/region dial plans. Tenant dial plans can be scoped at two levels:
    - **Tenant-scoped**: Applies to the entire organization
    - **User-scoped**: Applies to specific users

As Teams clients are provisioned, they receive an "effective dial plan," which is a combination of the service country/region dial plan and the relevant tenant-scoped dial plan.

To define a dial plan, go into the Teams admin center (TAC). Go to Voice and then "Dial plans." Select Add, and then enter a name and description for the dial plan. Under "Normalization rules," configure and associate one or more normalization rules for the dial plan (as shown in Figure 6-1).

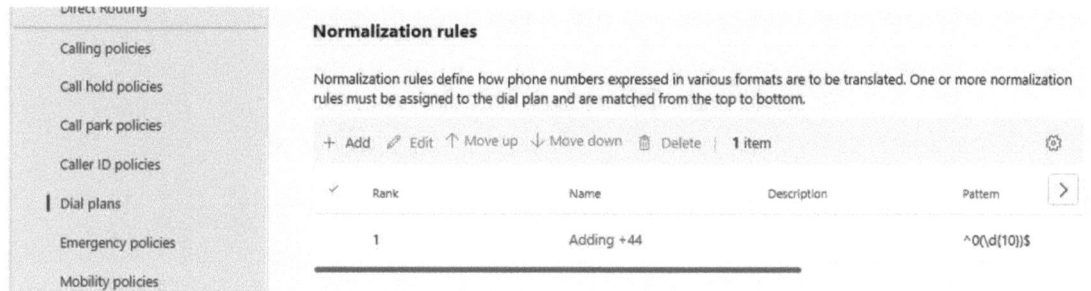

Figure 6-1. *Adding a dial plan*

Let's say, for an example, that a Teams user in the United Kingdom wants to make a call to a landline in the same country and he types 01234567890. The correct E.164 number is +441234567890. To get this output from the dialed number, we need to create a normalization rule like the next one:

Pattern: ^0(\d{10})$

- ^: Asserts the position at the start of the string.

- 0: Matches the leading zero, which is common in UK local numbers.

- (\d{10}): Captures exactly 10 digits following the initial zero. \d matches any digit (09), and {10} specifies exactly 10 digits.

- $: Asserts the position at the end of the string.

Translation: +44$1

- +44: This is the prefix we want to add, which is the international dialing code for the United Kingdom.

- $1: This refers to the first captured group from the pattern, which in this case is the 10-digit number following the leading zero.

Figure 6-2 shows how a normalization rule is added and tested in the TAC.

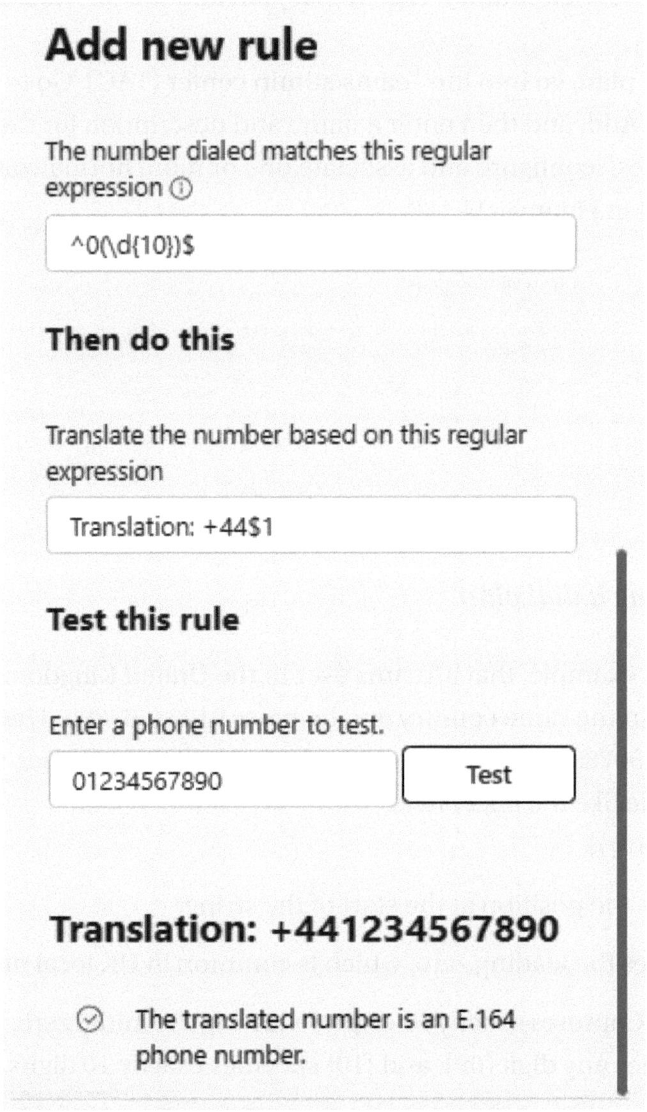

Add new rule

The number dialed matches this regular expression ⓘ

`^0(\d{10})$`

Then do this

Translate the number based on this regular expression

Translation: +44$1

Test this rule

Enter a phone number to test.

01234567890   [Test]

Translation: +441234567890

✓ The translated number is an E.164 phone number.

Figure 6-2. *Adding and testing a normalization rule*

Managing with PowerShell

To create a dial plan in Microsoft Teams with a normalization rule that adds the prefix +44 to UK numbers, you can use the following PowerShell commands. This example assumes that you have the Microsoft Teams PowerShell module installed and are connected to your Teams environment.

CHAPTER 6   CONFIGURING TEAMS PHONE

- Create a new normalization rule.

  ```
  $nr = NewCsVoiceNormalizationRule Identity Global/
  UKNormalizationRule Description "Add +44 prefix to UK
  numbers" Pattern '^0(\d{10})$' Translation '+44$1'
  ```

- Create a new tenant dial plan and add the normalization rule to it.

  ```
  NewCsTenantDialPlan Identity UKDialPlan Description
  "Dial Plan for UK" NormalizationRules @{add=$nr}
  SimpleName "UKDialPlan"
  ```

- To list all the dial plans in a tenant, you can use the `GetCsTenantDialPlan` PowerShell command. This command retrieves all the tenant dial plans that have been created in your Microsoft Teams environment.

6.1.2 Configure Calling Policies

In Microsoft Teams, calling policies control various features and functionalities related to calling and call forwarding for users. Here are the key features available in a Teams calling policy:

- **Make private calls**: Enable or disable all calling capabilities in Teams.
- **Cloud recording for calls**: Allow or prohibit recording of one-to-one Teams or PSTN calls.
- **Transcription**: Enable or disable post-call transcriptions.
- **Routing for PSTN calls**: Configure how calls are routed to the Public Switched Telephone Network (PSTN).
- **Routing for federated calls**: Determine how inbound federated calls are routed.
- **Call forwarding and simultaneous ring**: Set up call forwarding rules and simultaneous ringing to other users or external phone numbers.
- **Voicemail**: Manage voicemail settings for inbound calls, including enabling, disabling, or letting users decide.

- **Inbound calls can be routed to Call Groups**: Allow inbound calls to be routed to call groups.
- **Delegation**: Enable users to configure delegation for routing inbound calls to delegates and allowing delegates to make outbound calls on their behalf.
- **Prevent toll bypass**: Ensure calls are routed through the PSTN to avoid toll bypass.
- **Music on hold**: Enable or disable music played when a call is placed on hold.
- **Busy on busy**: Configure how incoming calls are handled when the user is already on a call.
- **Web PSTN calling**: Allow PSTN calls from the Teams web client.
- **Real-time captions**: Enable real-time captions for calls.
- **Spam filtering**: Enable spam call filtering.
- **SIP devices**: Allow users to use SIP devices for calling.
- **Popout for Incoming PSTN calls**: Configure a URL path to launch upon receiving an incoming PSTN call.

To manage calling policies in Microsoft Teams, you can use the TAC to go to Voice and then "Calling policies." To create a new policy, click Add. To edit an existing policy, select the policy you want to modify and click Edit.

Managing with PowerShell

The following are the main commands for calling policies in PowerShell:

- `NewCsTeamsCallingPolicy`
- `SetCsTeamsCallingPolicy`
- `GetCsTeamsCallingPolicy`
- `GrantCsTeamsCallingPolicy`
- `RemoveCsTeamsCallingPolicy`

Here are examples of how to use each of the PowerShell commands for managing Teams calling policies:

- NewCsTeamsCallingPolicy: This command creates a new Teams calling policy. The following example creates a new calling policy named CustomCallingPolicy with private calling, call groups, delegation enabled, and voicemail settings that users can override:

    NewCsTeamsCallingPolicy Identity "CustomCallingPolicy" AllowPrivateCalling $true AllowCallGroups $true AllowDelegation $true AllowVoicemail "UserOverride" Description "Custom calling policy for the organization"

- SetCsTeamsCallingPolicy: This command modifies an existing Teams calling policy. The following example modifies the CustomCallingPolicy to disable call groups and updates the description:

    SetCsTeamsCallingPolicy Identity "CustomCallingPolicy" AllowCallGroups $false Description "Updated policy without call groups"

- GetCsTeamsCallingPolicy: This command retrieves information about existing Teams calling.

- GrantCsTeamsCallingPolicy: This command assigns a specific Teams calling policy to a user. The following example assigns the CustomCallingPolicy to the user with the email adelev@m365x07896792.onmicrosoft.com:

    GrantCsTeamsCallingPolicy Identity "adelev@m365x07896792.onmicrosoft.com" PolicyName "CustomCallingPolicy"

- RemoveCsTeamsCallingPolicy: This command removes a specific Teams calling policy. The following example removes CustomCallingPolicy from the tenant:

    RemoveCsTeamsCallingPolicy Identity "CustomCallingPolicy"

CHAPTER 6 CONFIGURING TEAMS PHONE

6.1.3 Configure Call Park Policies

Call Park and Retrieve in Microsoft Teams allows users to place a call on hold, generating a unique code for retrieval. To use call park and retrieve, users must be Enterprise Voice users and be included in a call park policy. The parameters for a call park policy are shown in Figure 6-3.

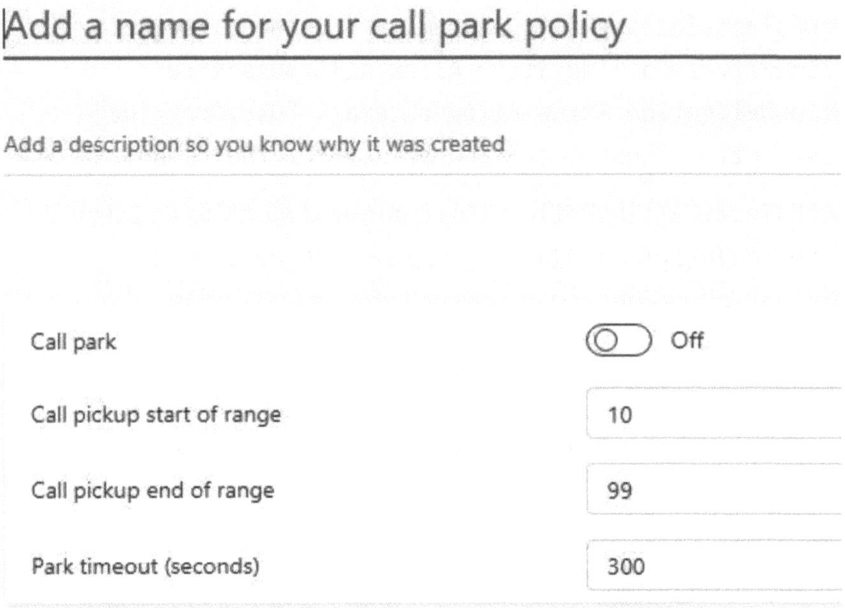

Figure 6-3. Settings in a call park policy

- **Call Pickup Range**: The default range is 10–99 and is customizable between 10–9999.

- **Timeout Setting**: This determines how long (120–1800 seconds, default 300 seconds) to wait before calling back when a parked call isn't picked up.

To set up and manage Call Park and Retrieve in the TAC, go to the left navigation pane and select Voice and then "Call Park policies."

Managing with PowerShell

The main commands to manage Call Park policies in PowerShell are:

- `NewCsTeamsCallParkPolicy`
- `SetCsTeamsCallParkPolicy`
- `GetCsTeamsCallParkPolicy`
- `RemoveCsTeamsCallParkPolicy`
- `GrantCsTeamsCallParkPolicy`

To create a new call park policy, use the `NewCsTeamsCallParkPolicy` cmdlet.
`NewCsTeamsCallParkPolicy Identity "CustomCallParkPolicy" Description "Custom Call Park Policy for the Organization" AllowCallPark $true CallParkTimeoutSeconds 300 PickupRangeStart 10 PickupRangeEnd 99`

This example creates a new call park policy named CustomCallParkPolicy with a timeout of 300 seconds and a pickup range from 10 to 99.

To modify an existing call park policy, use the `SetCsTeamsCallParkPolicy` cmdlet.
`SetCsTeamsCallParkPolicy Identity "CustomCallParkPolicy" CallParkTimeoutSeconds 600 PickupRangeStart 100 PickupRangeEnd 199`

This example modifies the CustomCallParkPolicy to set the timeout to 600 seconds and change the pickup range to 100199.

To remove a call park policy, use the `RemoveCsTeamsCallParkPolicy` cmdlet.
`RemoveCsTeamsCallParkPolicy Identity "CustomCallParkPolicy"`
This example removes the `CustomCallParkPolicy` from your tenant.

6.1.4 Configure Caller ID Policies

Implementing and managing caller ID policies in Microsoft Teams is important to maintain a professional image, ensuring privacy and security. The parameters available in a Caller ID policy are shown in Figure 6-4.

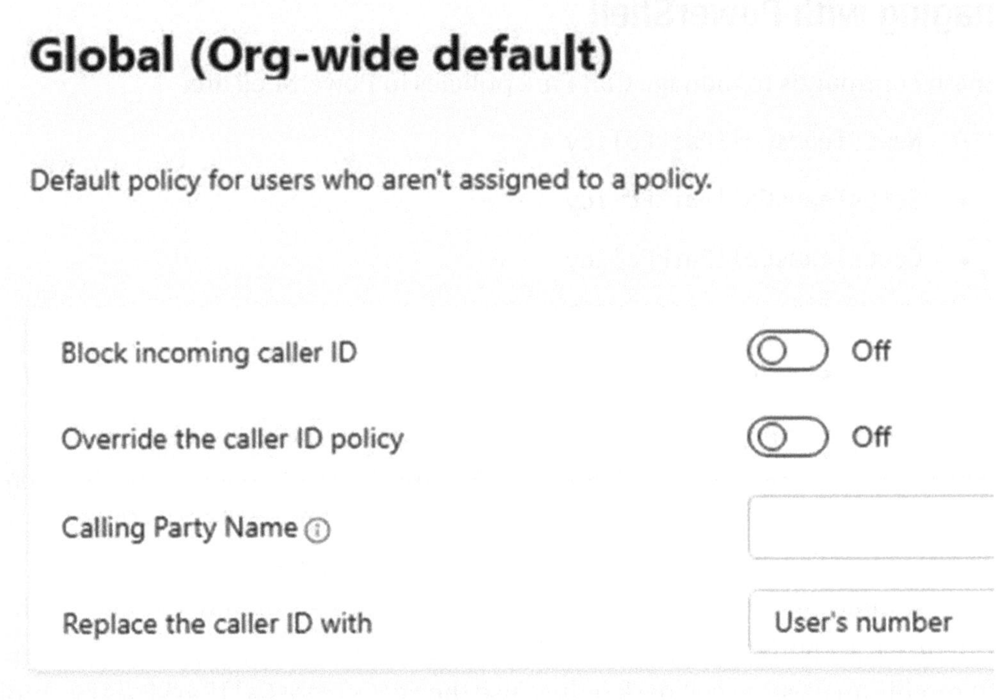

Global (Org-wide default)

Default policy for users who aren't assigned to a policy.

Block incoming caller ID	Off
Override the caller ID policy	Off
Calling Party Name ⓘ	
Replace the caller ID with	User's number

Figure 6-4. *Caller ID policy parameters*

Caller ID comprises two main components:

- **Calling line ID (CLID)**: The phone number displayed by the Public Switched Telephone Network (PSTN) as the caller's identity

- **Calling party name (CNAM)**: The name shown alongside the phone number, which could be a company's name, a user's name, or Anonymous.

For outbound PSTN caller ID in Microsoft Teams, the following options are available:

- **Default User Number**: The phone number assigned to the user

- **Anonymous**: Hides the user's PSTN number

- **Substitute Phone Number**: Can be either of the following:

- A number assigned to a resource account used by a Teams auto attendant or call queue through Operator Connect or Direct Routing.

- A service or toll-free number from the Calling Plans inventory assigned to a resource account for a Teams Auto attendant or Call queue.
  - **Calling Party Name (CNAM)**: The displays a custom name alongside the number (up to 200 characters, though downstream systems may support fewer).
  - **End User Control**: The `EnableUserOverride` parameter allows users to override the caller ID policy, e.g., setting the caller ID to Anonymous.
  - **Restrictions**: Certain phone numbers cannot be assigned as the outbound caller ID, including:
    - Userclassified numbers in Calling Plan or Operator Connect.
    - Onpremises numbers through Direct Routing assigned to a user.
  - **Skype for Business Server onpremises numbers:**

    Inbound Caller ID Options: Teams Phone shows the incoming external phone number as the caller ID. If the number matches a user or contact in Microsoft Entra ID or personal contacts, that information is displayed. If not, the telco-provided display name is shown if available.

    Block Incoming Caller ID: This setting blocks the caller ID on incoming PSTN calls, showing the call as Anonymous. This setting can be enabled but is not available to end users on the settings page.

The policies are managed in the TAC going to Voice and then "Caller ID policies" in the left navigation pane.

Managing with PowerShell

The following are the main commands to manage Caller ID policies in PowerShell:
- `NewCsCallingLineIdentity`
- `SetCsCallingLineIdentity`
- `RemoveCsCallingLineIdentity`

CHAPTER 6 CONFIGURING TEAMS PHONE

- GetCsCallingLineIdentity
- GrantCsCallingLineIdentity

Here are examples of how to use each of the PowerShell commands:

- NewCsCallingLineIdentity: This command creates a new Caller ID policy.

    NewCsCallingLineIdentity Identity "CustomCallerIDPolicy" CallingIDSubstitute Resource Description "Custom Caller ID Policy for the Organization" EnableUserOverride $true ResourceAccount ef50c30791414f14baf6055f452a31fe

    The command creates a new Caller ID policy in Microsoft Teams. This policy configures outbound calls to display the phone number of a specified resource account instead of the individual user's number. It also allows users to override the Caller ID settings if needed.

- SetCsCallingLineIdentity: This command modifies an existing Caller ID policy.

    SetCsCallingLineIdentity Identity "CustomCallerIDPolicy" CompanyName "New Company Name" EnableUserOverride $false

    This example modifies an existing Caller ID policy named CustomCallerIDPolicy in Microsoft Teams. It updates the company name displayed in the caller ID to New Company Name and disables the ability for users to override the Caller ID settings. RemoveCsCallingLineIdentity.

- GrantCsCallingLineIdentity: This command assigns a specific Caller ID policy to a user.

    GrantCsCallingLineIdentity Identity "adelev@m365x07896792.onmicrosoft.com" PolicyName "CustomCallerIDPolicy"

    This example assigns the CustomCallerIDPolicy to the user adelev@m365x07896792.onmicrosoft.com.

6.1.5 Configure Call Hold Policies for Users

A call hold policy in Microsoft Teams is a set of configurations that define how calls are managed when they are placed on hold. This includes what the person on hold experiences, such as whether they hear music, an announcement, or silence. The policies are available in the TAC, selecting Voice and then "Call hold policies" (see Figure 6-5).

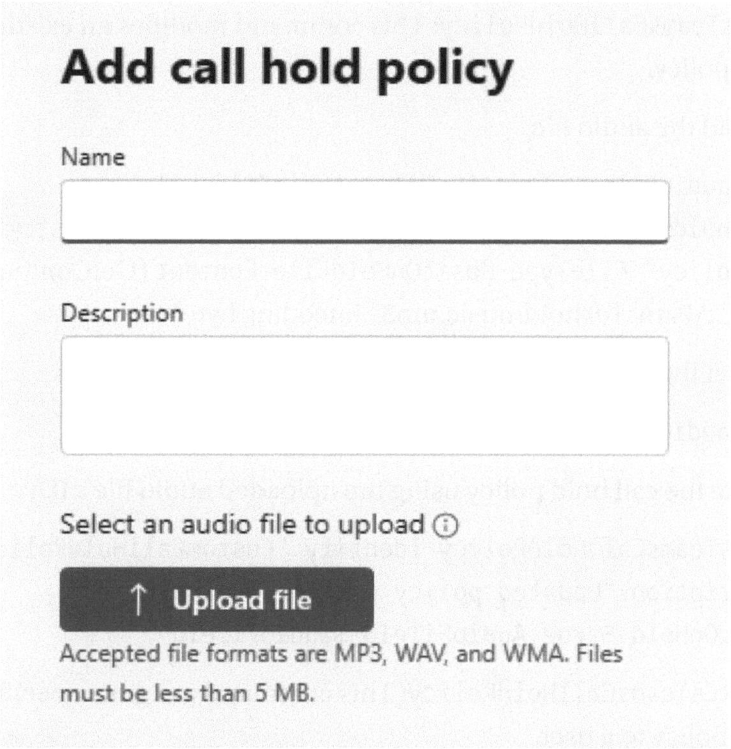

Figure 6-5. Configuring a call hold policy

Managing with PowerShell

The following are the main commands to manage call hold policies in PowerShell:

- `NewCsCallingLineIdentity`
- `SetCsCallingLineIdentity`
- `RemoveCsCallingLineIdentity`

- GetCsCallingLineIdentity
- GrantCsCallingLineIdentity

Here are some examples of how to use PowerShell commands for managing call hold policies in Microsoft Teams:

- GetCsTeamsCallHoldPolicy: This command retrieves information about existing call hold policies.
- SetCsTeamsCallHoldPolicy: This command modifies an existing call hold policy.
- Upload the audio file
  - $audioFile = ImportCsOnlineAudioFile FileName "holdmusic.mp3" Description "Hold music for custom policy" FileType MusicOnHoldFile Content (GetContent Path "C:\Path\To\holdmusic.mp3" Encoding byte)
- Extract the FileId
  - $audioFileId = $audioFile.Id
- Create the call hold policy using the uploaded audio file's ID:

  NewCsTeamsCallHoldPolicy Identity "CustomCallHoldPolicy" Description "Updated policy with new description" MusicOnHold $true AudioFileId $audioFileId

- GrantCsTeamsCallHoldPolicy: This command assigns a specific call hold policy to a user.

  GrantCsTeamsCallHoldPolicy Identity "adelev@m365x07896792.onmicrosoft.com" PolicyName "CustomCallHoldPolicy"

  This example assigns the CustomCallHoldPolicy to the user "adelev@m365x07896792.onmicrosoft.com".

- RemoveCsTeamsCallHoldPolicy: This command removes a specified call hold policy.

    RemoveCsTeamsCallHoldPolicy Identity "CustomCallHoldPolicy"

    This example removes the CustomCallHoldPolicy from your tenant.

6.1.6 Configure Outbound Call Restrictions

Outbound call restrictions are used to manage and restrict the types of audio conferencing and end-user Public Switched Telephone Network (PSTN) calls within your organization. There are two types of outbound call restrictions (by default, these controls are set to allow both international and domestic outbound calls).

- **Audio conferencing PSTN calls**: Limits the types of outbound calls that can be made from meetings organized by a user. The options include the following:
    - Any destination (default)
    - In the same country or region as the organizer
    - Zone A countries or regions only
    - Don't allow
- **Enduser PSTN calls**: Restricts the types of calls that individual users can make. The options include the following:
    - International and domestic (default)
    - Domestic
    - None

For the audio conferencing call restrictions, the settings are available in the TAC. Go to Users and then Manage Users and select one of the users. The Audio Conferencing settings will be on the right of the Account tab. If you click Edit, you will have access to the drop-down menu in Figure 6-6.

CHAPTER 6 CONFIGURING TEAMS PHONE

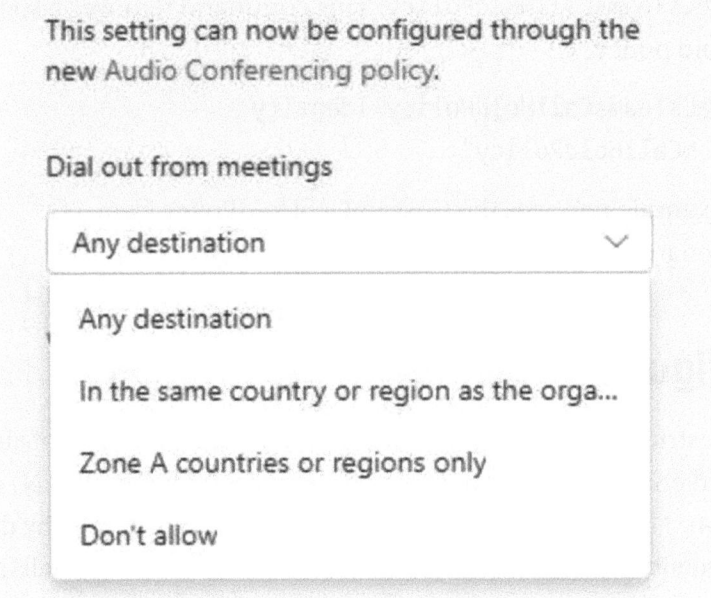

Figure 6-6. *Conferencing call restrictions in the user's settings*

That said, end-user PSTN calls restrictions are visible only from PowerShell. Also, it is not possible to create new policies or to edit the existing ones.

Managing with PowerShell

The following are the main commands to manage Outbound Call Restrictions policies in PowerShell:

- GetCsOnlineDialOutPolicy
- GrantCsDialoutPolicy

With the GetCsOnlineDialOutPolicy you can see a list of the available policies (see Table 6-1). The AllowPSTNConferencingDialOutType value is the one that restricts outbound calls from a meeting. The AllowPSTNConferencingDialOutType restricts the user's PSTN outgoing calls.

Table 6-1. *Outbound Call Restrictions Policies List*

Identity	AllowPSTNConferencingDialOutType	AllowPSTNOutboundCallingType
Global	InternationalAndDomestic	InternationalAndDomestic
DialoutCPCandPSTNInternational	InternationalAndDomestic	InternationalAndDomestic
DialoutCPCDomesticPSTNInternational	DomesticOnly	InternationalAndDomestic
DialoutCPCDisabledPSTNInternational	Disabled	InternationalAndDomestic
DialoutCPCInternationalPSTNDomestic	InternationalAndDomestic	DomesticOnly
DialoutCPCInternationalPSTNDisabled	InternationalAndDomestic	Disabled
DialoutCPCandPSTNDomestic	DomesticOnly	DomesticOnly
DialoutCPCDomesticPSTNDisabled	DomesticOnly	Disabled
DialoutCPCDisabledPSTNDomestic	Disabled	DomesticOnly
DialoutCPCandPSTNDisabled	Disabled	Disabled
DialoutCPCZoneAPSTNInternational	ZoneA	InternationalAndDomestic
DialoutCPCZoneAPSTNDomestic	ZoneA	DomesticOnly
DialoutCPCZoneAPSTNDisabled	ZoneA	Disabled

- `GrantCsTeamsCallingPolicy`: This command assigns an outbound call restrinctions policy to a user.

  `GrantCsTeamsCallingPolicy Identity "adelev@ m365x07896792.onmicrosoft.com" PolicyName "DialoutCPCZoneAPSTNDomestic"`

  This command ensures that the user `adelev@m365x07896792. onmicrosoft.com` will have the DialoutCPCZoneAPSTNDomestic policy applied, which restricts the type of outbound calls according to the policy settings.

6.1.7 Configure Inbound Call Blocking

All the available PSTN connectivity options for Teams support the capability to block inbound calls from a PSTN number. Administrators can create a list of number patterns and exceptions at the tenant level. Every incoming PSTN call's caller ID is checked against this list, and if a match is found, the call is rejected.

Inbound call blocking has the following features:

- **TenantLevel control**: The inbound call blocking feature is managed globally at the tenant level. Individual users cannot alter this list.

- **PSTN calls only**: This feature applies only to inbound calls originating from the PSTN.

- **User blocking**: While individual users cannot modify the global list, they can block PSTN calls directly through the Teams client. To block a PSTN number from the client, you have to select the call from your Teams client by going to Calls and then History. Click the call and select Block (see Figure 6-7).

CHAPTER 6 CONFIGURING TEAMS PHONE

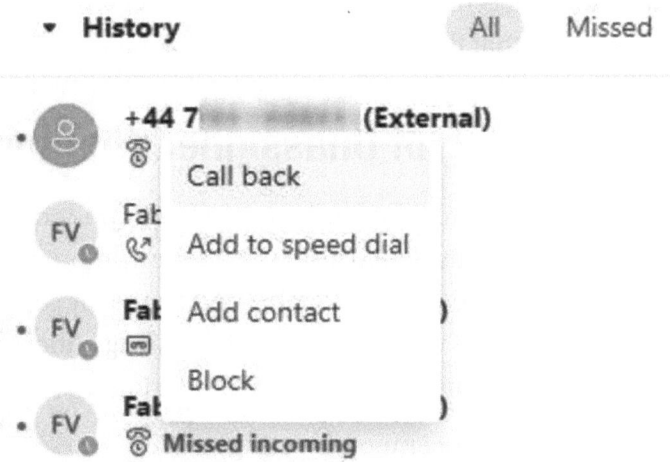

Figure 6-7. Blocking a PSTN number

Managing with PowerShell

The main commands to manage Inbound Call policies in PowerShell are divided in two categories, call blocking features and blocked number patterns.

The following commands are for managing the call blocking feature:

- GetCsTenantBlockedCallingNumbers
- SetCsTenantBlockedCallingNumbers

The following commands are for managing blocked number patterns:

- GetCsInboundBlockedNumberPattern
- NewCsInboundBlockedNumberPattern
- RemoveCsInboundBlockedNumberPattern
- SetCsInboundBlockedNumberPattern
- TestCsInboundBlockedNumberPattern

For example, to create a pattern that blocks all calls from +44123456789, you start by creating a pattern (based on regular expressions) like this:

```
NewCsInboundBlockedNumberPattern Name "BlockUKNumber"
Description "Blocks calls from +44123456789" Pattern
"^\+44123456789$" Enabled $true
```

CHAPTER 6   CONFIGURING TEAMS PHONE

Since inbound call blocking is managed at the tenant level and not directly assigned to individual users, make sure that the global setting for call blocking is enabled.

6.1.8 Configure Routing of Unassigned Numbers

Teams supports routing calls made to an unassigned number (phone numbers that are not currently allocated to a user or device) within your organization. Ensuring that calls to unassigned numbers are handled properly avoids dead ends for callers.

You can configure the routing of unassigned numbers using either the Teams admin center or PowerShell. These are some commonly used solutions:

- Route to a custom announcement (greeting)
- Route to the main switchboard (person in organization)
- Route to a user or resource account (voice application)

To set the configuration in the TAC, select Voice on the left, select Phone Numbers and then Routing Rules. To create a new rule, select "Add new rule." The configuration is executed in a screen like the one in Figure 6-8.

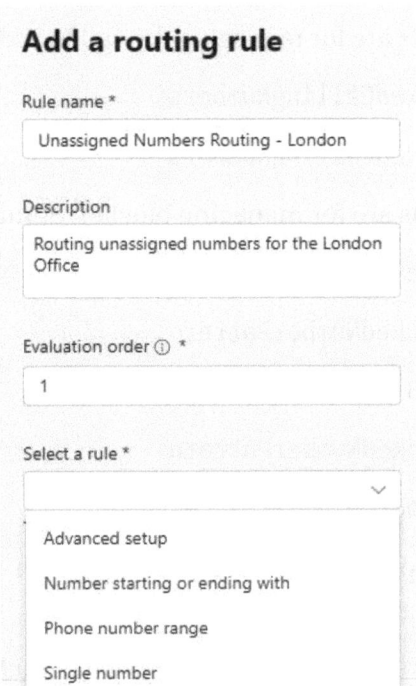

Figure 6-8. *Routing calls to unassigned numbers*

Selecting the advanced setup, you can use regular expressions to create a custom set of phone numbers.

Managing with PowerShell

The following are the main commands to manage Unassigned Numbers policies in PowerShell:

- NewCsTeamsUnassignedNumberTreatment
- GetCsTeamsUnassignedNumberTreatment
- SetCsTeamsUnassignedNumberTreatment
- RemoveCsTeamsUnassignedNumberTreatment

Let's assume you have an unassigned phone number in London (+4420123456789). You want to redirect the incoming calls to a resource account with the following configuration:

ObjectId: ef50c30791414f14baf6055f452a31fe

UserPrincipalName: TestRA@M365x07896792.onmicrosoft.com

The PowerShell to be used will be the following:

```
NewCsTeamsUnassignedNumberTreatment Identity
"RouteToTestRA" Pattern "^\+4420123456789$"
TargetType ResourceAccount Target
"ef50c30791414f14baf6055f452a31fe" Description "Route
calls to TestRA resource account"
```

The command provided will ensure that any calls made to the unassigned phone number will be routed to the resource account with the ObjectId ef50c30791414f14baf6055f452a31fe.

6.1.9 Assign Voice Policies Through Policy Packages

A policy package in Microsoft Teams is a set of policies and settings created to ease and streamline the process of managing policies for users who share similar roles within an organization. By using policy packages, administrators can ensure consistency and efficiency in how policies are applied across groups of users. A policy package bundles together various Teams policies such as messaging, meeting, and calling policies. These policies control features and behaviors in Teams, like who can start meetings, how messages are managed, and what calling features are available.

The policies within a package come with predefined settings tailored for specific roles. These settings are designed to meet the typical needs and responsibilities of those roles, ensuring that users have the appropriate permissions and capabilities.

The packages available in Teams at the moment of writing include the following:

- Education (higher education student)
- Education (primary school student)
- Education (secondary school student)
- Education (teacher)
- Education (primary school teacher using remote learning)
- Education (primary school student using remote learning)
- Frontline manager
- Frontline worker
- Healthcare clinical worker
- Healthcare information worker
- Healthcare patient room
- Public safety officer
- Small and medium business user (Business Voice)
- Small and medium business user (without Business Voice)

Note Custom user policy packages require a Teams Premium license.

To assign a policy package to one user, Go to "Manage users" in the TAC and select Users. Choose the user you want to assign the policy package to. On the user's page, select Policies and then click Edit next to "Policy package." In the Assign policy package pane, select the desired package and click Apply.

To assign a policy package to multiple users, go to "Policy packages" in the TAC. Select "Manage users"and then . In the "Manage users" pane, search for and add each user by the display name or username. Select Add for each user. Once all users are added, click Apply.

To assign a policy package to a group, go to "Policy packages" in the TAC. Select the "Group package assignment" tab. Add a group by clicking Add. In the "Assign policy package to a group" pane, so the following:

1. Search for and add the group.

2. Select the policy package.

3. Set the ranking for each policy type.

4. Click Apply (the screen used to assign policy packages to a group is shown in Figure 6-9).

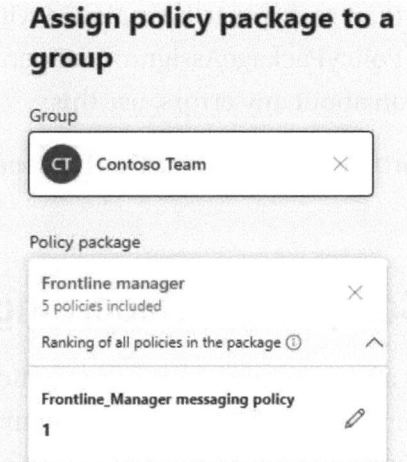

Figure 6-9. Assigning a policy package to a group

Managing with PowerShell

The following are the main commands to manage Policy Packages in PowerShell:

- NewCsBatchPolicyPackageAssignmentOperation
- GetCsBatchPolicyAssignmentOperation

For example, to apply the SmallMediumBusiness_BusinessVoice policy package to the user adelev@m365x07896792.onmicrosoft.com, you can use the NewCsBatchPolicyPackageAssignmentOperation cmdlet.

NewCsBatchPolicyAssignmentOperation Identity adelev@m365x07896792.onmicrosoft.com PolicyType TeamsVerticalPackagePolicy PolicyName SmallMediumBusiness_BusinessVoice OperationName "Assign_SMB_BusinessVoice_to_Adelev"

After running the command, you may want to check the status of the assignment operation.

```
# Get the OperationId from the assignment command output
$operationId = " 7b094c62c99346c68f4a6daa6323343a"
# Check the status of the batch assignment operation
GetCsBatchPolicyAssignmentOperation OperationId $operationId | fl
```

The $operationId value is an example to be replaced with the actual OperationId returned by the NewCsBatchPolicyPackageAssignmentOperation cmdlet.

To get detailed information about any errors, use this:

```
GetCsBatchPolicyAssignmentOperation OperationId $operationId | Select ExpandProperty UserState
```

6.1.10 Configure Compliance Recording Policies

To automatically record calls and meetings, Teams uses policy-based recording. Policy-based recording ensures compliance with corporate or regulatory requirements by capturing and retaining communications as needed.

Admin policies can determine when calls and meetings should be automatically recorded. Teams support integration with partner recording solutions, enhancing platform functionality, user experience, and administrative controls for recording, storing, and analyzing communications.

Teams supports different types of recording:

- Convenience (regular Teams recording)
  - **Initiator**: User
  - **Target**: Percall/meeting

- **Storage Owner**: User
- **Notification**: Required
- **Access Owner**: User
- **Retention Policy**: Optional
- Organizational (Compliance Recording)
  - **Initiator**: Admin (system)
  - **Target**: Peruser
  - **Storage Owner**: Compliance
  - **Notification**: Required
  - **Access Owner**: Compliance
  - **Retention Policy**: Mandatory

The user experience will include the following:

- **Visual Notifications**: Desktop/web, mobile (iOS/Android), Teams Phones, Teams Rooms
- **Audio Notifications**: SIP phones, Skype for Business, audio conferencing, PSTN callers

Managing with PowerShell

There are a few steps required to implement compliance recording policies. This example assumes that the application has the following parameters:

AcsResourceId:
ApplicationId: abc123456789def01234f2e1f609d511
DisplayName: M365x07896792 Compliance Recorder
ObjectId: 55491f4641b64df3b08ccb09c2b9134e
UserPrincipalName: recorder.bot@M365x07896792.OnMicrosoft.com

1. Create an application instance:

   ```
   NewCsOnlineApplicationInstance UserPrincipalName
   recorder.bot@M365x07896792.OnMicrosoft.com DisplayName
   ComplianceRecordingBotInstance ApplicationId
   abc123456789def01234f2e1f609d511
   ```

2. Sync the application instance:

   ```
   SyncCsOnlineApplicationInstance ObjectId
   55491f4641b64df3b08ccb09c2b9134e ApplicationId
   abc123456789def01234f2e1f609d511
   ```

3. Create a compliance recording policy:

   ```
   NewCsTeamsComplianceRecordingPolicy Identity
   TestComplianceRecordingPolicy Enabled $true Description
   "Test recording policy"
   ```

4. Set the compliance recording policy:

   ```
   SetCsTeamsComplianceRecordingPolicy
   Identity TestComplianceRecordingPolicy
   ComplianceRecordingApplications
   @(NewCsTeamsComplianceRecordingApplication
   Id 55491f4641b64df3b08ccb09c2b9134e Parent
   TestComplianceRecordingPolicy)
   ```

5. Assign the compliance recording policy to a user:

   ```
   GrantCsTeamsComplianceRecordingPolicy Identity
   adelev@m365x07896792.onmicrosoft.com PolicyName
   TestComplianceRecordingPolicy
   ```

6. Verify the policy assignment:

   ```
   GetCsOnlineUser Identity adelev@m365x07896792.
   onmicrosoft.com | select SipAddress, TenantId,
   TeamsComplianceRecordingPolicy | fl
   ```

6.2 Configure Dynamic Emergency Calling

6.2.1 Design Dynamic Emergency Calling Scenarios

Dynamic emergency calling in Microsoft Teams is designed to ensure that emergency calls are routed correctly and that accurate location information is provided to emergency services. This capability is critical in various scenarios where the user's location may change frequently. Here are the primary scenarios for dynamic emergency calling:

- Office buildings with multiple floors and zones

    - **Scenario**: Employees working in a multifloor office building or large campus.

    - **How it works**: Network elements like Ethernet switches, Wi-Fi access points, and subnets are mapped to specific locations within the building. When a user moves to a different floor or zone, their device connects to different network elements. The Teams client updates the user's location information dynamically based on the network connectivity.

- Remote work and hot desking

    - **Scenario**: Employees working remotely or using hot desks in different locations.

    - **How it works**: As remote workers or hot desking employees connect to different networks (home, coworking spaces, different offices), the Teams client sends location requests to the LIS. The LIS updates the user's current location based on the network they are connected to.

- Manufacturing and industrial sites

    - **Scenario**: Workers in large manufacturing plants or industrial sites with extensive network coverage.

    - **How it works**: Network elements such as Ethernet switches and Wi-Fi access points within the industrial site are mapped to specific emergency locations. The Teams client dynamically updates location information as workers move through different areas of the site.

6.2.2 Configure Emergency Calling Locations

Emergency locations allow emergency services to correctly identify the location of a caller during an emergency call. Regardless of the PSTN connectivity option, an emergency location may be assigned to a phone number.

You can add emergency locations for your organization using the TAC. In the left navigation, click Locations and then Emergency addresses. Then add a new location.

- Enter the location details.
    - Enter a name and description for the location.
    - Select the country or region and then enter the address.

For activating a phone number in Microsoft 365 in Belgium, France, Germany, Ireland, Netherlands, and Spain, the address set up in the emergency location must match the phone number's area code. This ensures compliance with local regulations and proper routing of emergency calls.

Managing with PowerShell

The following are the main commands to manage emergency calling locations in PowerShell:

- New-CsOnlineLisLocation
- Set-CsOnlineLisLocation
- Get-CsOnlineLisLocation
- Remove-CsOnlineLisLocation

For example, let's to create an emergency location for the Contoso HQ in London

```
New-CsOnlineLisLocation -CompanyName "Contoso"
-CivicAddressId 489d0130-2956-11ef-95ed-0df60e2a7b24
-Location "London HQ"
```

This command helps administrators define specific physical locations associated with network elements.

6.2.3 Configure Emergency Calling Policies

Microsoft Teams provides several policies to configure and manage emergency calling. These policies can be managed through the Microsoft Teams admin center or by using PowerShell.

- Emergency Call Routing Policy

  - This policy is specifically for Direct Routing and is used to configure how emergency calls are routed. It defines the emergency numbers, applies masks to these numbers if needed, and specifies the PSTN route for each number.

  - This policy can be assigned to individual users, network sites, or both.

- Emergency Calling Policy

  - This policy applies to Calling Plans, Operator Connect, Teams Phone Mobile, and Direct Routing. It configures the security desk notification experience when an emergency call is made, detailing who should be notified and how.

  - Security Desk Notification defines how and who to notify within the organization when an emergency call is placed.

Both policies are managed from the TAC in Voice under "Emergency policies." For emergency calling policy, do the following:

1. Enter a name and description for the policy.

2. Set the External location lookup mode to on to allow your end users to configure their emergency address when they are working from a network location outside the corporate network.

3. Emergency service disclaimer shows a banner to remind end users to confirm their emergency location.

4. Configure one or more emergency numbers.

CHAPTER 6 CONFIGURING TEAMS PHONE

5. Enter the emergency dial string that people in your organization will dial to contact emergency services. You are able to select how the notification is managed:

   - **Send notification only**: A Teams chat message is sent to the users and groups that you specify.

   - **Conferenced in but are muted**: A Teams chat message is sent to the users and groups that you specify. They can listen (but not participate) in the conversation between the caller and the PSAP operator.

   - **Conferenced in and are unmuted**: A Teams chat message is sent to the users and groups that you specify. They can unmute to listen and participate in the conversation between the caller and the PSAP operator.

Figure 6-10 shows the configuration screen.

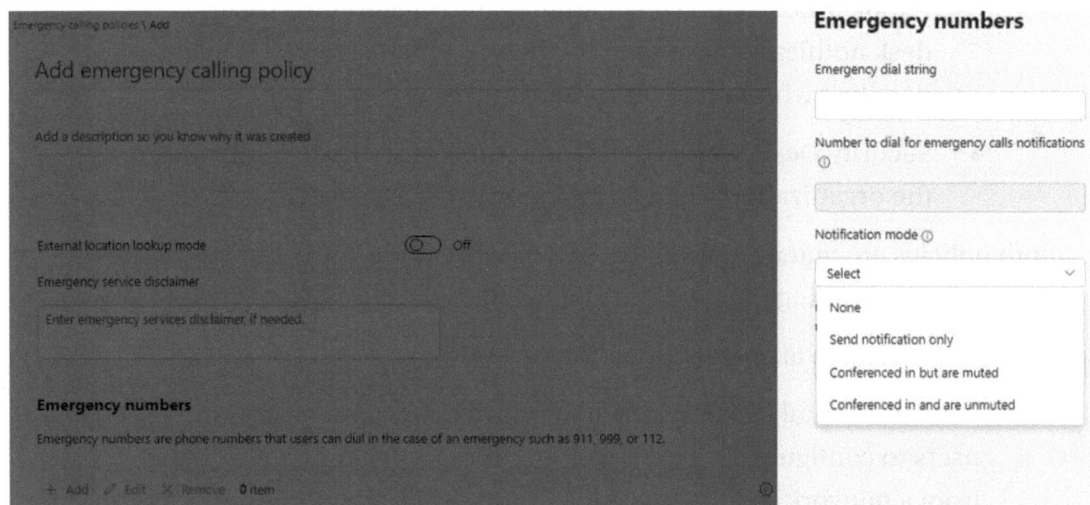

Figure 6-10. *Emergency calling policy and notification modes*

For emergency call routing policies:

1. Enter a name and description for the policy.

2. Turn on "Dynamic emergency calling" to enable dynamic emergency calling. Teams will retrieve policy and location information from the service and include that information as part of the emergency call.

3. Under Emergency numbers, click Add, and then do the following:

   - **Emergency dial string**: Enter the emergency dial string. This dial string indicates that a call is an emergency call, and the route pattern must match this dial string exactly.

   - **Emergency dial mask**: A dial mask is the number that you want to translate into the value of the emergency dial string.

   - **PSTN usage record**: PSTN usage record is used to determine which route is used to route emergency calls from users who are authorized to use them.

Managing with PowerShell

The following are the main commands to manage emergency calling policies in PowerShell:

- NewCsTeamsEmergencyCallingPolicy
- SetCsTeamsEmergencyCallingPolicy
- GrantCsTeamsEmergencyCallingPolicy
- NewCsTeamsEmergencyCallRoutingPolicy
- SetCsTeamsEmergencyCallRoutingPolicy
- Grant CsTeamsEmergencyCallRoutingPolicy

For example, let's add a new emergency calling policy named ECP2 for the emergency dial string 112. The policy includes notifications to the group security@contoso.com with a dialout number of +44123456789. The notification mode is set to conference with muted participants, and external location lookup is disabled. The extended notification for the emergency dial string 112 is added to the policy.

```
$en1 = NewCsTeamsEmergencyCallingExtendedNotification
EmergencyDialString "112"
```

```
NewCsTeamsEmergencyCallingPolicy Identity ECP2
Description "Test ECP2" NotificationGroup "adelev@
m365x07896792.onmicrosoft.com" NotificationDialOutNumber
"+441632960961" NotificationMode ConferenceMuted
ExternalLocationLookupMode Disabled
ExtendedNotifications @{add=$en1}
```

Let's create a new emergency call routing policy for the European emergency number 112, with an alternative dial mask of 999, and associate it with the specified PSTN usage. The policy is named EU_Test and allows enhanced emergency services.

```
$emergencyNumber = NewCsTeamsEmergencyNumber
EmergencyDialString "112" EmergencyDialMask "999"
OnlinePSTNUsage "EUPSTNUsage"

NewCsTeamsEmergencyCallRoutingPolicy Identity
"EU_Test" EmergencyNumbers @{add=$emergencyNumber}
AllowEnhancedEmergencyServices $true Description
"Emergency routing policy for EU"
```

6.2.4 Configure Networks and Locations (Location Information Service)

The network administrator configures network settings and the location information service (LIS) to map network elements (such as subnets, switches, and wireless access points) to specific emergency addresses.

Teams clients send network connectivity information to the LIS at startup, periodically, and whenever a network change is detected.

The key components are sites, subnets, and trusted IP addresses.

- **Sites**: These represent collections of subnets and are used exclusively for dynamic policy assignment to users.

- **Subnets**: These define specific network segments within a site.

- **Trusted IP addresses**: These consist of the collection of external IP addresses for the enterprise network. The dynamic policy or location determination based on the endpoint's IP address will occur only if the user's external IP address matches an address in the trusted IP addresses list.

CHAPTER 6 CONFIGURING TEAMS PHONE

To configure the network information for emergency calling, go to the TAC and select Locations. Click "Networks & locations." You can select Subnets, "WiFi access points," Switches, or Ports (see Figure 6-11).

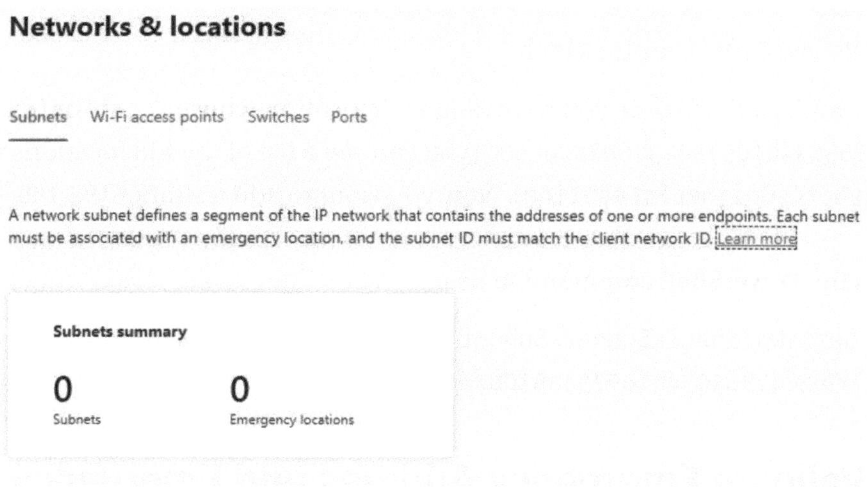

Figure 6-11. Adding network locations

If you add a subnet, for example, you can map it to an emergency location that you have already defined (or define a new one). A similar process is used to add trusted IP addresses, select Locations, and then click "Network topology." Here you can add network sites and trusted IPs.

Managing with PowerShell

The following are the main commands to manage policy packages in PowerShell:

- GetCsOnlineLisSubnet
- SetCsOnlineLisSubnet
- RemoveCsOnlineLisSubnet
- GetCsOnlineLisPort
- SetCsOnlineLisPort
- RemoveCsOnlineLisPort
- GetCsOnlineLisWirelessAccessPoint
- SetCsOnlineLisWirelessAccessPoint

- RemoveCsOnlineLisWirelessAccessPoint
- GetCsOnlineLisSwitch
- SetCsOnlineLisSwitch
- RemoveCsOnlineLisSwitch

For example, let's assume you have defined a location whose LocationId is "99bec42865034bfd9754a910b2dcac50" (you can see a list of the LIS locations with the command GetCsOnlineLisLocation). Now you want to add a subnet 192.168.10.0 to that location.

This is the PowerShell command to use:

- SetCsOnlineLisSubnet Subnet 192.168.10.0 LocationId 99bec42865034bfd9754a910b2dcac50

6.2.5 Validate Emergency Address and Emergency Calling from Teams Clients

To verify that an emergency calling policy has been applied correctly, you can check the user's Teams client. For example, a policy that enables location lookup mode and a disclaimer will show the behavior in Figure 6-12 in the dial pad.

CHAPTER 6 CONFIGURING TEAMS PHONE

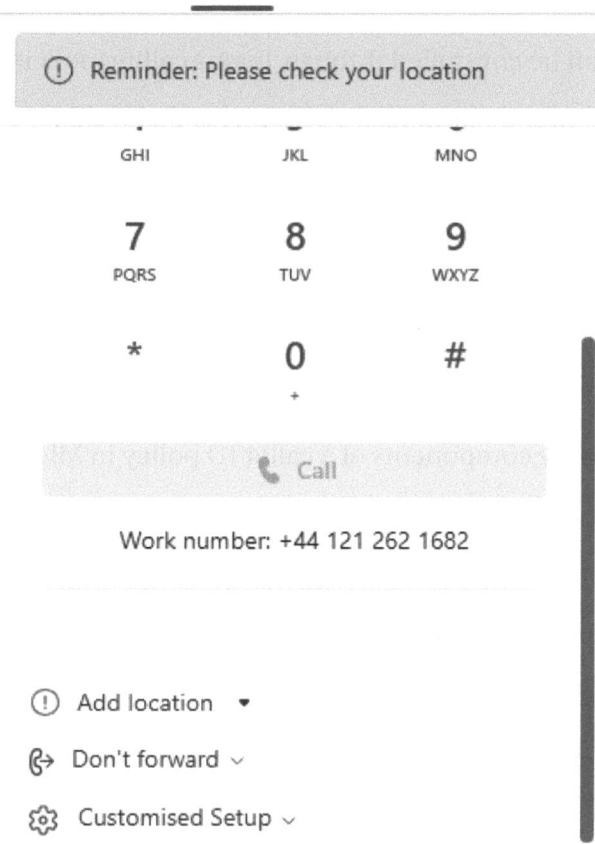

Figure 6-12. Emergency calling policies user experience

6.2.6 Knowledge Check

Question 1:

What is the format for international telephone numbers as per the E.164 standard?

1. A maximum of 15 digits.

2. A country code of one to three digits.

3. A subscriber number of a maximum of 12 digits.

4. Must include a + sign at the beginning.

5. A country code of exactly two digits.

CHAPTER 6   CONFIGURING TEAMS PHONE

Question 2:
Which features can be controlled through Teams calling policies?

1. Allow or prohibit recording of 1:1 Teams or PSTN calls.
2. Enable or disable real-time captions.
3. Manage call forwarding rules and simultaneous ringing.
4. Control how inbound federated calls are routed.
5. Customize call hold experience for Teams clients.

Question 3:
What are the primary components of a caller ID policy in Microsoft Teams?

1. Calling line ID (CLID).
2. Calling party name (CNAM).
3. Caller location information.
4. Call routing details.
5. Spam call filtering settings.

Question 4:
What is required to manage emergency calling locations in Microsoft Teams?

1. Define specific physical locations associated with network elements.
2. Ensure the emergency location address matches the phone number's area code.
3. Assign an emergency location to a phone number.
4. Enable external location lookup mode.
5. Integrate with third-party location services.

Question 5:

Which commands are used to manage unassigned number treatments in Microsoft Teams using PowerShell?

1. `New-CsTeamsUnassignedNumberTreatment`
2. `Get-CsTeamsUnassignedNumberTreatment`
3. `Set-CsTeamsUnassignedNumberTreatment`
4. `Remove-CsTeamsUnassignedNumberTreatment`
5. `Test-CsTeamsUnassignedNumberTreatment`

Answers

Question 1: 1, 2, 3
Question 2: 1, 2, 3, 4
Question 3: 1, 2
Question 4: 1, 2, 3
Question 5: 1, 2, 3, 4

CHAPTER 7

Call Queues, Auto Attendants, and Users

In this chapter, we will talk about features that are essential for completing the services offered by Microsoft Teams Phone. Configuring auto attendants, call queues, and resource accounts ensures efficient call routing and management and improves customer service and operational efficiency. Customizing features like Music on Hold and caller ID adds branding to the service. Proper user and policy management for the additional phone features like dial-out conferencing, on top of what we have already seen, ensures that the Microsoft Teams services are tailored on the specific usages.

In this chapter, the following required skills and exam topics are described:

Configure auto attendants and call queues:

- Design call flows for auto attendants and call queues.
- Configure auto attendants and call queues.
- Deploy channel-based call queues.
- Configure resource accounts.
- Assign licenses to resource accounts.
- Assign phone number to resource accounts.
- Assign a resource account to an auto attendant or call queue.
- Configure Microsoft 365 groups for voicemail.
- Interpret call queue conference mode.
- Interpret call queue routing methods.
- Configure holidays for auto attendants.

- Configure custom Music on Hold (MoH).
- Assign a dynamic caller ID policy for call queues.
- Configure voice applications policies for auto attendants and call queues.

Configure and Manage Users for Teams Phone:

- Assign a Teams Phone Standard license.
- Assign a Teams Calling Plan.
- Assign user dial plans.
- Assign phone numbers to users by using the Microsoft Teams admin center.
- Assign phone number to users by using PowerShell.
- Assign a verified emergency address location.
- Assign a calling policy to a user.
- Assign a voice routing policy to a Direct Routing user.

Configure and Manage Calling Features for Teams Phone:

- Configure voicemail for users.
- Configure group call pickup for users.
- Configure Call Forwarding.
- Configure Simultaneous Ring.
- Configure call delegation for users.
- Enable and configure audio conferencing for a user.
- Assign a Dial-out from meetings policy for a user.
- Assign a call hold policy for a user.
- Configure Shared Calling.

CHAPTER 7 CALL QUEUES, AUTO ATTENDANTS, AND USERS

7.1 Configure Auto Attendants and Call Queues

Teams offers a complete set of tools to manage customers' service and route phone calls that are managed by a group of operators or agents. Auto attendants in Teams act as virtual receptionists and have the capability to direct callers to the appropriate agent or service. Call queues manage incoming calls to agents with the objective that no caller is left waiting without support.

7.1.1 Design Call Flows for Auto Attendants and Call Queues

Teams Phone provides auto attendants as an automated system to manage incoming calls and route them based on time (business hours, weekday, and calendar events) and/or using choices in a menu system (callers can make their menu choice by using a phone keypad or speech recognition).

Auto attendants include the following features:

- **Call routing**: Auto attendants can direct callers to specific individuals, call queues, external numbers, other auto attendants, or voicemail based on the time of day (business hours, off-hours, holidays).

- **Menu prompts**: Prompts can be created using text-to-speech or prerecorded audio files. Speech recognition allows for hands-free navigation, while the keypad can also be used.

- **Customization**: Each auto attendant can be tailored with specific languages and time zones to accommodate global business needs.

Call queues in Teams Phone are used to handle incoming calls (usually routed from an auto attendant).

Call queues include the following features:

- **Queue management**: Call queues can route callers to available agents in the queue (based on the selected distribution methos), holding them on the line until an agent is free.

- **Exceptions handling**: Call queues allow specific routing when no agents are logged in or when the queue exceeds specified wait times or caller limits. Calls can be redirected to individuals, voicemail, other call queues, or auto attendants.

171

- **Agent management**: Agents can be allowed to opt out of a call queue based on their work schedule. Also, call queues can be enabled to respect the agents presence in Teams, ensuring efficient call distribution.

Unlike auto attendants, call queues do not have separate routing for off-hours and holidays.

To design the call flows, business requirements must be mapped to technical specifications, as shown here:

Business Requirement	Feature in Call Queues or Auto Attendants
Caller Access	
How will callers reach you?	Auto attendants (internal/external/click-to-call)
What languages are needed?	Auto attendants and call queues (language settings)
Will you allow voice inputs from callers or only keypad dialing inputs?	Auto attendants (input method settings)
Call Routing	
Do you need separate routing for off-hours or holidays?	Auto attendants (business hours and holidays routing)
What are your defined business hours and holidays?	Auto attendants (business hours and holidays configuration)
Agent Call Management	
Should agents in a call queue have the option to opt out of taking calls?	Call queues (agent opt-out settings)
Voice Prompts	
Do you prefer to record your own voice prompts or use the system-generated voice?	Auto attendants (custom or system-generated voice prompts)

(*continued*)

Business Requirement	Feature in Call Queues or Auto Attendants
Caller ID for Outgoing Calls	
Should agents in call queues or the operator use a specific caller ID when dialing out?	Call queues and auto attendants (caller ID settings for outbound calls)

7.1.2 Configure Auto Attendants and Call Queues

In this paragraph we will explain how to set up auto attendants to provide callers with options and direct them to the right department or individual. We will also cover the configuration of call queues to manage multiple incoming calls.

Prerequisites

To set up auto attendants and call queues in Microsoft Teams, the following prerequisites are necessary:

- Resource accounts:
  - One for each auto attendant and each call queue.
  - Each must have a free Microsoft Teams Phone Resource Account license.
- External phone calls:
  - At least one DDI (Microsoft service number, Operator Connect number or Direct Routing number) for direct dialing from external phone numbers.
  - Service numbers can be toll or toll-free.
- Agents requirements:
  - Agents must be Enterprise Voice enabled (online or on-premises).
  - If using Direct Routing or Operator Connect numbers, agents require the following:
    - An online voice routing policy (if using transfer mode).

CHAPTER 7   CALL QUEUES, AUTO ATTENDANTS, AND USERS

- ○ An Audio Conferencing license or online voice routing policy (if using conference mode).
- ○ Agents using the Microsoft Teams app must be in TeamsOnly mode.
- Resource Account Configuration for caller ID:
  - Each resource account must have a Teams Phone Resource Account license and one of the following:
    - ○ A Calling Plan license and a phone number
    - ○ An Operator Connect phone number
    - ○ Direct Routing: an online voice routing policy and a phone number assignment (required if you want to transfer incoming call to an external phone number)
- Licensing Details:
  - All resource accounts must have a free Microsoft Teams Phone Resource Account license.

Additional Notes

- Resource accounts are disabled for sign-in and must remain so.
- Chat and presence are not available for these accounts.
- Transfers between Calling Plan, Operator Connect, and Direct Routing trunks are not supported.

Configuring Auto Attendants

For auto attendants, execute the following implementation steps:

- Creating an auto attendant.
  - Go to the Teams admin center (TAC) and under Voice select "Auto attendants."
  - Create a new auto attendant and configure the following (see Figure 7-1):
    - ○ Name.

CHAPTER 7 CALL QUEUES, AUTO ATTENDANTS, AND USERS

- ○ Operator.
- ○ Time zone.
- ○ Language.
- ○ Enable voice inputs to allow voice commands in menus.
- Set up the call flow.
  - ○ Greeting Message.
  - ○ Routing Calls.
  - ○ Directory Search: Enable Dial by Name.
  - ○ Configure for outside business hours and holidays.

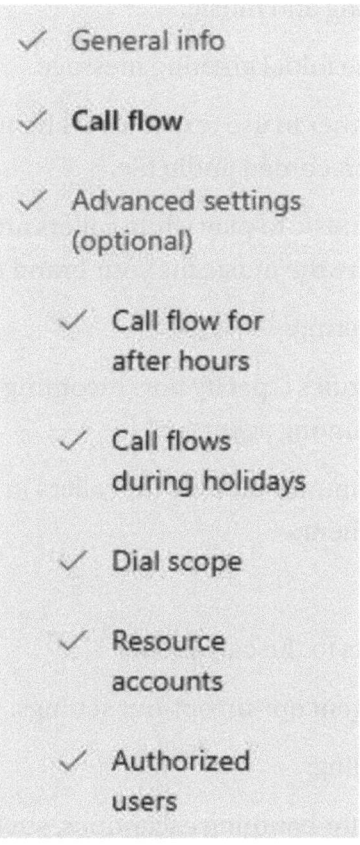

Figure 7-1. Configuration steps for an auto attendant

CHAPTER 7   CALL QUEUES, AUTO ATTENDANTS, AND USERS

Configuring Call Queues

For call queues, execute the following implementation steps:

- Create a call queue.
    - Go to the TAC and under Voice select "Call queues."
    - Create a new call queue and configure the following (see Figure 7-2):
        - Provide a name for the call queue.
        - Assign a resource account for the call queue.
        - Set the time zone.
    - Set up the greeting and music.
        - Configure the initial greeting message.
        - Choose whether to use text-to-speech for the greeting or upload a prerecorded audio file.
        - Select hold music to play while callers are waiting in the queue. Ensure the music fits your brand and is not irritating.
    - Set up call answering.
        - Call answer rules (specify how incoming calls should be distributed among agents)
        - Set the maximum wait time for callers in the queue before redirecting them.
    - Agent selection:
        - Assign agents to the call queue.
        - Configure agent opt-in/opt-out settings.
    - Exception handling:
        - Set up rules for handling exceptions, such as when no agents are available.
        - Define actions for overflow scenarios.

CHAPTER 7 CALL QUEUES, AUTO ATTENDANTS, AND USERS

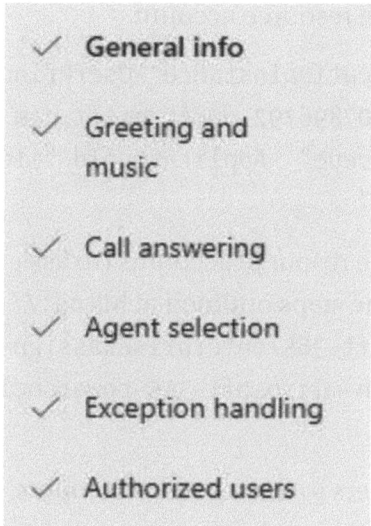

Figure 7-2. Configuration steps for a call queue

Managing with PowerShell

To set up an auto attendant for a company reception that routes incoming calls to a call queue with two receptionists as agents during business hours using the domain @M365x07896792.onmicrosoft.com, follow these steps:

- Create resource accounts for the auto attendant and call queue.
- Assign phone numbers to these resource accounts.
- Create the call queue and assign the receptionists as agents.
- Create the auto attendant with appropriate greetings and routing rules.
- Create the auto attendant resource account.

    ```
    New-CsOnlineApplicationInstance -UserPrincipalName
    receptionAA@M365x07896792.onmicrosoft.com -DisplayName
    "Reception Auto attendant" -ApplicationId
    "ce933385-9390-45d1-9512-c8d228074e07"
    ```

CHAPTER 7   CALL QUEUES, AUTO ATTENDANTS, AND USERS

- Create the call queue resource account.

    New-CsOnlineApplicationInstance -UserPrincipalName receptionCQ@M365x07896792.onmicrosoft.com -DisplayName "Reception Call Queue" -ApplicationId "11cd3e2e-fccb-42ad-ad00-878b93575e07"

- Assign licenses to the resource accounts (to assign licenses in PowerShell follow the steps outlined at https://learn.microsoft.com/en-us/microsoft-365/enterprise/assign-licenses-to-user-accounts-with-microsoft-365-powershell?view=o365-worldwide).

- Assign phone numbers to the resource accounts.

    Set-CsPhoneNumberAssignment -Identity receptionAA@M365x07896792.onmicrosoft.com -PhoneNumber +1234567890 -PhoneNumberType CallingPlan

    Set-CsPhoneNumberAssignment -Identity receptionCQ@M365x07896792.onmicrosoft.com -PhoneNumber +1234567899 -PhoneNumberType CallingPlan

- Define receptionists.

    $agents = @("receptionist1@M365x07896792.onmicrosoft.com", "receptionist2@M365x07896792.onmicrosoft.com")

- Create a call queue.

    $callQueue = New-CsCallQueue -Name "Reception Call Queue" -PrimaryUri "sip:receptionCQ@M365x07896792.onmicrosoft.com" -Agents $agents -DistributionMethod "Serial" -WelcomeMessageEnabled $true -MusicOnHoldEnabled $true

- Retrieve a call queue ID.

    $callQueueId = (Get-CsCallQueue -Identity "Reception Call Queue").Identity

- Create an auto attendant.

  ```
  $autoAttendant = New-CsAutoAttendant -Name "Reception Auto 
  attendant" -PrimaryUri "sip:receptionAA@M365x07896792.
  onmicrosoft.com" -TimeZone "Pacific Standard Time" 
  -CallFlows @(@{Type = "BusinessHours"; CallFlow = 
  @(@{TargetType = "Queue"; Target = $callQueueId})})
  ```

- Retrieve an auto attendant ID.

  ```
  $autoAttendantId = (Get-CsAutoAttendant -Identity 
  "Reception Auto attendant").Identity
  ```

- Add a greeting prompt.

  ```
  Set-CsAutoAttendantPrompt -Identity $autoAttendantId 
  -Prompt @{"TextToSpeechPrompt" = "Welcome to our company. 
  Please wait while we connect you to the next available 
  receptionist."}
  ```

Deploy Channel-Based Call Queues

In the call answering section of the call queue configuration, it is possible to select a Teams channel as the source of the agents list (up to 200 agents), as shown in Figure 7-3. Only users in the channel that are enabled to Phone System will be enabled as agents.

CHAPTER 7   CALL QUEUES, AUTO ATTENDANTS, AND USERS

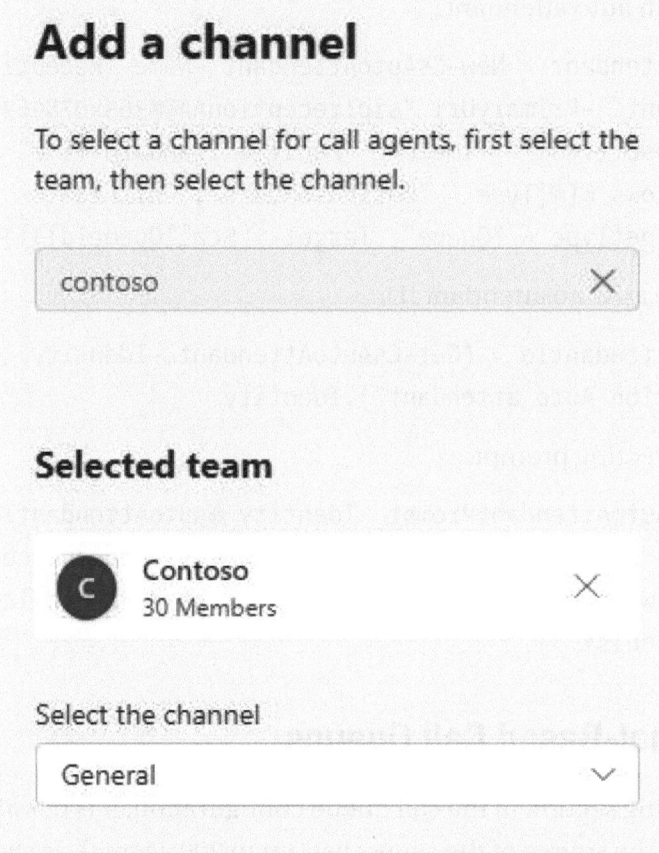

Figure 7-3. *Choosing a channel to answer incoming calls for a call queue*

When a Teams channel is enabled for a call queue, the user experience will be as follows:

- **Notification of incoming calls**: Agents will receive notifications of incoming calls directly within the Teams channel. This notification includes caller ID information and any relevant details about the call.

- **Joining the call**: Agents can answer the call with a single click. If multiple agents are available, the call may ring for all, and the first to answer will handle the call.

- **Call handling**: Once an agent answers, they can use all standard Teams calling features such as hold, transfer, and consult before transferring. They can also use chat to collaborate with other team members if needed.

CHAPTER 7   CALL QUEUES, AUTO ATTENDANTS, AND USERS

- **Presence and availability**: The call queue takes into account the presence status of agents. If an agent is set to Do Not Disturb or is already on another call, the call will be routed to the next available agent.

- **Missed calls**: If a call is not answered by any available agents within a specified timeframe, it is marked as a missed call. Agents and administrators can view missed call notifications within the Teams channel and their activity feed. Missed call notifications may include caller ID information, the time of the call, and any message left by the caller, allowing agents to follow up promptly.

- **Voicemail**: If the call queue is configured to redirect unanswered calls to voicemail, callers will be given the option to leave a message. Voicemail messages are transcribed (if transcription is enabled) and sent to the designated Teams channel or individual agents (as shown in Figure 7-4). The transcription and audio file are accessible directly within Teams.

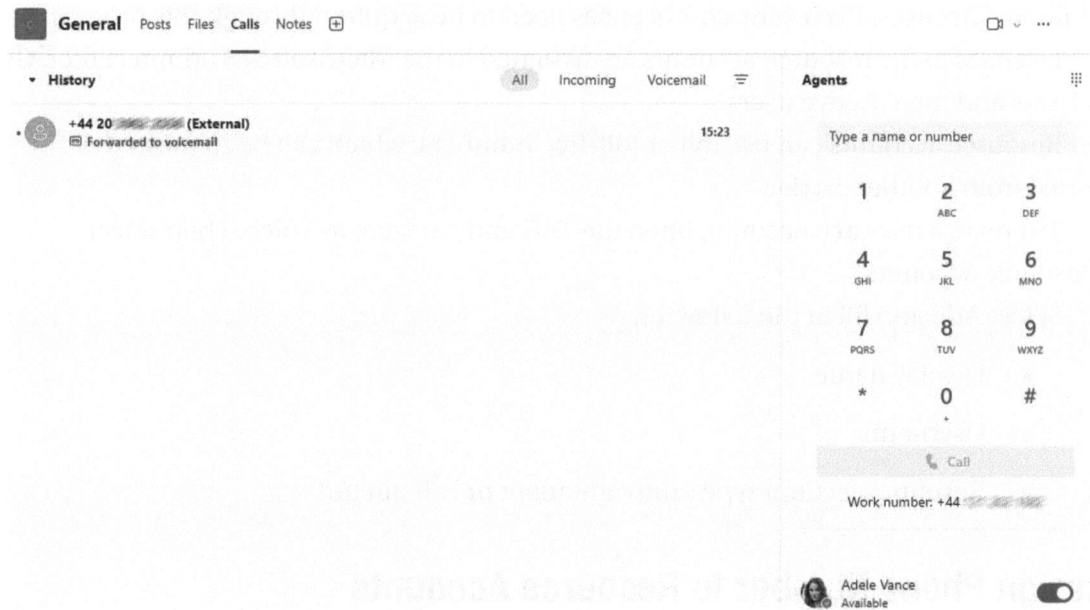

Figure 7-4. *Voice-enabled Teams channel*

Configure Resource Accounts

In Microsoft Teams, to be active, each auto attendant or call queue is required to be associated to (at least) one resource account.

Assign Licenses to Resource Accounts

Resource accounts require Teams Phone Resource Account licenses. These licenses are free, but the quantity available depends on the number of Phone System licenses purchased by the organization.

Organizations with subscriptions that include Phone System features, such as Teams Phone Standard, Teams Phone with Calling Plan, or Teams Shared Devices licenses, receive an allocation of 25 Teams Phone Resource Account licenses at no additional cost. Additionally, for every 10 user licenses of Teams Phone Standard, Teams Phone with Calling Plan, or Teams Shared Devices held by the organization, an extra Teams Phone Resource Account license is granted.

To obtain the Teams Phone Resource Account licenses, open the Microsoft 365 admin center and go to Billing. Select "Purchase services" and "Add-ons" to purchase additional licenses. Even zero-cost licenses need to be acquired through this process.

Licenses to the resource accounts are assigned in the Microsoft 365 admin center. Go to Users and then "Active users."

Resource accounts can use toll or toll-free numbers, which can be requested or ported from another carrier.

To create a resource account, open the TAC and navigate to Voice. Then select "Resource accounts."

Select Add and fill in the following:

- Display name
- Username
- Resource account type (auto attendant or call queue)

Assign Phone Number to Resource Accounts

To assign a phone number, open the TAC and go to Voice. Select "Resource accounts," select your resource account, and click "Assign/unassign."

CHAPTER 7 CALL QUEUES, AUTO ATTENDANTS, AND USERS

Assign a Resource Account to an Auto Attendant or Call Queue

To assign a resource account to an auto attendant or call queue in Microsoft Teams, follow these steps:

- Open the TAC.
- Navigate to Voice and then "Auto attendant" (or "Call queue").
- Select the auto attendant (or call queue).
- On the "General info" tab, add the required resource account (see Figure 7-5).

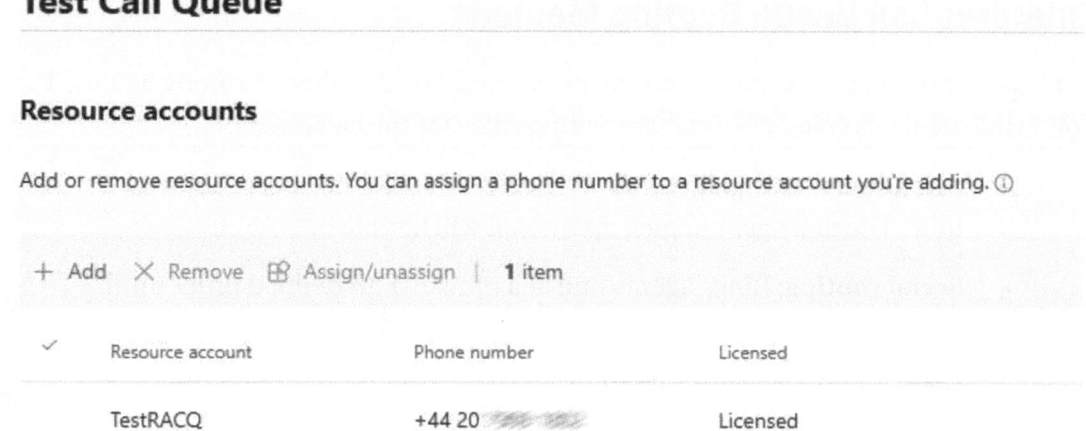

Figure 7-5. *Adding a resource account*

For an auto attendant or call queue that have more than one phone number, it is possible to associate a resource account for each number.

Configure Microsoft 365 Groups for Voicemail

To use a shared voicemail in an auto attendant or call queue, you must define an Office 365 group. The Office 365 group will include the members who will receive the voicemail messages.

To create an office 365 group, sign in to the Microsoft admin center, and click Teams & Groups.

Select "add a group" and choose Office 365. In the "Active teams and groups" tab, select "Teams & Microsoft 365 Groups" and click "Add a Microsoft 365 group."

Set a name, a description, the owners, the members' email addresses, and the privacy.

Interpret Call Queue Conference Mode

The ConferenceMode parameter specifies whether conference mode will be enabled for calls in this call queue. Enabling conference mode significantly reduces the time it takes to connect a caller to an agent once the agent accepts the call. Note that this setting applies only to Microsoft Teams and does not include Skype for Business (SfB).

Interpret Call Queue Routing Methods

Call answer rules specify how incoming calls should be distributed among agents. The following are the typologies of call answering rules for the call queue:

- **Attendant routing:** Rings all call agents in the queue at the same time. The first agent to pick up the call will handle it.

- **Serial routing**: Rings agents one at a time in a predefined order until someone answers the call.

- **Round robin routing**: Distributes calls evenly among agents by cycling through them. Each agent gets an equal opportunity to answer calls.

- **Longest idle routing**: Routes the call to the agent who has been idle (i.e., not on a call) for the longest period.

- **Parallel routing**: Like attendant routing, but allows more control over the number of agents it rings simultaneously.

Configure Holidays for Auto Attendants

Holidays for auto attendants in Microsoft Teams refer to specific dates and times when the usual call routing and handling rules are overridden to accommodate nonworking days, such as public holidays, company holidays, or any other designated nonworking days. During these periods, the auto attendant can be configured to handle calls differently to inform callers about the holiday and provide alternative options if needed.

To set up holidays for auto attendants, follow these steps:

- Open the Microsoft TAC and go to Voice. Select "auto attendants."
- Select the auto attendant to configure.
- Click "Call flows during holidays."
- Click Add for "Holiday call settings."
- Select a name for the holiday call settings. From the drop-down menu, you can select a previously defined holiday or add a new one. Select the greetings and call routing options (holiday call settings are shown in Figure 7-6).

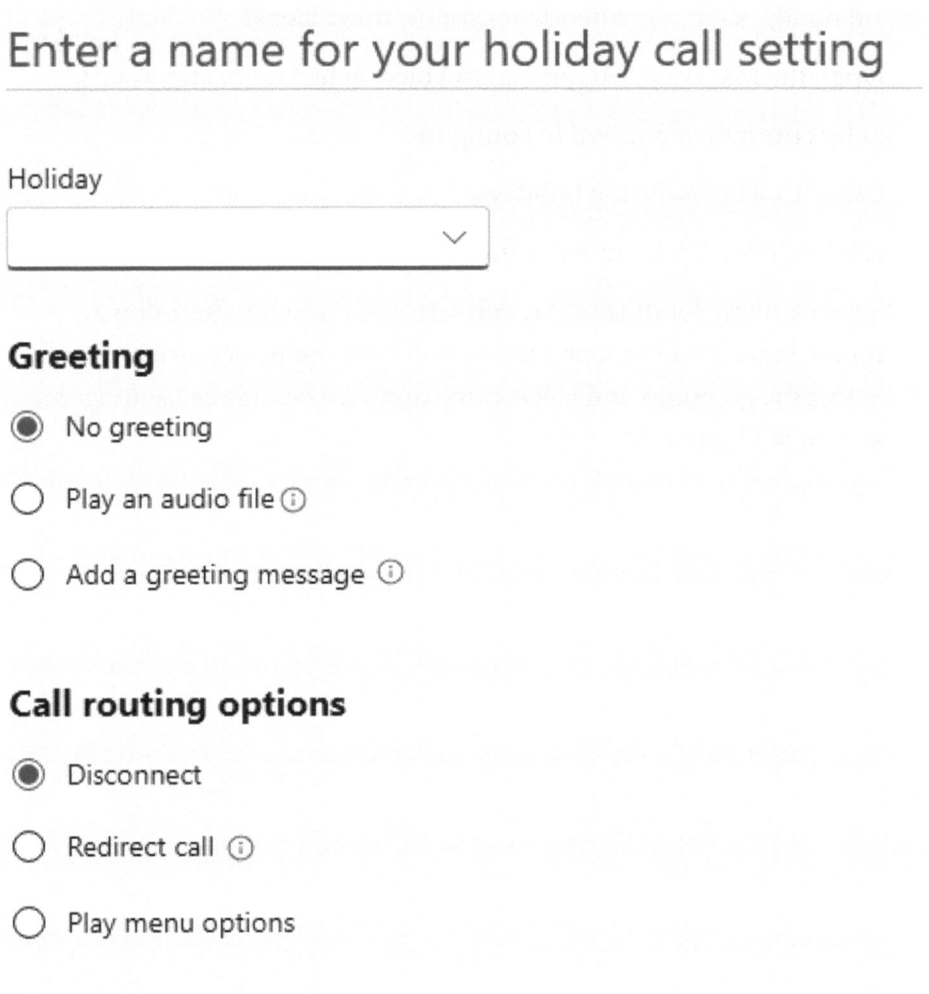

CHAPTER 7   CALL QUEUES, AUTO ATTENDANTS, AND USERS

Enter a name for your holiday call setting

Holiday

Greeting

◉ No greeting

○ Play an audio file ⓘ

○ Add a greeting message ⓘ

Call routing options

◉ Disconnect

○ Redirect call ⓘ

○ Play menu options

Figure 7-6. Holiday call settings

Disconnect the call.

Configure Custom Music on Hold

You can configure custom Music on Hold for your call queues in Microsoft Teams. This setup allows you to provide a customized experience for callers, ensuring they hear the appropriate music or messages while on hold.

To prepare your audio file, ensure your audio file is in one of the accepted formats: MP3, WAV, or WMA. The file must be less than 5 MB.

CHAPTER 7   CALL QUEUES, AUTO ATTENDANTS, AND USERS

- To apply the custom MoH, open TAC, go to Voice, and select "call queues."

- Select the call queue to configure.

- Select "Greeting and music."

- Under the "Music on hold" section, choose "Play an audio file."

- Click "Upload file" to upload your custom MoH audio file.

- Select the audio file from your computer.

Assign a Dynamic Caller ID Policy for Call Queues

Caller ID policies in Microsoft Teams are used to manage and customize the caller ID information that is displayed to recipients when calls are made from within the Teams environment.

To configure the caller ID policy for Teams users to use a call queue, follow these steps:

- Open the TAC, go to Voice, and select "caller ID policies."

- Click Add to create a new caller ID policy.

- Add a name and a description and select "Resource account" from the "Replace the caller ID with" drop-down menu.

- Select the resource account from "Replace the caller ID with this resource account." See Figure 7-7.

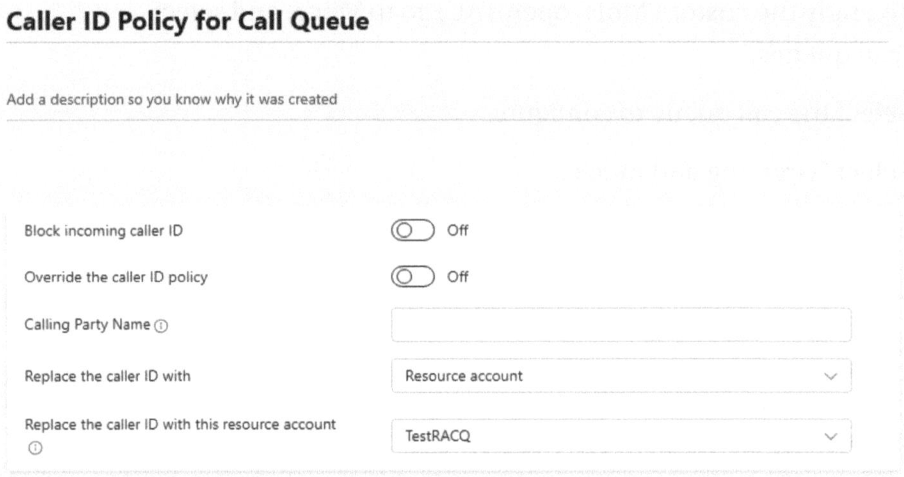

Caller ID Policy for Call Queue

Add a description so you know why it was created

Block incoming caller ID	Off
Override the caller ID policy	Off
Calling Party Name	
Replace the caller ID with	Resource account
Replace the caller ID with this resource account	TestRACQ

Figure 7-7. *Caller ID policy for call queues*

Apply the new caller ID policy to users or groups.

Configure Voice Applications Policies for Auto Attendants and Call Queues

Voice application policies enable the creation and assignment of these policies to authorized users, determining the configuration changes they can make to the auto attendants and call queues they manage. Voice application policies can be managed through the Microsoft Teams admin center or by using PowerShell. By default, users receive the global policy unless a custom policy is created and assigned to them.

Managing with PowerShell

To manage voice application policies with PowerShell, use the following cmdlets:

- `Set-CsTeamsVoiceApplicationsPolicy`: Update Teams voice applications policy settings.

- `Get-CsTeamsVoiceApplicationsPolicy`: Retrieve information on Teams voice applications policies.

- `Grant-CsTeamsVoiceApplicationsPolicy`: Assign a Teams voice applications policy to one or more users.

CHAPTER 7 CALL QUEUES, AUTO ATTENDANTS, AND USERS

- `New-CsTeamsVoiceApplicationsPolicy`: Create a new Teams voice applications policy.

- `Remove-CsTeamsVoiceApplicationsPolicy`: Delete an existing Teams voice applications policy.

- For example, let's create a new Teams voice applications policy (auto attendant delegation):

  ```
  New-CsTeamsVoiceApplicationsPolicy -Identity
  "AutoAttendantDelegation" -Description "Policy for
  delegating Auto attendant management"
  ```

- Let's assign the new policy to adelev@m365x07896792.onmicrosoft.com.

  ```
  Grant-CsTeamsVoiceApplicationsPolicy -Identity
  adelev@m365x07896792.onmicrosoft.com -PolicyName
  "AutoAttendantDelegation"
  ```

7.1.3 Configure and Manage Users for Teams Phone

Microsoft Teams Phone is a feature within Microsoft Teams that allows integration with PSTN telephony. The following are the main steps to deploy Teams Phone to users:

- Licensing.

- Assign phone numbers to users.

- Set up voice routing (configuring dial plans, voice routes, and PSTN usage records).

- Define call policies.

- Configure user settings within Teams, including voicemail settings, call answering rules, and outbound caller ID.

Assign a Teams Phone Standard License

As explained in Section 4.1, to enable a user to Teams Phone, the following are the minimum requirements for PSTN connectivity:

- A Teams Phone add-on license (that requires for the user to already have a Microsoft Teams license)
- A PSTN provider to give the incoming and outgoing connectivity to the PSTN network (Microsoft with Calling Plans or a telco of your choice)

To assign Microsoft Teams Phone Standard, navigate to the Microsoft 365 Admin center, assign the license to each user that requires it.

Assign a Teams Calling Plan

To assign a Teams Calling Plan (for example Domestic Calling Plan) to a user (for example Adele Vance), open the Microsoft 365 admin center, go to Users, and select "Active users."

From the list of active users, select Adele Vance. This will bring up her user details pane on the right side. In the user details pane, you can see a list of available licenses. Check the box next to Microsoft Teams Domestic Calling Plan.

Assign User Dial Plans

To assign a dial plan to a user, open the TAC, go to Users, click "Manage users," and select the user you want to configure. Click Policies and select Edit. On the "Edit policy assignment" tab, select "Dial plan" from the drop-down menu.

To assign to a group, open the TAC, go to Voice, select "Dial plans," and click "Group policy assignment." Click Add. On the "Assign policy to group" tab, select the group, the dial plan (from the drop-down menu), and the rank for the policy.

Assign Phone Numbers to Users by Using the Microsoft Teams Admin Center

To assign a phone number to a user, open the TAC, go to Users, select "Manage users," and select the user you want to configure. On the General tab, click Edit. The "Phone number type" drop-down menu will have Calling Plan, Direct Routing, and Operator Connect, depending on the licenses assigned to the user. See Figure 7-8.

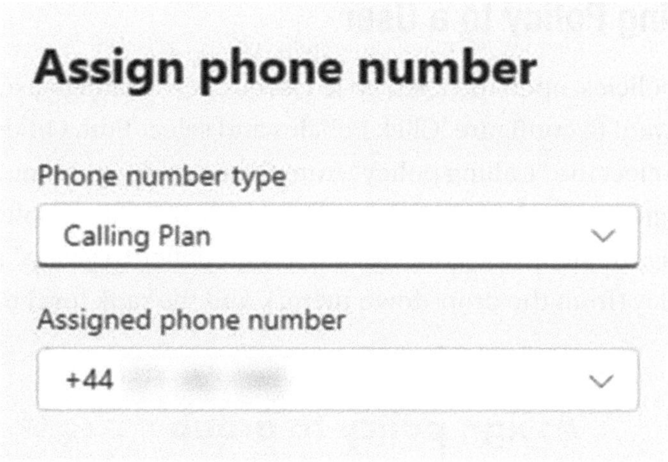

CHAPTER 7   CALL QUEUES, AUTO ATTENDANTS, AND USERS

Figure 7-8. Assigning a phone number

Assign a Phone Number to Users by Using PowerShell

To assign a phone number to a user in Microsoft Teams using PowerShell, you can use the `Set-CsPhoneNumberAssignment` cmdlet. For example, you want to assign a phone number (+44 123 4567 8910) to the user `AdeleV@M365x07896792.OnMicrosoft.com` with a calling plan.

- `Set-CsPhoneNumberAssignment -Identity AdeleV@M365x07896792.OnMicrosoft.com -PhoneNumber +4412345678910 -PhoneNumberType CallingPlan`

Assign a Verified Emergency Address Location

To assign a phone number to a user, open the TAC, go to Users, select "Manage users," and select the user you want to configure. On the General tab, click Edit and on the "Assign phone number" tab, under "Emergency location," select "Search by city" or "Search by location description." Select one of the configured emergency address locations.

Assign a Calling Policy to a User

To assign calling policies, open the TAC, go to Users, click "Manage users," and select the user that you want to configure. Click Policies and select Edit. On the "Edit policy assignment" tab, select the "Calling policy" from the drop-down menu.

To assign to a group, open the TAC, go to Voice, select "Calling policies," and click "Group policy assignment." Click Add. On the "Assign policy to group" tab, select the group, the policy (from the drop-down menu), and the rank for the policy (see Figure 7-9).

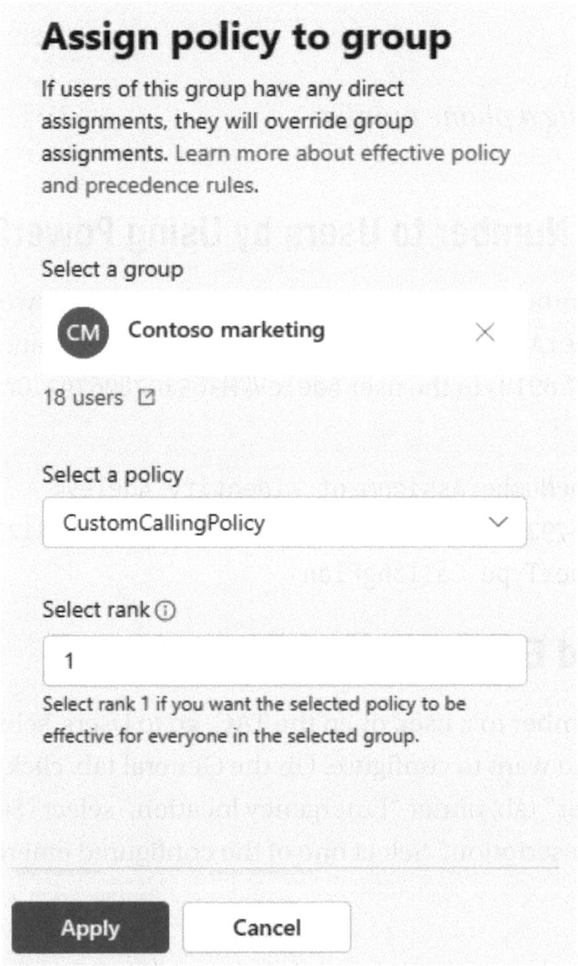

Figure 7-9. Assigning a policy to group

CHAPTER 7   CALL QUEUES, AUTO ATTENDANTS, AND USERS

To assign calling policies using PowerShell, you have to use the command `Grant-CsTeamsCallingPolicy`. For example, to assign a custom calling policy named CustomCalling to the user AdeleV@M365x07896792.OnMicrosoft.com using PowerShell, use this:

```
Grant-CsTeamsCallingPolicy -Identity AdeleV@M365x07896792.OnMicrosoft.com -PolicyName CustomCalling
```

Assign a Voice Routing Policy to a Direct Routing User

To assign a voice route to a user, open the TAC, go to Users, click "Manage users," and select the user you want to configure. Click Policies and select Edit. On the "Edit policy assignment" tab, select the "Voice routing policy" from the drop-down menu.

To assign to a group, open the TAC, go to Voice, select "Voice routing policies," and click "Group policy assignment." Click Add. On the "Assign policy to group" tab, select the group, the voice routing policy (from the drop-down menu), and the rank for the policy.

7.1.4 Configure and Manage Calling Features for Teams Phone

Microsoft Teams Phone provides a wide-ranging suite of calling functionalities designed to deliver communication and collaboration within an organization. In this chapter, we will see how to configure them.

Configure Voicemail for Users

To set up the voicemail for a user, open the TAC, go to Users, select "Manage users," and select the user you want to configure. This Voicemail section (as shown in Figure 7-10) allows the configuration of voicemail settings for Adele Vance.

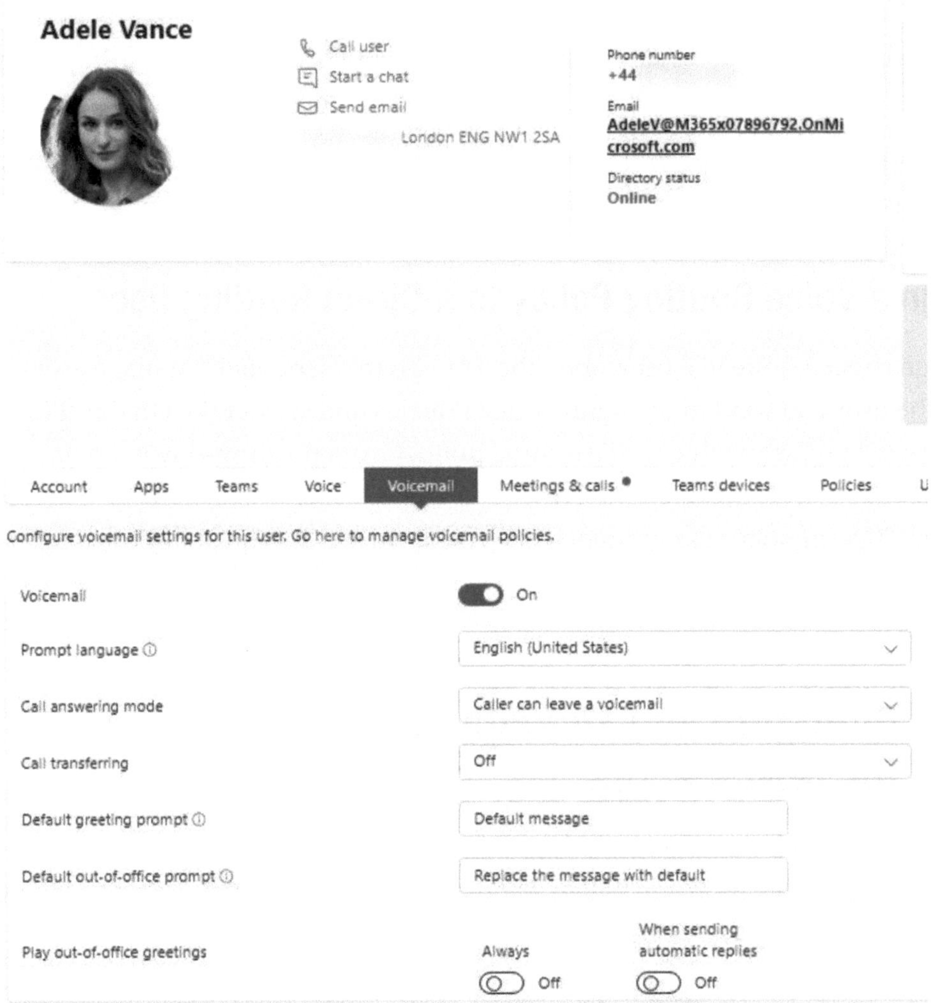

CHAPTER 7   CALL QUEUES, AUTO ATTENDANTS, AND USERS

Figure 7-10. Voicemail settings for a user

Here are the options available:

- **Voicemail Toggle**: This turns voicemail on or off for the user.

- **Prompt Language**: This specifies the language in which voicemail prompts will be played. It is currently set to English (United States).

CHAPTER 7   CALL QUEUES, AUTO ATTENDANTS, AND USERS

- **Call Answering Mode:** In the drop-down menu, the options are "Caller can leave a voicemail," "Play an outgoing message to the caller," or "Service declines the call with no message."

- **Call Transferring**: In the drop-down menu the options are "Off," "Transfer to a user," or "Transfer to a number."

- Default greeting prompt.

- Default out-of-office prompt.

- Play out-of-office greetings.

    - Always (on/off switch).

    - When sending automatic replies (on/off switch).

Configure Group Call Pickup for Users

Group call pickup is a feature in Microsoft Teams that allows members of a predefined group to answer each other's calls. This feature is particularly useful in scenario such as in customer service centers or support teams.

To configure group call pickup for a user, open the TAC, go to Users, click "Manage users," and select the user you want to configure. Open the Voice tab.

In "Call answering rules," select "Be immediately forwarded" and from the "Call forward type" drop-down menu select "Group call pickup." Click the "Manage call group" button to open the screen that allows you to manage group membership and to set the notification/ringing method (as shown in Figure 7-11).

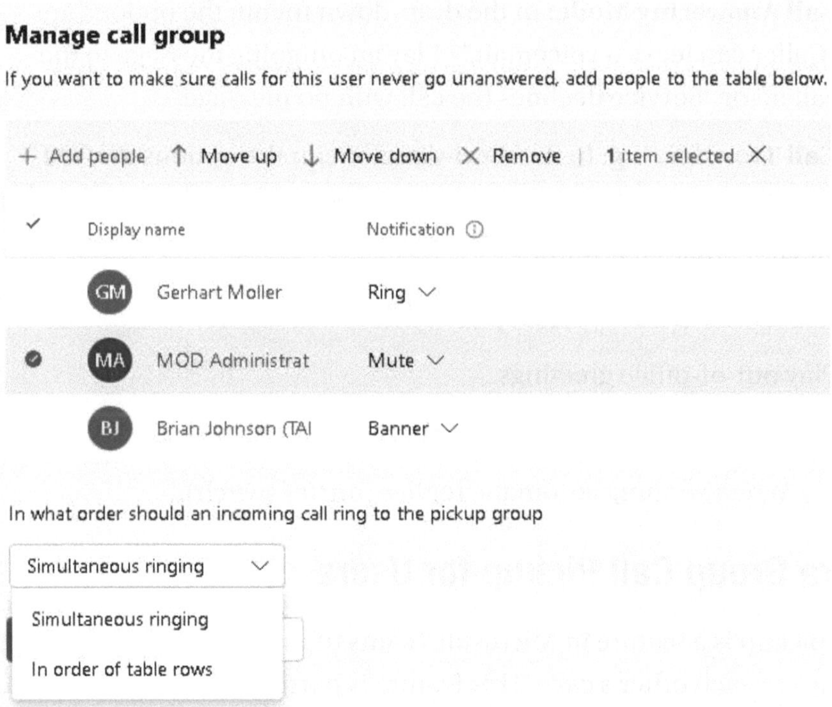

CHAPTER 7   CALL QUEUES, AUTO ATTENDANTS, AND USERS

Figure 7-11. Manage call group screen

The options available for configuring group call pickup in Microsoft Teams are the following:

Notification settings for each member:

- **Ring**: This option will make the phone ring when a call comes in, notifying the user with an audible ringtone.

- **Mute**: This option will mute the call notification, meaning the user will not hear a ringtone but may still receive visual notifications.

- **Banner**: This option will display a banner notification on the user's screen, alerting them to the incoming call without making an audible sound.

Call ringing order:

- **Simultaneous Ringing**: All members of the call pickup group will be notified of the incoming call at the same time. Any member can then choose to answer the call.

CHAPTER 7   CALL QUEUES, AUTO ATTENDANTS, AND USERS

- **In Order of Table Rows**: Calls will be distributed to the group members in the order they appear in the table. The call will be offered to the first member on the list, and if they do not answer, it will move to the next member, and so on.

Configure Call Forwarding

To configure group call forwarding for a user, open the TAC, got to Users, click "Manage users," and select the user you want to configure. Open the Voice tab.

In "Call answering rules," select "Be immediately forwarded." The drop-down menu "Call forward type" offers different options:

- **Voicemail**: This option will forward incoming calls directly to the user's voicemail. The caller will be able to leave a voice message if the user is unavailable.

- **Forward to a Person**: This option allows the user to forward incoming calls to another specific person within the organization. The user can select a person from the directory to receive the calls.

- **Another Number**: This option allows the user to forward incoming calls to another phone number. The user can specify an external number (such as a mobile or landline) where calls will be directed.

- **Delegate**: This option allows the user to designate a delegate who will receive and manage incoming calls on their behalf. The delegate is usually an assistant or colleague who can answer calls for the user.

- **Group Call Pickup**: This option enables group call pickup, allowing a predefined group of users to answer the call. If the user is unavailable, any member of the group can pick up the call, ensuring it does not go unanswered.

Configure Simultaneous Ring

To configure group simultaneous ringing for a user, open the TAC, go to Users, select "Manage users," and select the user you want to configure. Open the Voice tab.

CHAPTER 7   CALL QUEUES, AUTO ATTENDANTS, AND USERS

In "Call answering rules," select "Ring "user's" Devices." Under Also Allow there are a few additional options including the following:

- **None**: No additional actions will be allowed. Calls will follow the primary call answering rule set above.

- **Simultaneous Ring a User**: This option allows another specified user to ring simultaneously with the user's devices. Both the first user and the other user will receive the call notification at the same time, allowing either of them to answer the call.

- **Simultaneous Ring a Number**: This option allows an additional phone number to ring simultaneously with the user's devices. The specified number can be an external phone number, such as a mobile or landline.

- **Call Delegation**: This option allows the user to delegate call answering to another user. The delegate will have the ability to answer calls on the first user's behalf.

- **Group Call Pickup**: This option enables a predefined group of users to pick up calls.

The options listed here are also available in the "If unanswered" menu, which specifies the duration (in seconds) that the user's devices will ring before the call is redirected according to the call forwarding rules. The default is 20 seconds, but this can be adjusted as needed.

Configure Call Delegation for Users

Call delegation in Microsoft Teams allows a user to assign another person (delegate) the ability to make and receive calls on their behalf. This is useful for scenarios where a user might need assistance in managing their calls, such as executives who have assistants managing their schedules and communications. To configure group simultaneous ringing for a user, open the TAC, go to Users, click "Manage users," and select the user that you want to configure. Open the Voice tab. In "Call answering rules," select "Ring "user's" Devices." In the Also Allow section, select "Call delegation."

CHAPTER 7 CALL QUEUES, AUTO ATTENDANTS, AND USERS

The configuration options include the following:

- **Add People**: This allows the user to add individuals to the call group who will act as delegates. These people will receive calls on behalf of the user and can handle calls according to the permissions set.

  - **Make calls**: The delegate can make calls on behalf of the user.

  - **Receive calls**: The delegate can receive calls on behalf of the user.

  - **Make and receive calls**: The delegate can both make and receive calls on behalf of the user.

  - **Can't make or receive calls**: The delegate cannot make or receive calls on behalf of the user.

- **Allow Changing Call Settings**: This is used to allow or disallow the delegate from changing call settings.

Enable and Configure Audio Conferencing for a User

You can adjust the audio conferencing settings for individual users in your organization. These settings include options like the conferencing provider, default toll or toll-free numbers, conference IDs, and PINs.

To configure audio conferencing for a user, open the TAC, go to Users, select "Manage users," and select the user that you want to configure. On the General tab, near "Audio Conferencing," and click Edit (see Figure 7-12).

CHAPTER 7   CALL QUEUES, AUTO ATTENDANTS, AND USERS

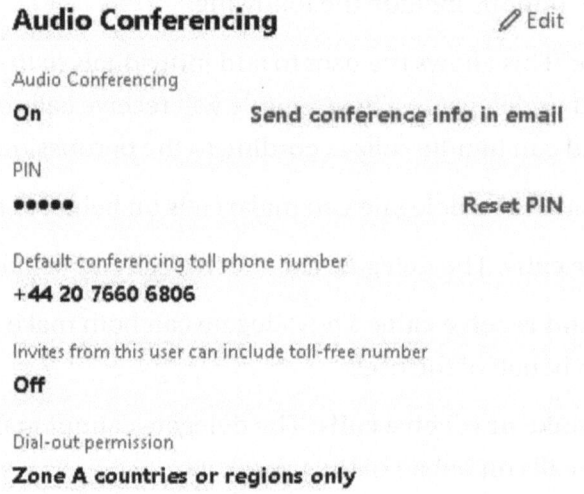

Figure 7-12. Audio Conferencing settings

Audio Conferencing Settings

- **Audio Conferencing On/Off**: To enable or disable audio conferencing for a user, click Edit next to Audio Conferencing. In the pane that appears, toggle the Audio Conferencing setting to On or Off.

- **Sending Conference Info via Email**: Use this option to send the user's audio conferencing phone number through email immediately. Note that this email will not include the PIN.

- **Resetting the PIN**: If you need to reset the user's PIN, select Reset PIN.

- **Default Conferencing Toll Phone Number**: These numbers are set on the audio conferencing bridge and can be formatted as desired in Teams meeting requests. To change the default toll number, click Edit next to Audio Conferencing and choose a number under "Toll number" in the pane. Alternatively, you can set phone numbers via the TeamsAudioConferencingPolicy, which will override the default toll number settings if applied.

- **Including Toll-Free Numbers in Invites**: This setting can be altered using TeamsAudioConferencingPolicy.

- **Unauthenticated Users in Meetings**: Toggle the setting "Unauthenticated users can be the first person in the meeting" to On or Off to control this feature.

- **Dial-Out Permissions**: To change dial-out permissions, click Edit next to Audio Conferencing and select the desired option under "Dial-out from meetings."

Assign a Dial-Out from Meetings Policy for a User

You can specify the destinations where users are allowed to dial out during meetings.

To configure a dial-out from meetings policy for a user, open the TAC, go to Users, select "Manage users," and select the user that you want to configure. In the General tab near Audio Conferencing, click Edit

The options available for this setting are as follows:

- **Any destination**: This option allows users to dial out to any international or domestic destination during a meeting. There are no restrictions on the geographic location of the call recipient.

- **In the same country or region as the organization**: Users can only dial out to numbers within the same country or region where the organization is based. This option restricts international dialing and limits calls to domestic destinations.

- **Zone A countries or regions only**: Users are restricted to dialing out only to specific countries or regions categorized under Zone A. This typically includes a predefined list of countries where dialing is permitted, which might be based on business needs or regulatory compliance.

- **Don't allow**: This option disables the ability to dial out from meetings altogether. Users will not be able to initiate outbound calls during a meeting using the Teams dial-out feature.

Assign a Call Hold Policy for a User

Call hold policies control the audio file that is played when a Teams user puts a caller on hold. You can upload an audio file to define custom music on hold. Accepted file formats are MP3, WAV, and WMA. The file size must be less than 5 MB.

To assign a dial plan to a user, open the TAC, go to Users, select "Manage users," and select the user you want to configure. Click Policies and select Edit. On the "Edit policy assignment" tab, select the "Call hold" policy from the drop-down menu.

To assign to a group, open the TAC, go to Voice, select "Call hold policies" and "Group policy assignment," and select the group and the policy you want to apply.

Configure Shared Calling

Shared calling in Microsoft Teams Phone is a solution for users who do not require a dedicated phone number. This feature leverages shared phone numbers associated with auto attendants, reducing costs.

To enable a user, follow these steps:

- Assign Teams Phone licenses.
- Enable users for voice without assigning them individual phone numbers.

To configure a resource account, follow these steps:

- Assign a phone number to the resource account for both inbound and outbound calls.
- Associate the resource account with the auto attendant for inbound calling.
- Assign a location to the resource account for emergency calling.

To create a shared calling policy, follow these steps:

- To create a shared calling policy, open the TAC, select Voice, and select "Shared calling policies."
    - Add the name and description, and use Search for Resource Account to find and select the resource account that will be used for making calls.

CHAPTER 7   CALL QUEUES, AUTO ATTENDANTS, AND USERS

- Click the "Add emergency callback number" button to specify one or more emergency callback numbers.
- Assign the Shared Calling policy to users.

If using PowerShell, use the `TeamsSharedCallingRoutingPolicy` cmdlets to create and manage Shared Calling policies.

7.1.5 Knowledge Check

Question 1:

What are the key components needed to set up auto attendants in Microsoft Teams?

1. Resource accounts.
2. Business hours configuration.
3. Greeting messages.
4. User dial plans.
5. Call forwarding rules.

Question 2:

Which features are supported by auto attendants in Microsoft Teams?

1. Call routing based on time of day.
2. Customizable menu prompts.
3. Speech recognition for hands-free navigation.
4. Queue management for incoming calls.
5. Agent presence monitoring.

Question 3:

What prerequisites are necessary for configuring call queues in Microsoft Teams?

1. Resource accounts for each call queue.
2. At least one DDI for external phone calls.
3. Enterprise Voice–enabled agents.
4. Teams Phone Resource Account license.
5. Agent opt-in/opt-out settings.

CHAPTER 7   CALL QUEUES, AUTO ATTENDANTS, AND USERS

Question 4:

What settings are involved in the configuration of auto attendants for Microsoft Teams?

1. Name, operator, time zone, and language.
2. Greeting message and call routing.
3. Directory search and holiday call settings.
4. Emergency callback numbers.
5. Agent call management.

Question 5:

How do call queues handle incoming calls in Microsoft Teams?

1. Distribute calls based on selected distribution methods.
2. Hold callers on the line until an agent is free.
3. Redirect calls when no agents are logged in.
4. Enable agents to opt-out based on their work schedule.
5. Provide separate routing for off-hours and holidays.

Question 6:

What are the steps to create a resource account for an auto attendant using PowerShell?

1. Use `New-CsOnlineApplicationInstance` cmdlet.
2. Assign a Teams Phone Resource Account license.
3. Assign a phone number using `Set-CsPhoneNumberAssignment`.
4. Configure call routing with `New-CsAutoAttendant`.
5. Set up emergency callback numbers.

Question 7:

Which call answering rules are available for configuring call queues in Microsoft Teams?

1. Attendant Routing.
2. Serial Routing.

CHAPTER 7 CALL QUEUES, AUTO ATTENDANTS, AND USERS

3. Round Robin Routing.
4. Longest Idle Routing.
5. Parallel Routing.

Question 8:

What options are available for configuring group call pickup in Microsoft Teams?

1. Ring.
2. Mute.
3. Banner.
4. Simultaneous Ringing.
5. In Order of Table Rows.

Question 9:

What policies can be assigned to a user for managing calling features in Microsoft Teams?

1. Calling policy.
2. Voice routing policy.
3. Call hold policy.
4. Dynamic caller ID policy.
5. Voicemail policy.

Question 10:

What are the key benefits of configuring Shared Calling in Microsoft Teams?

1. Simplifies phone number management.
2. Reduces costs by not requiring dedicated phone numbers.
3. Utilizes phone numbers associated with Auto Attendants.
4. Enhances scalability and flexibility.
5. Provides emergency callback number configuration.

CHAPTER 7   CALL QUEUES, AUTO ATTENDANTS, AND USERS

Answers
Question 1: 1, 2, 3
Question 2: 1, 2, 3
Question 3: 1, 2, 3, 4
Question 4: 1, 2, 3
Question 5: 1, 2, 3, 4
Question 6: 1, 2, 3, 4
Question 7: 1, 2, 3, 4, 5
Question 8: 1, 2, 3, 4, 5
Question 9: 1, 2, 3, 4, 5
Question 10: 1, 2, 3, 5

CHAPTER 8

Teams Rooms and Devices

This chapter is focused on Microsoft Teams Rooms and devices. The exam topics include planning, designing, and maintaining Teams-certified device solutions, ensuring integration and optimal performance within various meeting spaces.

The emphasis is on recommend room configurations based on meeting spaces and customer requirements. The certification exam syllabus also requires knowledge on deploying various phones (common area, user, and conference), remote deployment of Android devices, and configuring the SIP Gateway.

In this chapter, the following required skills and exam topics are described:

Plan and design Teams-certified device solutions:

- Recommend a room configuration based on the meeting space.
- Recommend a room configuration based on customer and business requirements.
- Compare capabilities and features of Teams Rooms Basic and Teams Rooms Pro.
- Recommend a Teams Rooms device platform (Android vs. Windows vs. Surface Hub).
- Recommend Teams-certified devices.
- Recommend Teams Rooms certified components.
- Recommend when to use coordinated meetings.
- Recommend when to use Cloud Video Interop (CVI) or Direct Guest Join.

CHAPTER 8 TEAMS ROOMS AND DEVICES

- Recommend an update strategy for Teams Meeting Room devices.
- Identify the requirements for a Microsoft Exchange Online resource account.
- Identify the enrollment requirements for Microsoft Intune.
- Plan for advanced features on shared devices.

Maintain Teams Rooms and devices:

- Configure device settings.
- Configure IP phone policies.
- Configure local network settings.
- Configure security and updates.
- Configure Conditional Access Policy MFA exception for Resource accounts.
- Configure meeting room settings by using the Microsoft Teams admin center or the local Teams application settings.
- Create and configure device configuration profiles for Android-based devices.
- Manage Teams Rooms from the Microsoft Teams Rooms Pro Management portal.
- Configure Intune policies for Teams devices.
- Configure Intune Configuration profiles (for Windows MTRs).
- Enable advanced voice capabilities for shared space devices.
- Enable hotline for shared space devices.
- Configure Virtual Front Desk.
- Deploy common area phones, user phones, conference phones.
- Create and manage Teams device tags.
- Deploy Android devices remotely.
- Configure SIP Gateway.

CHAPTER 8   TEAMS ROOMS AND DEVICES

- Monitor Teams device health.
- Troubleshoot authentication issues.
- Troubleshoot update issues.
- Troubleshoot remote provisioning issues.
- Troubleshoot Bluetooth beaconing.

8.1 Plan and Design Teams-Certified Device Solutions

Microsoft Teams Rooms offers a comprehensive meeting experience with HD video, audio, and content sharing, suitable for any meeting space from small areas to large conference rooms.

Microsoft Teams Rooms includes the following essential components:

- Touchscreen console
- Compute module
- Microsoft Teams Rooms application
- Peripheral devices (camera, microphone, speaker)
- External screens (up to two)
- HDMI input

For more details on certified systems and peripherals, refer to Teams Rooms certified systems and peripherals.

8.1.1 Recommend a Room Configuration Based on the Meeting Space

The Microsoft Teams Rooms Pro Management Portal is a comprehensive tool designed to help organizations effectively manage and optimize their Microsoft Teams Rooms (MTR) deployments. As part of the portal there are room-planning capabilities. The portal allows administrators to get a detailed overview of the current equipment in each Teams Room and to plan for new ones.

CHAPTER 8   TEAMS ROOMS AND DEVICES

The portal is accessible using Microsoft Teams Rooms Pro Management Portal. On the left side, select Planning and then Standards to see a list of standard room types (and the capability to create custom ones), as shown in Figure 8-1.

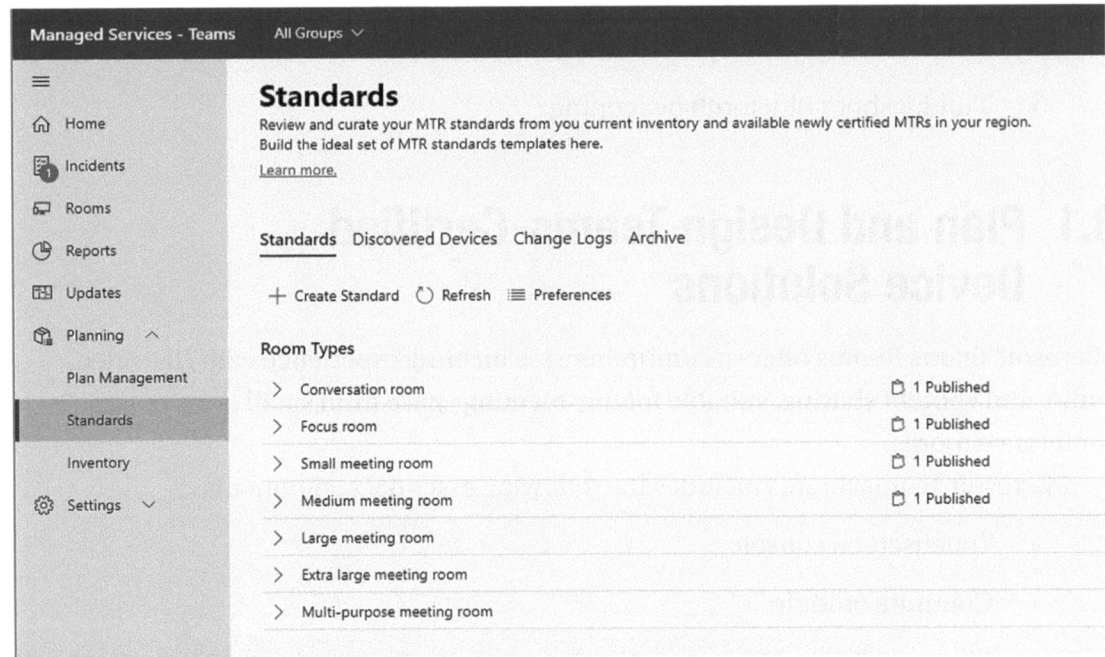

Figure 8-1. *Rooms standards inside the Pro Management portal*

Each standard is paired with a room capacity, as shown in Table 8-1.

Table 8-1. *Rooms Standards and Capabilities*

Room Type	Capacity
Conversation room	2–3
Focus room	4–5
Small meeting room	6–8
Medium meeting room	9–14
Large meeting room	15–20
Extra large meeting room	21–32
Multipurpose meeting room	33+

CHAPTER 8 TEAMS ROOMS AND DEVICES

Each standard includes a list of devices that are suggested for that specific meeting space. For example, for a medium meeting room, the list includes devices like Neat-Neat Board, Jabra-PanaCast 50 Room System, Poly-Poly Studio X52 + TC10, Cisco-Room Bar Pro - First Light, and Yealink-MVC S60.

8.1.2 Recommend a Room Configuration Based on Customer and business requirements

As part of the room planning process, it is essential to consider additional requirements beyond just room size.

- **Business requirements**: Determine the primary use of the room, whether for regular team meetings, executive briefings, training sessions, or collaborative work.
- **Budget**: Establish the budget allocation for the equipment and furnishings.
- **Technical requirements**: Assess compatibility with existing infrastructure, Internet bandwidth, and any specific software or hardware needs.

Each of these factors influences the selection of hardware and accessories. Additionally, Teams Rooms have architectural requirements that must be addressed. These include the shape of the room, available network cabling, sound insulation, and lighting. Proper planning in these areas is crucial to ensure the room meets customer requirements and provides an optimal user experience.

8.1.3 Compare Capabilities and Features of Teams Rooms Basic and Teams Rooms Pro

Microsoft Teams Rooms Basic and Pro are the licensing options that replaced the former Teams Rooms Standard and Premium licenses.

Microsoft Teams Rooms Basic offers essential conferencing features suitable for smaller meeting spaces, while Teams Rooms Pro provides advanced functionalities and AI-powered management ideal for larger, more complex environments. Your choice should depend on your room size, business requirements, technical needs, and budget considerations.

CHAPTER 8   TEAMS ROOMS AND DEVICES

Teams Rooms Basic License:

- **Cost**: Free, bundled with certified Teams Rooms devices (cannot be purchased separately)
- **License Limit**: Up to 25 rooms per customer environment
- **Features**: See Table 8-2

Teams Rooms Pro License:

- **Cost**: Paid (price varies by country)
- **Features**: See Table 8-2

Table 8-2. Teams Rooms Basic and Teams Rooms Pro Features

Feature	Teams Rooms Basic	Teams Rooms Pro
Cost	Free (with certified Teams device up to 25 rooms)	$40 room/month (annual subscription)
Teams Rooms on Windows	Yes	Yes
Teams Rooms on Android	Yes	Yes
Teams Rooms on Surface Hub	Yes	Yes
One-touch join	Yes	Yes
Proximity join	Yes	Yes
Meeting ID	Yes	Yes
Meet now (start ad hoc meetings)	Yes	Yes
Direct guest join for Zoom and Webex meetings	Yes	Yes
Join meetings across Teams clouds		Yes
Check-in with Teams panel		Yes
Share and view all Teams content types	Yes	Yes
Share an analog whiteboard with intelligent content capture		Yes

(continued)

Table 8-2. (*continued*)

Feature	Teams Rooms Basic	Teams Rooms Pro
Teams video gallery with multiple layout options	Yes	Yes
Front row		Yes
Together mode		Yes
Large gallery (up to 50 videos)		Yes
Split gallery across two screens		Yes
Engage with chat and Loop components		Yes
Make and receive peer-to-peer and group calls	Yes	Yes
Microsoft 365 Phone System	Yes	Yes
Make and receive calls with Microsoft Teams Phone	Requires calling plan	Requires calling plan
Intelligent speaker support for live transcript with speaker identification		Yes
Intelligent camera support with multiple video streams		Yes
Support for multiple cameras		Yes
Panoramic room view		Yes
Remote PTZ controls		Yes
AI noise suppression		Yes
People counting		Yes
Secure operating system	Yes	Yes
System-level security (such as secure boot and assigned access)	Yes	Yes
Endpoint management with Microsoft Intune and Microsoft Configuration Manager		Yes

(*continued*)

Table 8-2. (*continued*)

Feature	Teams Rooms Basic	Teams Rooms Pro
Microsoft Entra ID (formerly Azure Active Directory) advanced grouping and conditional access		Yes
Teams admin center enrollment and inventory	Yes	Yes
Automatic software updates	Yes	Yes
Detailed system and configuration information		Yes
Peripheral health management		Yes
Remote settings configuration		Yes
Device history and activity		Yes
Device alerting		Yes
Device analytics		Yes
Custom tagging		Yes
App updates and AI-powered remediation service		Yes

8.1.4 Recommend a Teams Rooms Device Platform (Android vs. Windows vs. Surface Hub)

The choice between Windows Teams Rooms and Android Teams Rooms depends on your organization's specific needs and priorities. Windows Teams Rooms offer more advanced features, greater customization, and robust integration with the Microsoft ecosystem, making them suitable for larger and more complex environments. Android Teams Rooms, on the other hand, provide a cost-effective, simple, and user-friendly solution ideal for smaller businesses or less demanding setups.

Windows previously offered better supportability and remote support options, whereas Android faced challenges in providing the same ease and compatibility. However, recent updates have improved Android significantly, making it a more viable option. Currently, Windows still excels in meeting engagement, device controls, and

CHAPTER 8 TEAMS ROOMS AND DEVICES

collaboration tools. While this might suggest Windows is ahead, both platforms have unique features. For instance, Windows supports the Surface Hub, whereas Android does not, but Android is compatible with the Microsoft Whiteboard App, which Windows is not. Table 8-3 compares the features available to the two MTR solutions.

Table 8-3. Features Comparison Between Android MTRs and Windows MTRs

Features		Windows	Android
Meeting join	One-touch-join	Available	Available
	Proximity join	Available	Available
	QR code meeting join	Available	Available
	Meet now	Available	Available
	Teams Meeting with ID	Available	Available
	Direct guest join	BlueJeans: Available	BlueJeans: Not available
		Webex: Available	Webex: Available
		Zoom: Available	Zoom: Available
	Direct guest join with ID	BlueJeans: Not available	BlueJeans: Not available
		Webex: Not available	Webex: Not available
		Zoom: Available	Zoom: Not available
	SIP/H.323 calling	Available	Not available
	PSTN calling	Available	Available
	Admins can require meeting ID and passcode on meeting join	Available	Available
	Cross cloud meeting join (for example, Commercial and then GCC or GCC High and then GCC)	Available	Not available

(continued)

Table 8-3. (*continued*)

Features		Windows	Android
Meeting engagement and collaboration	Intuitive, purpose-built app experience	Available	Available
	Video and content layouts (Front Row, Together Mode, Large Gallery, etc.)	Available	Available
	Front Row unified background	Available	Not available
	Configure default meeting layout	Available	Available
	View chat in all layouts	Available	Available
	Chat bubbles	Available	Available
	Raise hand, lower all hands	Available	Available
	Pin multiple participants	Available	Not available
	Spotlight multiple participants	Available	Available
	Live reactions	Available	Available
	PowerPoint Live	Available	Available
	Live closed captions	Available	Available
	Participate in breakout rooms	Not available	Not available
	Teams Premium meeting protection policies (watermark, E2E encryption for meetings, and sensitivity labels)	Available	Available
	Start meeting recording and transcription	Not available	Not available
	Teams Town Hall (Presenter role)	Not available	Not available
	Teams Town Hall (Attendee role)	Not available	Not available
	Teams Live Event (Presenter role)	Available	Not available
	Teams Live Event (Attendee role)	Available	Not available
	Overflow Meeting Join (1k+ meeting participants)	Available	Not available
	Microsoft Whiteboard during Teams Meeting (with touch display)	Available	Available

(*continued*)

CHAPTER 8 TEAMS ROOMS AND DEVICES

Table 8-3. (*continued*)

Features		Windows	Android
	Microsoft Whiteboard outside a meeting (with touch display)	Not available	Available
	Intelligent content capture (content camera)	Available	Available
	Meeting Lock	Available	Available
	Automatically disconnect if room is the only participant 5 minutes after meeting time ends	Available	Available
	Cloud IntelliFrame	Available	Not available
	Multi-stream IntelliFrame	Available	Not available
	Spatial Audio	Available	Not available
	People Recognition	Available	Not available
	Intelligent Speaker	Available	Not available
	Room Capacity Notifications	Available	Available
	User accessible device language change	Available	Not available
	Rate my call report	Available	Not available
	Net promoter score (NPS) at meeting end	Available	Not available
	Meeting controls on touch enabled front of room displays	Not available	Available
	Smart Camera Controls	Available	Available
	Local pan tilt zoom (PTZ) controls	Not available	Not available
	Remote Pan tilt zoom (PTZ) control	Available	Available
	Switch between multiple in-room cameras	Available	Available
	Coordinated meetings	Available	Not available

(*continued*)

CHAPTER 8 TEAMS ROOMS AND DEVICES

Table 8-3. (*continued*)

Features		Windows	Android
	Third party custom room control	Available	Not available
	Companion mode	Available	Available
	Automatically hide room video from in-room desktop participants	Available	Available
	Room remote (Desktop & Mobile)	Available	Available
	Teams Casting (Desktop & Mobile)	Available	Available
Front of Room Configurations	Single Screen	Available	Available
	Dual Screen	Available	Available
	Touch board form factor (no console)	Available	Available
	Front of Room (16:9) (1920x1080 or 3840x2160)	Available	Available
	Front of Room (21:9) (2560x1080 or 5120x2160) (Single Display Only)	Available	Not available
Security	Secure mounting, security lock slot (Kensington lock), I/O ports access	Available	Available
	Operating System	Windows 10 / Windows 11	Android 9+
	Kiosk mode	Available	Available
	Microsoft Defender for Endpoint	Available	Not available
Device Management	Built-in backgrounds	Available	Available
	Custom background	Available	Not available
	Unauthenticated proxy support	Available	Available
	Authenticated proxy support	Not available	Not available
Teams Admin Center	Automatic onboarding	Available	Available
	Device inventory views	Available	Available

(*continued*)

CHAPTER 8   TEAMS ROOMS AND DEVICES

Table 8-3. (*continued*)

Features		Windows	Android
	Overall device health monitoring	Available	Available
	Connected peripheral health monitoring	Available	Not available
	Remote configuration (restart, settings, & log collection)	Available	Available
	Automatic Teams app updates	Available	Available
	Real-time and call quality analytics	Available	Available
Pro Management Portal	Automatic onboarding	Available	Available
	Overall device health monitoring	Available	Available
	Connected peripheral health monitoring	Available	Not available
	Remote Access	Available	Not available
	Partner Delegation	Available	Available
	Autopilot + Autologin	Available	Not available
	One Time Passcode	Available	Not available
	ServiceNow Integration	Available	Available
	Device grouping & Role-based access control	Available	Available
	Device Settings Management	Available	Not available
	Update Management	Available	Not available
	Log Collection	Available	Available
	Incident Management	Available	Available
	Health and usage reports	Available	Available
	Events	Available	Available
	Standards and Rooms Planner	Available	Available

As part of the list of available solutions for MTR, you have also to consider Surface Hub (that is now sold on its version 3), which is the solution manufactured directly by Microsoft. The Microsoft Surface Hub 3 is a significant innovation for collaborative workspaces, with advanced features and seamless Microsoft integration, making it ideal for boosting team collaboration and productivity, especially in remote and hybrid work scenarios. Table 8-4 summarizes the pros and cons of Surface Hub.

Table 8-4. *Specific Pros and Cons for Surface Hub*

Pros	Cons
Smart rotation and AI tools enhance user experience.	High price
Improved performance for multitasking	Dependency on Microsoft ecosystem limits third-party compatibility
Revamped Teams Rooms for effective remote meetings	
Sleek design suitable for various work environments	

8.1.5 Recommend Teams-Certified Devices

Microsoft has created a Teams Devices Certification Program to ensure that certified devices meet standards for performance and quality across audio, video, and user interface experiences. The program involves collaboration between Microsoft and OEM partners to meet certification requirements, including security, audio/video quality, Teams experience, and accessibility. Certification ensures devices run the required operating system version for Teams and the Teams admin center. Microsoft supports the latest Teams client version on certified devices for two years post-certification period.

It is possible to search for certified devices in the Teams device store. The device store is accessible in two different ways (the availability depends on the country).

- In the Teams admin center
- Inside the Teams app

A list of the certified devices is also available online at https://www.microsoft.com/en-us/microsoft-teams/across-devices/. The devices are listed in these categories: Headsets, Speakerphones, Web cameras, Desk phones and Teams displays, Teams Rooms, Teams Rooms accessories.

CHAPTER 8   TEAMS ROOMS AND DEVICES

In addition to the category of device that you need, different parameters have to be considered:

- Audio quality (including noise cancellation capability, speaker quality and echo) reduction.

- Video quality (including resolution, frame rate and field of view)

- Connectivity (USB, Bluetooth, or wireless options)

- Security features

- Accessibility

- Price range

By evaluating these parameters, you can suggest the most appropriate Teams-certified device tailored to specific user needs and organizational requirements.

8.1.6 Recommend Teams Rooms Certified Components

For MTRs there are a few categories of additional accessories that can be used to improve the user experience, including additional cameras, additional speakers, additional and expanded control panels, and Teams panels.

Microsoft Teams panels are compact touchscreen devices mounted outside meeting spaces, typically next to entrances. These panels provide a quick view of location and meeting details and allow for on-the-spot meeting space reservations. With large text and color-coded indicators, meeting space availability can be seen from a distance (see Figure 8-2).

CHAPTER 8 TEAMS ROOMS AND DEVICES

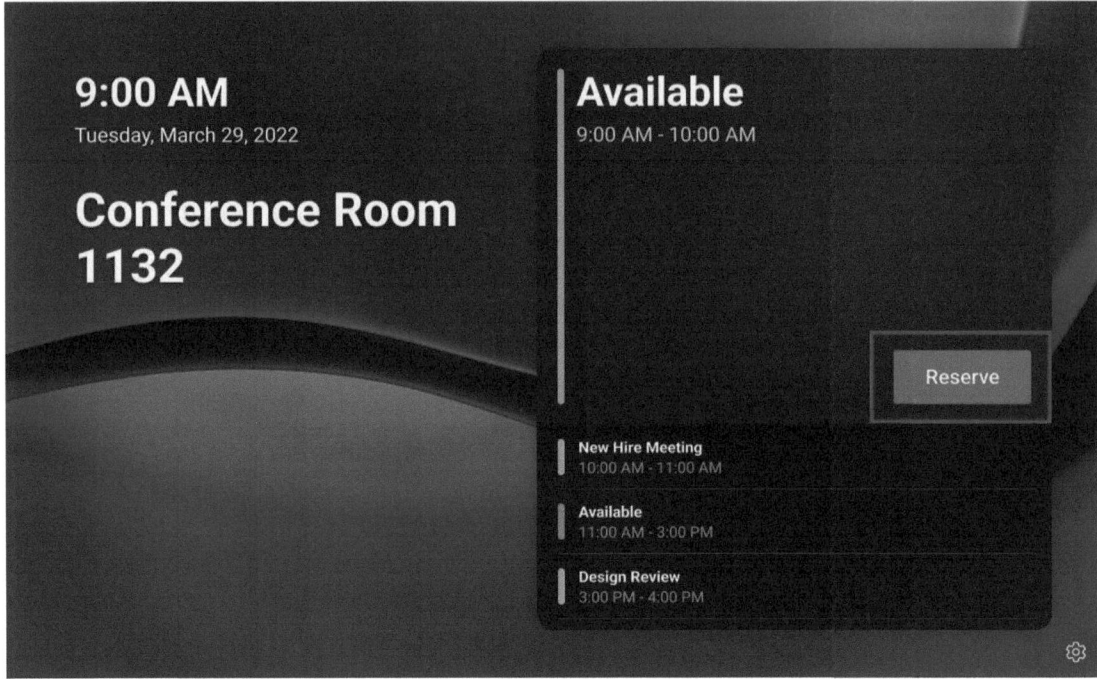

Figure 8-2. A Teams panel

8.1.7 Recommend When to Use Coordinated Meetings

Coordinated meetings allow Microsoft Teams Rooms on Windows devices and Surface Hubs in a meeting room to join the same meeting simultaneously. This setup optimizes the use of cameras, speakers, and microphones to avoid echo and feedback noise.

- Decide the roles of each device in a meeting room (e.g., which device will use the active microphone, camera, and whiteboard).

- Get your devices' user principal names (UPNs). You can find them in the Microsoft 365 admin center by going to Users and then "Active users."

- Create a deployment worksheet to document your configuration settings for each device.

- Configure Teams Rooms on Windows Device or Select Surface Hubs. Select More and then Settings on the device, enter the administrator password, select Coordinated Meetings, and turn it on. As an alternative, you can use an XML configuration file.

8.1.8 Recommend When to Use Cloud Video Interop (CVI) or Direct Guest Join

Cloud Video Interop (CVI) allows third-party SIP and H.323 video room devices (VTCs) to join Microsoft Teams meetings. CVI supports audio, video, and content sharing through desktop, web clients, and many partner devices that integrate natively with Teams.

CVI is ideal for organizations with the following characteristics:

- **Large deployment**: More than 50 meeting room and personal video devices that are not directly compatible with Microsoft Teams.

- **Investment retention**: Desire to retain the value of current meeting room and personal video devices while transitioning to a native Microsoft Teams solution.

CVI provides an interim solution; however, it's recommended to consider native Teams Meeting solutions like Teams Rooms Systems for long-term use.

MTRs support a one-touch experience, called Direct Guest Join, to join third-party online meetings such as those hosted on Cisco Webex and Zoom (as shown in Figure 8-3).

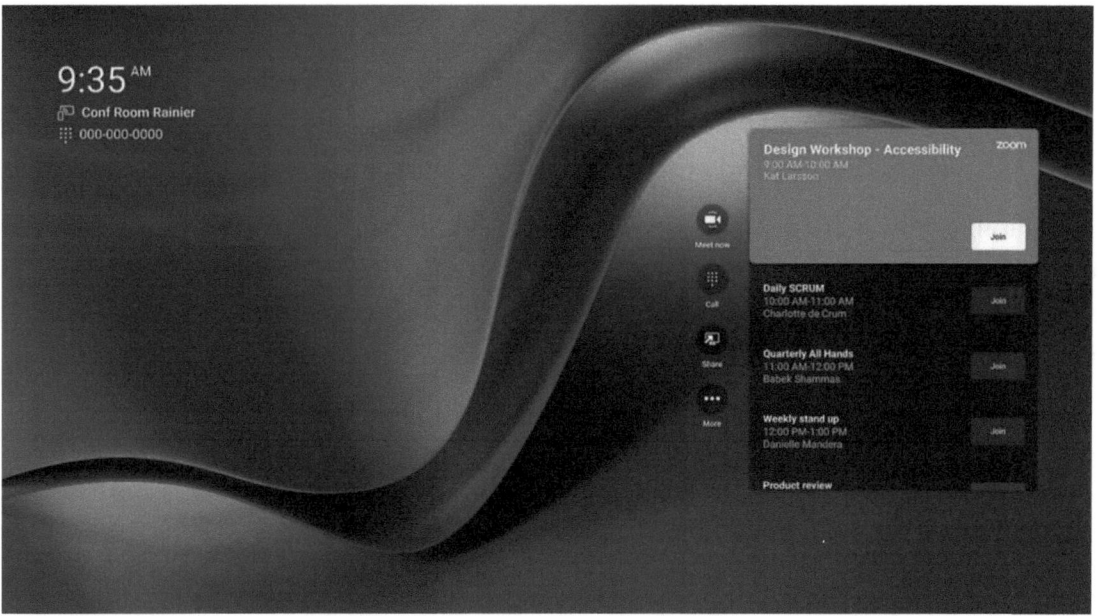

Figure 8-3. Direct Guest Join for an MTR

Participants experience the meeting as intended by the third-party service, with all the functionalities (audio, video, content sharing) provided by Zoom or Webex.

The device ensures that the best possible configurations (like disabling other microphones to avoid echo) are in place.

- **Webex Meetings**: Meetings must be hosted in Webex Meetings Pro using version WBS 40.7 or later.

- **Zoom Meetings**: Regular Zoom meetings are supported, but Zoom Webinars and Zoom Events are not.

8.1.9 Recommend an Update Strategy for Teams Meeting Room Devices

As we have seen before, an MTR is potentially built using different devices and accessories. The consequence is that both software and firmware require an update process. Microsoft Teams Rooms Pro Management provides update management in two main ways.

- **Automatically Managed**: Updates are installed on your devices automatically based on Pro Management's assessment, requiring no user intervention.

- **Ring Validated**: A ring system is used to preview updates on selected devices, allowing for monitoring and ensuring quality before a wider rollout. This method provides an extra layer of precaution.

Automatically managed does not require any additional action. Ring validation involves creating different groups, or "rings," where updates are initially tested on a small set of devices before being rolled out to a larger set. The process typically includes the following steps:

- **Staging ring**: This is the first group where updates are deployed. It acts as a test group and includes a diverse range of devices to ensure compatibility and catch any potential issues early.

- **General ring**: After successful validation in the staging ring, updates are deployed to this group, which includes most MTRs across the enterprise.

- **Executive ring:** This ring consists of high-profile rooms where minimal disruption is essential, such as large conference rooms used for executive meetings.

Even with ring validation, a room might receive "catch-up" updates mandated by Microsoft to ensure it complies with the latest recommendations.

8.1.10 Identify the Requirements for a Microsoft Exchange Online Resource Account

Microsoft 365 offers resource accounts as mailbox and Teams accounts that are dedicated to specific resources, such as an MTR. The Exchange Online mailbox is used for activities like automatically respond to meeting invites. Microsoft 365 resource accounts are different from Teams resource accounts (that we have seen in Chapter 7). Microsoft 365 resource accounts are linked to an Exchange Online mailbox and allow for the booking of shared resources like rooms and projectors. Each resource account you want to associate with an MTR needs a Teams Rooms license.

The Microsoft 365 account can be created from the Microsoft 365 admin portal or using PowerShell. From the admin portal, click Resources in the left panel, and then select Rooms & equipment.

Select "Add resource" to create a new resource account. Enter a display name and email address for the account and then select Save. From PowerShell, follow these steps:

- Connect to Exchange Online with this:
  - `Connect-ExchangeOnline`

- Add an account when you create a room mailbox so it can authenticate with Microsoft Teams.

- For example, let's create a Microsoft 365 resource account for the MTR called Crystal (Crystal@M365x07896792.OnMicrosoft.com),
  - `New-Mailbox -MicrosoftOnlineServicesID Crystal@M365x07896792.OnMicrosoft.com -Name "Conf Room Crystal" -Alias ConfRoomCrystal -Room -EnableRoomMailboxAccount $true -RoomMailboxPassword (ConvertTo-SecureString -String '<Password>' -AsPlainText -Force)`

- New-Mailbox: This cmdlet is used to create a new mailbox in Exchange Online.

- -MicrosoftOnlineServicesID Crystal@M365x07896792.OnMicrosoft.com: This parameter specifies the Microsoft Online Services ID for the new mailbox. This is essentially the email address that will be assigned to the resource account.

- -Name "Conf Room Crystal": This parameter sets the display name of the mailbox. In this case, it is set to Conf Room Crystal.

- -Alias ConfRoomCrystal: This parameter sets the alias for the mailbox. An alias is an alternate email address that can be used to reference the mailbox.

- -Room: This switch parameter specifies that the mailbox being created is a room mailbox, which is used for scheduling and reserving rooms.

- -EnableRoomMailboxAccount $true: This parameter enables the room mailbox account, allowing it to be used as a resource account.

- -RoomMailboxPassword (ConvertTo-SecureString -String '<Password>' -AsPlainText -Force): This parameter sets the password for the room mailbox account. The ConvertTo-SecureString cmdlet converts the plain text password to a secure string, which is required for setting the password securely. Replace <Password> with the actual password you want to assign to the account.

It is possible to customize the previously created MTR resource account. For example:

```
Set-CalendarProcessing -Identity Crystal@M365x07896792.
OnMicrosoft.com -AutomateProcessing AutoAccept
-AddOrganizerToSubject $false -DeleteComments $false
-DeleteSubject $false -ProcessExternalMeetingMessages $true
-RemovePrivateProperty $false -AddAdditionalResponse $true
-AdditionalResponse "This is a Microsoft Teams Meeting
room! Please ensure to leave the room clean after use."
```

- **AutomateProcessing: AutoAccept**: The room mailbox will automatically accept meeting invitations.

- **AddOrganizerToSubject: $false**: The organizer's name will not be added to the subject line.

- **DeleteComments: $false**: Comments in the meeting request will be kept.

- **DeleteSubject: $false**: The subject of the meeting request will be kept.

- **ProcessExternalMeetingMessages: $true**: External meeting requests will be processed.

- **RemovePrivateProperty: $false**: The private flag in the meeting request will be preserved.

- **AddAdditionalResponse: $true**: Additional text will be added to the meeting acceptance response.

- **AdditionalResponse: "This is a Microsoft Teams Meeting room! Please ensure to leave the room clean after use."**: In addition to the basic message, this response includes a reminder for users to leave the room clean after use, which helps maintain the room's condition and promotes considerate use.

8.1.11 Identify the Enrollment Requirements for Microsoft Intune

To enroll an Android- or a Windows-based MTR to Intune, there are two different processes.

- Teams Android-based MTRs are managed by Intune via Android Device Administrator (DA) management. An Intune license is required (that could be part of the license you are already using). You need to set the MDM authority before you can enroll devices. For the Android device administrator enrollment:

- Sign in to the Microsoft Intune admin center, go to Devices and then Android and then Enrollment.
- Under "Android device administrator," choose "Personal and corporate-owned devices with device administration privileges."
- Select the checkmark next to "Use device administrator to manage devices." By enabling this feature, you grant Microsoft permission to send both user and device information to Google.
- Open the Compliance tab and create an Android Device Administrator compliance policy.
- Assign the policy it to a Microsoft Entra group that contains the users who are signing into the Teams devices.

- To enroll Windows MTR devices in Intune, you can use automatic MDM enrollment.

  - Name your MTR with a standard naming format (for example, a name starting with MTR).
  - Create a dynamic device group in Intune. From the Microsoft Intune admin center, open Groups and then "New Group." Select Security for the group type. Select a name and a description. For the Membership type, choose Dynamic Device.
  - Add a dynamic query and then (device.displayName -startsWith "MTR"). After the validation completes, select Save and then Create.
  - Create enrollment rules for the dynamic group.
  - On the device, from the Windows Start menu, open Settings and then Accounts and then "Access work or school." You should use an Intune device enrollment manager (DEM) account specifically because Teams Room devices are shared.

8.1.12 Plan for Advanced Features on Shared Devices

Microsoft Teams Shared Devices is an add-on license dedicated to devices not in the MTR category that allows you to designate those devices as shared. Using this license, devices like common area phones can support features like call queues and auto attendants, call park, and voicemail. This license also supports Microsoft Teams displays and Microsoft Teams panels.

The Microsoft Teams Shared Devices license includes the following service plans:

- Microsoft Teams
- Microsoft Teams Phone
- Microsoft Intune (Microsoft Intune Plan 1 and Plan 2)
- Microsoft Entra ID P1
- Exchange Online Plan (voicemail only)

By default, the basic calling experience will be on the common area phone's home screen, but you can turn on an advanced calling experience.

The following advanced calling features are available for supported Teams phone device models with a Teams Shared Devices license:

- Call park and retrieve.
- Cloud-based voicemail through Exchange Online Plan 2.
- To disable cloud-based voicemail, see Voicemail user settings using PowerShell.
- Call queues.
- Auto attendants.
- Group call pickup.
- Forwarding rules.

Turning on advanced calling capabilities requires you to purchase hardware models that can support all required capabilities. Table 8-5 shows what phone device features are available with each license.

Table 8-5. Workloads and Teams Licenses Matching

	Calls	Contacts	Voicemail	Walkie Talkie	Calendar
Teams Phone license	Yes	Yes	Yes	Yes	Yes
Teams Shared Device license	Yes	Yes	Yes	Yes	No
Teams Rooms Pro license	Yes	Yes	No	No	Yes

8.2 Maintain Teams Rooms and Devices

Maintaining Teams Rooms and devices involves several key activities to ensure optimal performance and reliability like the following:

- Keeping the Teams Rooms app and device firmware up-to-date
- Configuring device settings and policies through Intune
- Configuring conditional access policies for resource accounts
- Configuring the SIP gateway for interoperability with other communication systems

Certain maintenance tasks included on the MS-721 exam will be discussed next.

8.2.1 Configure Device Settings

The first tool to manage Teams devices is the Teams admin center; it supports Teams Rooms on Windows, Teams Rooms on Android, Surface Hubs (Legacy), panels, phones, displays, and SIP devices (see Figure 8-4).

CHAPTER 8 TEAMS ROOMS AND DEVICES

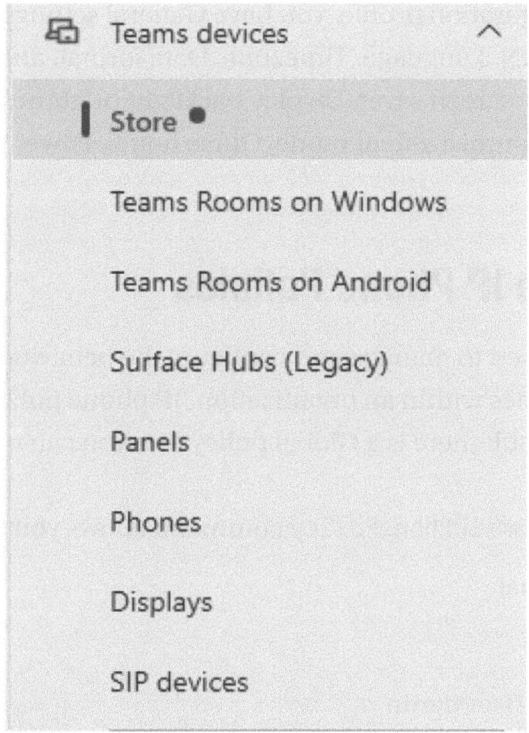

Figure 8-4. The Teams devices panel

For each device, you'll see details such as device name, manufacturer, model, user, status, action, last seen, and history. You can customize this view to display the information that best suits your needs. If you've signed up for Microsoft Intune, then phones, Teams Rooms on Android, Teams displays, and Teams panels are automatically enrolled. Once enrolled, device compliance is verified, and conditional access policies are applied.

The TAC supports the execution of tasks on Teams devices including changing device information, managing software updates, assigning or changing configuration policies, adding or removing device tags, restarting devices, filtering devices using device tags, scheduling device actions, viewing device history and diagnostics, viewing device action details, canceling device actions, and performing actions on multiple devices.

Teams uses configuration profiles for devices to manage Teams-certified devices. To manage configuration profiles, from the TAC go to the "Teams devices" section on the left, select the type of device (for example, Phones), and then select the "Configuration profiles" tab.

231

CHAPTER 8 TEAMS ROOMS AND DEVICES

As part of the configuration profile, you have General settings (Set device lock Timeout, Device lock PIN, Language, Timezone, Date format, and Time format) and Device settings (Display screen saver, Display backlight brightness, Display backlight timeout, Display high contrast, Silent mode, Office hours, Power saving, and Screen capture).

8.2.2 Configure IP Phone Policies

IP phone policies are used to manage and configure the behavior and features of Teams-certified IP phones within an organization. IP phone policies are managed via PowerShell, and by default there is a Global policy that you can modify (or you are able to define new ones).

Using the `get-CsTeamsIPPhonePolicy` command allows you to see the Global policy:

> Identity: Global
>
> Description:
>
> SignInMode: UserSignIn
>
> SearchOnCommonAreaPhoneMode: Enabled
>
> AllowHomeScreen: EnabledUserOverride
>
> AllowBetterTogether: Enabled
>
> AllowHotDesking: True
>
> HotDeskingIdleTimeoutInMinutes: 120

The following options are available for `New-CsTeamsIPPhonePolicy` and `Set-CsTeamsIPPhonePolicy`:

- `AllowBetterTogether`: Determines whether Better Together mode is enabled, allowing phones to lock and unlock in an integrated fashion with a Windows PC running a 64-bit Teams desktop client.

- `AllowHomeScreen`: Determines whether the Home Screen feature of the Teams IP Phones is enabled.

- `AllowHotDesking`: Determines whether hot desking mode is enabled.

- `HotDeskingIdleTimeoutInMinutes`: Determines the idle timeout value in minutes for the signed-in user account.

- Identity: The identity of the policy to be created.
- SearchOnCommonAreaPhoneMode: Determines whether a user can search the Global Address List in Common Area Phone Mode.
- SignInMode: Determines the sign-in mode for the device when signing in to Teams.

For example, with the following command, you can create a custom policy (CommonAreaPhonePolicy) with idle timeout for hot desking set to 30 minutes:

- ```
  New-CsTeamsIPPhonePolicy -Identity CommonAreaPhonePolicy
  -SignInMode CommonAreaPhoneSignIn -AllowBetterTogether
  Disabled -AllowHomeScreen Enabled -AllowHotDesking $true
  -HotDeskingIdleTimeoutInMinutes 30 -Description "Policy
  for common area phones"
  ```

8.2.3 Configure Local Network Settings

Configuration profiles include Network settings. To manage configuration profiles, from the TAC go to the "Teams devices" section on the left, select the type of device (for example, Phones), and then select the "Configuration profiles" tab.

The following options are available: DHCP enabled, Logging enabled, Host name, Domain name, IP address, Subnet mask, Default gateway, Primary DNS, Secondary DNS, Device's admin password, and Network PC port.

8.2.4 Configure Security and Updates

To manage the device updates, you can use the configuration profiles.

In the General settings you can modify "Maintenance window," "Update frequency," and "Restart Teams automatically" (see Figure 8-5).
  ```

CHAPTER 8 TEAMS ROOMS AND DEVICES

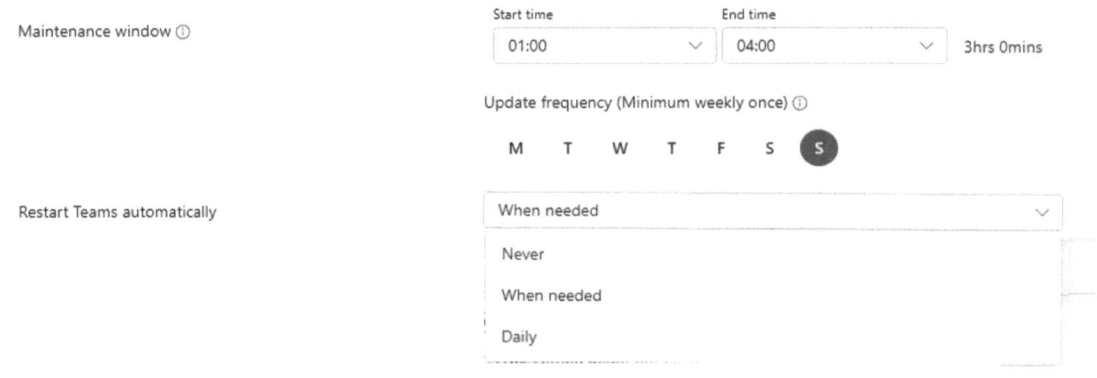

Figure 8-5. Maintenance options for Teams devices

8.2.5 Configure Conditional Access Policy MFA Exception for Resource Accounts

One of the most common security configurations for a Microsoft 365 tenant is to use Microsoft Entra Conditional Access to require multifactor authentication (MFA) and limit authentication requests to specific networks or devices. That said, certain accounts (like resource accounts for MTRs) must be excluded from MFA requirements. These accounts are used to sign in and provide essential meeting functionalities without direct human intervention. Enforcing MFA on these accounts would require manual input for every sign-in attempt, which is unusable.

Conditional Access policies must include a user, group, or workload identity assignment as one of the signals in the decision process. You can configure exclusions using a Microsoft Entra group to make the management easier.

So, for example, you could create a group containing the MTR's resource accounts to manage the exclusions in the Microsoft Entra admin center. After that, still in the Entra admin center, you can go to Protection and then "Conditional Access" and then Policies to manage your policies. Select the Conditional Access policy to which you want to add an exclusion, and under Assignments, select Users. Click Exclude and then "Users and groups" (see Figure 8-6). Add the group that contains the resource accounts and click the Save button.

CHAPTER 8　TEAMS ROOMS AND DEVICES

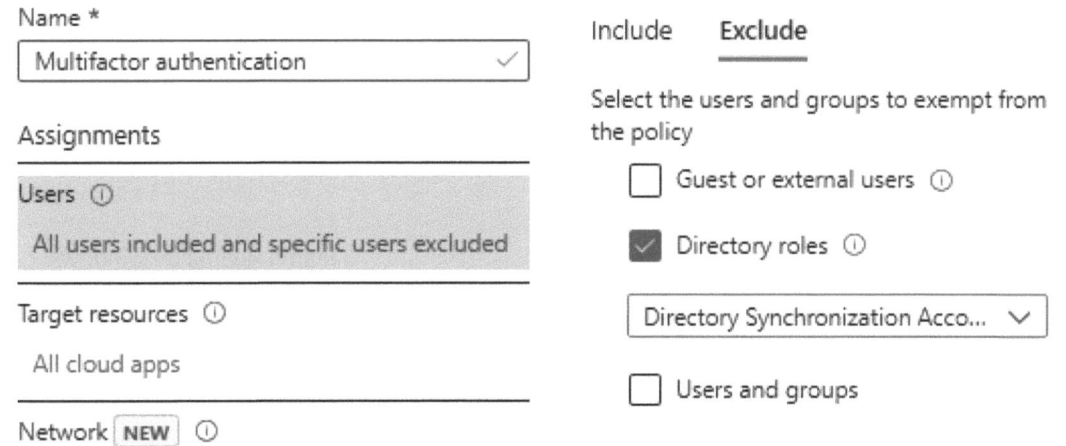

Figure 8-6. Adding exclusions to a Conditional Access policy

8.2.6 Configure Meeting Room Settings by Using the Microsoft Teams Admin Center or the Local Teams Application Settings

For MTRs and Surface Hubs, you can manage the devices from the TAC or using the Teams application installed locally in the device. To manage MTRs in TAC, go to Teams Devices and then Teams Rooms on Windows or Surface Hubs. Then select "Edit settings."

The available settings are listed in Table 8-6.

Table 8-6. Settings for Windows and Surface Hubs

Setting	Accepted Values	Supported Device Types
Account		Teams Rooms on Windows
Email	Email address	Teams Rooms on Windows
Supported meeting mode	Microsoft Teams only	Teams Rooms on Windows
	Skype for Business (default) and Microsoft Teams	
	Skype for Business and Microsoft Teams (default)	
	Skype for Business Only	

(*continued*)

235

CHAPTER 8 TEAMS ROOMS AND DEVICES

Table 8-6. (*continued*)

Setting	Accepted Values	Supported Device Types
Modern authentication	On	Teams Rooms on Windows
	Off	
Exchange address	Email address	Teams Rooms on Windows
Domain\username (optional)	Account domain and user name	Teams Rooms on Windows
Configure domain	Comma-separated list	Teams Rooms on Windows
Meetings		Teams Rooms on Windows, Surface Hubs
Automatic screen sharing	On	Teams Rooms on Windows
	Off	
HDMI ingest audio sharing	On	Teams Rooms on Windows
	Off	
Show meeting names	On	Teams Rooms on Windows
	Off	
Auto-leave if everyone else left meeting	On	Teams Rooms on Windows
	Off	
Join third-party meetings	Cisco Webex	Teams Rooms on Windows, Surface Hubs
	Zoom	
Join with room info	Selected	Teams Rooms on Windows, Surface Hubs
	Unselected	
Join with custom info	Selected	Teams Rooms on Windows
	Unselected	

(*continued*)

Table 8-6. (*continued*)

Setting	Accepted Values	Supported Device Types
Name (required)	Name of room or space	Teams Rooms on Windows
Email (required)	Email address	Teams Rooms on Windows
Device		Teams Rooms on Windows
Dual monitor mode	On	Teams Rooms on Windows
	Off	
Allow content duplication	Selected	Teams Rooms on Windows
	Unselected	
Bluetooth beaconing	On	Teams Rooms on Windows, Surface Hubs
	Off	
Automatically accept proximity-based meeting invitations	Selected	Teams Rooms on Windows, Surface Hubs
	Unselected	
Send logs with feedback	On	Teams Rooms on Windows
	Off	
Email address for logs and feedback	Email address	Teams Rooms on Windows
Coordinate Meetings		Teams Rooms on Windows
Coordinated Meetings	On	Teams Rooms on Windows, Surface Hubs
	Off	
Turn on this device's microphone	On	Teams Rooms on Windows, Surface Hubs
	Off	

(*continued*)

Table 8-6. (*continued*)

Setting	Accepted Values	Supported Device Types
Let people enable when joining a meeting	Selected	Teams Rooms on Windows, Surface hubs
	Unselected	
Turn on this device's camera	On	Teams Rooms on Windows, Surface Hubs
	Off	
Let people enable when joining a meeting	Selected	Teams Rooms on Windows, Surface Hubs
	Unselected	
Turn on whiteboarding for this device	On	Teams Rooms on Windows, Surface Hubs
	Off	
Trusted device accounts (separate with commas)	List of devices	Teams Rooms on Windows, Surface Hubs
Peripherals		Teams Rooms on Windows
Conferencing microphone	List of available microphones	Teams Rooms on Windows
Conferencing speaker	List of available speakers	Teams Rooms on Windows
Default volume	0-100	Teams Rooms on Windows
Default speaker	List of available speakers	Teams Rooms on Windows
Default volume	0-100	Teams Rooms on Windows
Content camera	List of available cameras	Teams Rooms on Windows
Content Camera Enhancements	On	Teams Rooms on Windows
	Off	
Rotate Content Camera 180 degrees	On	Teams Rooms on Windows
	Off	

(*continued*)

CHAPTER 8 TEAMS ROOMS AND DEVICES

Table 8-6. (*continued*)

Setting	Accepted Values	Supported Device Types
Theming		Teams Rooms on Windows
	Default	Teams Rooms on Windows
	No theme	
	Custom	
	List of built-in themes	

The MTR Home screen supports some configuration and operations that are different between Windows and Android based rooms (see Table 8-7).

Table 8-7. *Actions Available in the MTR Home*

Setting	Windows MTRs	Android MTRs
Meet now	Available	Available
Call	Available	Available
Share	Available	Available
Teams cast	Enabled/Disabled (Settings and then Device)	Enabled/Disabled (Teams Admin Settings)
HDMI input	Various options (Settings and then Meetings)	Various options (Teams Admin Settings)
Whiteboard	Supported on touch board form factor	Disable via Teams Admin Settings
Join with an ID	Available	Available
Room Controls	Available	Not Available
Accessibility	High contrast mode, external keyboard	Controlled by device manufacturer
Language	Changeable via home screen	Controlled by device manufacturer
Help: Report a problem	Enabled with Pro license or email setup	Not available outside preview

(*continued*)

Table 8-7. (*continued*)

Setting	Windows MTRs	Android MTRs
Help: Give feedback	Available	Available
Calendar	Join meetings, show/hide meeting names	Join meetings, show/hide meeting names
QR code	Available	Available
Background	Customizable with Pro license	Default backgrounds only

8.2.7 Create and Configure Device Configuration Profiles for Android Based Devices

To manage Android devices configuration profiles, from the TAC, go to the "Teams devices" section on the left, select Teams Rooms on Android, and then select the "Configuration profiles" tab. As we have seen for other devices, the available settings are divided into General, Meeting Settings, Device Settings and Network Settings.

8.2.8 Manage Teams Rooms from the Microsoft Teams Rooms Pro Management Portal

We introduced the Teams Rooms Pro Management Portal in Section 8.1.1.

The Pro Management Portal supports the following:

- **Intelligent Operations**: Utilizes software and machine learning for automated updates, problem detection, and resolution
- **Update Management**: Automates updates for meeting applications and Windows, based on customer-defined deployment rings
- **Enhanced Insights**: Provides rich analytics, reporting, and insights from large-scale usage data

The management capabilities include the following:

- Room planning and rollout
- Monitoring

- Troubleshooting and remediation
- Update management
- Insights and recommendations
- Compliance and certifications

8.2.9 Configure Intune Policies for Teams Devices

Intune app protection policies (APP) define which apps are allowed and the actions they are allowed to execute. The APP data protection framework consists of three levels, each building on the previous one:

- Enterprise Basic Data Protection (Level 1):
    - Features:
        - PIN protection and encryption
        - Selective wipe operations
        - Android device attestation validation
- Enterprise Enhanced Data Protection (Level 2):
    - Features:
        - Data leakage prevention mechanisms
        - Minimum OS requirements
- Enterprise High Data Protection (Level 3):
    - Features:
        - Advanced data protection mechanisms
        - Enhanced PIN configuration
        - APP mobile threat defense

Teams on Android supports app settings that allow customizations via Microsoft Intune.

App configuration can be delivered using mobile device management (MDM) or through the Intune App Protection Policy (APP) channel.

To configure the policies, open the `Microsoft Intune admin center.` Go to Apps and then "App protection policies." Click Create Policy and select a platform (as shown in Figure 8-7).

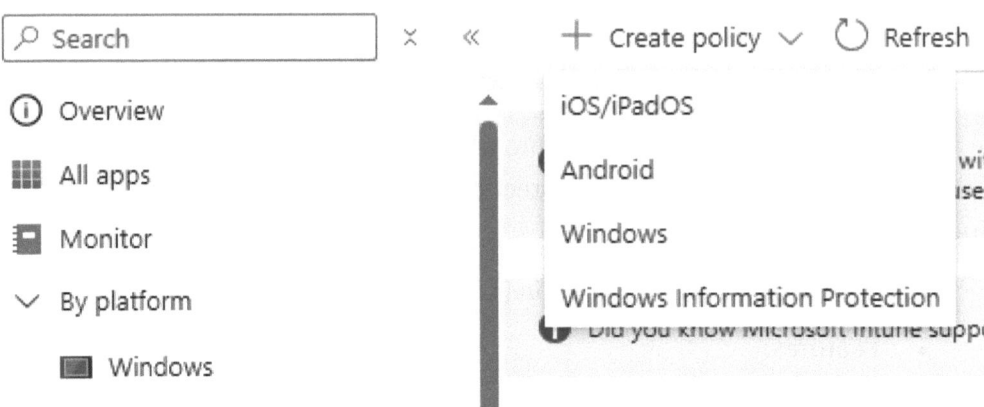

Figure 8-7. Creating an APP

1. On the Basics tab, type a name and description. Click Next.

2. On the Apps page, click Select "Public apps," and then find and select the Microsoft Teams apps. Click Next.

3. The "Data protection page" includes the Data Loss Prevention (DLP) controls, like cut, copy, paste, and save-as restrictions. You can customize the settings as required and click Next.

4. The "Access requirements" page is used to set the PIN and credential requirements that users must meet to access apps in a work context. Again, you can customize the settings as required and click Next.

5. The "Conditional launch" page includes the sign-in security requirements for your access protection policy. Customize the settings as required and click Next.

6. The Assignments page is used to assign or exclude an APP for specific groups. Select the required groups and click Next.

7. On the "Review + create" page, check the final configuration and click the Create button to confirm it.

8.2.10 Configure Intune Configuration Profiles (for Windows MTRs)

Teams Rooms use a specially configured Windows 10 image from the original equipment manufacturer (OEM). Configuration profiles in Intune enable you to manage various aspects of the Windows operating system like managing the Start menu, enabling or disabling connectivity, options and so on. MTRs, which are scoped as meeting room appliances, already limit the user access to the software strictly required for Teams meetings, and standard configuration policies are not a good fit for them. A use case for configuration profiles in MTRs is to enable BitLocker to encrypt the local drive for enhanced security.

To create the configuration profile, open the Microsoft Intune admin center and select Devices and then Manage devices; then select Configuration, Create, and then New policy. Select "Windows 10 and later" from the "Platform" drop-down menu. From the "Profile type" drop-down menu, select Templates and click Endpoint Protection. Click the Create button. In the Basics page, enter a name for the profile and click Next. Under "Configuration settings," expand Windows Encryption.

Select Require in the "Encrypt devices" toggle. Select Enable in the "Configure encryption methods" toggle (see Figure 8-8).

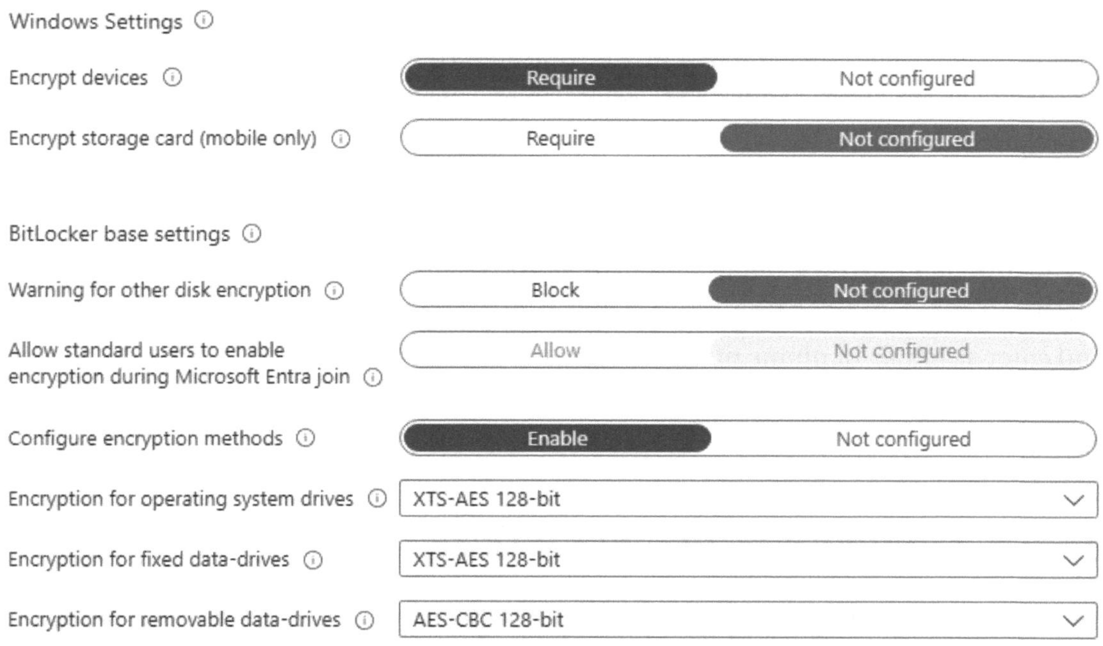

Figure 8-8. Configuration profile, BitLocker for an MTR

Click Next on all the remaining pages up to the "Review + create" page. On this page, check the final configuration and click the Create button to confirm it.

8.2.11 Enable Advanced Voice Capabilities for Shared Space Devices

We listed the advanced voice features in Section 8.1.12. You can enable the features from the Teams admin center or on your Teams phone device that is signed in to your Teams Shared Devices account.

From the TAC, on the left side, navigate to "Teams devices" and then Phones and then select the Configuration profiles tab.

Select the configuration profile assigned to your common area phone (or add a new one).

In the Calling settings section, turn on the "Advanced calling" toggle; then select the Save button.

8.2.12 Enable Hotline for Shared Space Devices

In some scenarios the requirement for a Teams common area phone is to ring to a single, specific location or a directory contact when the phone handset is picked up. This feature is called a hotline phone or private line auto ringdown (PLAR) phone.

To enable the feature, in the TAC, select "Teams devices" and then Phones and then "Configuration profiles."

Select a configuration profile and under Calling settings, turn on the Enable the Hotline toggle and then click the Save button.

To turn on PLAR on a Teams phone, sign into your Teams device and select Settings and then Device settings. Next select "Admin only" and then Calling. Then select Hotline and enter a contact or phone number to be autodialed.

Enter the display name you want to show on the phone's home screen and then select Save.

8.2.13 Configure Virtual Front Desk

Virtual Front Desk (VFD) is a feature on Teams display devices that enables the device to act as a virtual receptionist via a video call on Teams.

CHAPTER 8 TEAMS ROOMS AND DEVICES

When you log in to a Teams display with an account that has the Microsoft Teams Shared license assigned, the display will show the Teams hot desk UI. To change to Teams VFD, click Settings. Go to "Device settings" and then Teams, and then select "Teams admin settings." In the next screen select Virtual Front Desk. The settings on the VFD page include "Virtual front desk mode," "Configured contact," "Display message," "Call button message," and Video. When the settings are complete, select "Restart Teams app."

8.2.14 Deploy Common Area Phones, User Phones, Conference Phones

A common area phone is typically placed in a common area like a lobby or another area to allow different people to make a phone call. To set up a common area phones (CAPs) for Microsoft Teams, the following steps are required:

1. Create a new user account and assign licenses (common area phones consume Microsoft Teams Shared Devices license). Enter a username and manually set the password for your CAP. Manually setting a password for common area phones is recommended to prevent sign-in issues for your end users.

2. Set policies for common area phones (IP phone policies, voice routing policies, and calling policies). If Conditional Access policies are used for Android devices in the organization, evaluate the need to create exclusions for Teams CAPs.

3. Assign phone numbers.

4. Depending on how many phones you're deploying, you have three sign-in options:

    - Local sign-in.

    - Sign in from another device.

    - Sign in using the Teams admin center.

You can sign into to a CAP from another device using a code. In this scenario you will enter the username and password on another device, rather than on the phone itself:

- On your common area phone, find the code displayed on the sign-in screen.
- On another device, go to https://www.microsoft.com/devicelogin.
- Enter the code and follow the instructions to complete signing in.

As an admin, you can remotely provision and sign into common area phones from the Teams admin center. For more details, refer to Section 8.2.16.

User phones are paired with a Teams using one of the login methods, similarly to CAPs. However, the device interface will contain the information referred to the specific user.

8.2.15 Create and Manage Teams Device Tags

In the TAC, you can add one or more tags to devices and use them to filter the view of your devices. The same tag can be used on different type of devices, but in that scenario each specific device view (phones, MTRs and so on) will be filtered using the tag.

To manage tags, in the TAC, go to Teams Devices and then choose any device. Select Actions in the upper-right corner of the page and select "All device tags."

To create a device tag, select + Add and select the Save icon.

8.2.16 Deploy Android Devices Remotely

In Teams it is possible to remotely provision Teams Android devices using their Media Access Control (MAC) IDs. MAC IDs or MAC addresses are unique identifiers assigned to network interfaces for communications on the physical network segment. A MAC address is typically represented as six pairs of hexadecimal digits, separated by colons or hyphens.

Each MAC address is intended to be unique to a specific piece of hardware, assigned by the manufacturer of the network interface card (NIC).

To add a MAC address, go to the TAC and select Teams Devices. Open Phones and select "Provision devices" from the Actions tab. You can add the MAC address and a location for the device manually (as shown in Figure 8-9) or upload a file.

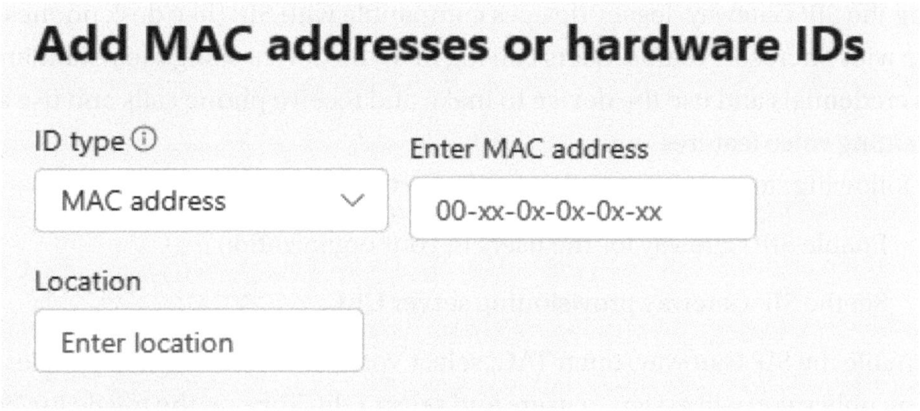

CHAPTER 8   TEAMS ROOMS AND DEVICES

Figure 8-9. Adding Android device MAC address

When the device is added to the list, you are able to click "Generate verification code" (see Figure 8-10).

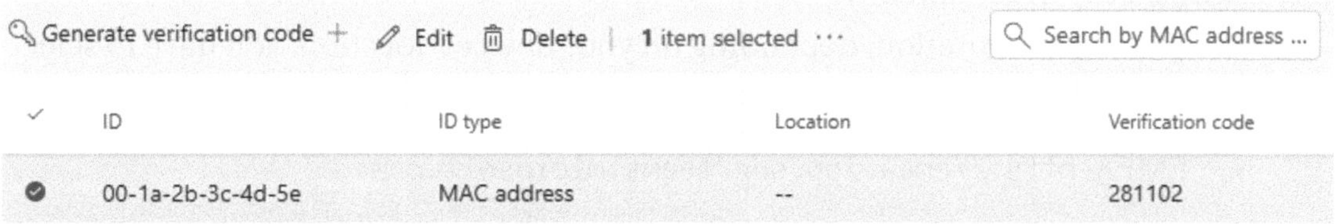

Figure 8-10. Generating a verification code

When the device is powered on and connected to the network, on the Teams device select "Provision device" from Settings. The verification code generated in the TAC has to be provided,

Once the device is provisioned successfully, the tenant's name appears on the sign-in page.

The provisioned device appears in the Waiting for sign in tab. Start the remote sign-in process as shown in Section 8.2.14.

8.2.17 Configure SIP Gateway

A SIP-compatible device is a communication device that supports the Session Initiation Protocol (SIP) for initiating, maintaining, and terminating real-time sessions, such as voice and video calls, over IP networks.

Using the SIP Gateway, legacy devices compatible with SIP (like desk phones) can integrate with Microsoft Teams. Users can log in to the device using their standard tenant's credentials and use the device to make and receive phone calls and use a part of the remaining voice features.

The following steps are required to configure the SIP Gateway:

- Enable SIP Gateway for the users in your organization.
- Set the SIP Gateway provisioning server URL.

To enable the SIP Gateway, open TAC, select Voice and then "Calling policies." Select the calling policy you will assign to users and select Edit. Turn on the toggle for "SIP devices can be used for calls" and then click Save.

SIP devices need a provisioning URL to automatically download their firmware and configuration settings from the Teams SIP Gateway. To set the SIP Gateway provisioning server URL, you can use a Dynamic Host Configuration Protocol (DHCP) server on your network or set the URL manually.

In the DHCP configuration, depending on your devices' location, you have to select one of the URLs in the following list:

- EMEA: `http://emea.ipp.sdg.teams.microsoft.com`
- Americas: `http://noam.ipp.sdg.teams.microsoft.com`
- APAC: `http://apac.ipp.sdg.teams.microsoft.com`

Depending on the maker of the device, you could have to use different option numbers for the provisioning URL (like option 66 for Yealink and/or Option 160 for Poly). Devices within your organization will connect to the SIP Gateway provisioning server. Once provisioned successfully, SIP phones will show the Teams logo and a soft button for signing in.

To manually configure the provisioning server URL into a SIP device, depending on the device, you could connect to the embedded web interface and set the parameters or use different configuration methods.

8.2.18 Monitor Teams Device Health

TAC offers a health status feature, available in the Teams Devices panel, under the specific device type list (like Phones). The health status also indicates the issue severity.

CHAPTER 8　TEAMS ROOMS AND DEVICES

Teams administrators are able to customize the severity of the issues to differ from the standard proposed by Microsoft. You can set alerts related to the health status of devices. In the left navigation of TAC, select "Notifications & alerts" and then Rules. Every M365 tenant has a default rule "Device state rule" that you can connect to Teams channels or webhooks to send an alert and then enable (see Figure 8-11).

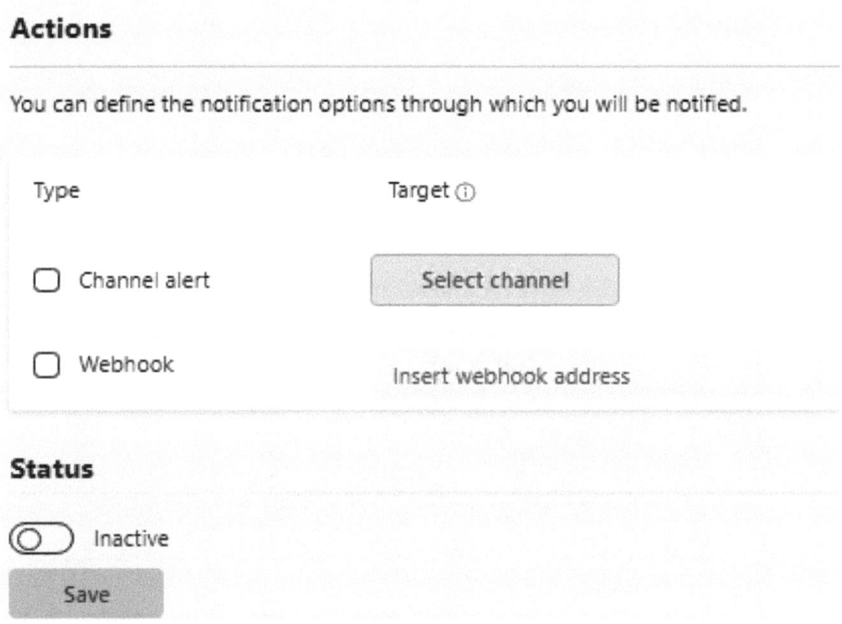

Figure 8-11. Setting an alert for devices health

8.2.19 Troubleshoot Authentication Issues

There are different tools you can use to resolve sign-in errors in Teams. The first one is the "Teams Sign-in diagnostic." To open it, use https://aka.ms/TeamsSignInDiag and then fill the "Provide the username or email of the user reporting this issue" field (see Figure 8-12).

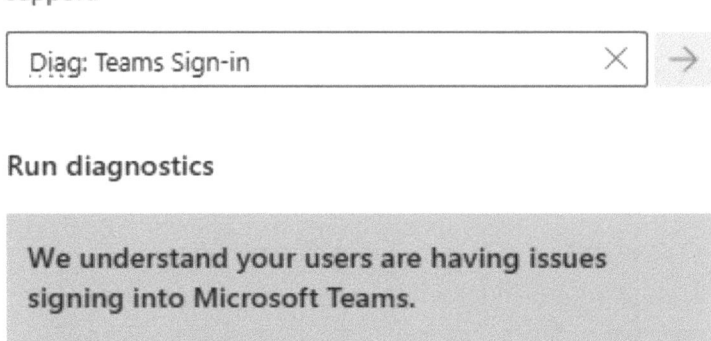

Figure 8-12. Teams sign-in diagnostic

You can use the Microsoft Remote Connectivity Analyzer diagnostic, a diagnostic tool that helps you troubleshoot and resolve connectivity issues related to Microsoft services.

To use it, open a web browser, open the URL, and select Microsoft Teams (see Figure 8-13).

Figure 8-13. Microsoft Remote Connectivity Analyzer

Click "Teams Sign in" and test the account that is presenting issues.
To manually fix the issue, do the following:

- Check whether the user's Teams client is running the latest update. Select the ellipsis (…) and then Settings. Click About Teams to check the client version.

- Check the error code on the Teams sign-in screen. If the code is listed here, follow the provided guidance to fix the error.

- Finally, you could try to uninstall Teams and delete the Teams folders in `%appdata%\Microsoft` folder.

8.2.20 Troubleshoot Update Issues

A useful tool to fix issues with Teams updates are the Teams client logs. When Teams is successfully installed, you have two different logs you can use to troubleshoot the update issues.

- `%LocalAppData%\Microsoft\Teams\SquirrelSetup.log`: This log is written by `Update.exe`, which is an executable that services the Teams app.

- `%AppData%\Microsoft\Teams\logs.txt`: This log is used by the Teams app (specifically `Teams.exe`) to record significant application events.

Teams can automatically start the update process or users can manually check for updates by going to the ellipsis (…) menu next to their profile picture and selecting "Check for updates." When running an update (as in https://learn.microsoft.com/en-us/microsoftteams/troubleshoot-installation), do the following:

- Teams makes a web request and includes the current app version and deployment ring information. The goal of this step is to get the download link. A failure at this step is logged in `%AppData%\Microsoft\Teams\logs.txt`.

- Download update. Teams downloads the update by using the download link obtained from step 1. When the download is complete, Teams calls `Update.exe` to stage the download. A download failure is also logged in `%AppData%\Microsoft\Teams\logs.txt`.

- Stage the update. The downloaded content is verified and unpacked into an intermediate folder, %LocalAppData%\Microsoft\Teams\stage, which is done by Update.exe. Failures at this step are logged in %LocalAppData%\Microsoft\Teams\SquirrelSetup.log.

- Install the update. There are multiple ways to start Teams. The system automatically starts Teams when a user logs in or you can start Teams through a shortcut. In this step, Update.exe checks for the presence of the staging folder, verifies the content again, and performs file operations to unstage the app. The old application folder in %LocalAppData%\Microsoft\Teams\current is backed up to %LocalAppData%\Microsoft\Teams\previous and the stage folder is renamed to current. Failures at this step are logged in %LocalAppData%\Microsoft\Teams\SquirrelSetup.log.

- If %LocalAppData%\Microsoft\Teams\SquirrelSetup.log or %AppData%\Microsoft\Teams\logs.txt don't contain sufficient information to determine the underlying cause and you need more information to troubleshoot the issue, go to Collect, and analyze application and system logs.

8.2.21 Troubleshoot Remote Provisioning Issues

When remote provisioning of a device fails, often the issue is related to a wrong connectivity configuration. Check the connection requirements at https://learn.microsoft.com/en-us/microsoftteams/prepare-network.

Also, confirm that the conditional access policies applied are compatible with a Teams device. You can check for errors in the Entra Admin Center. Open the Microsoft Entra admin center and select the "User sign-ins (non-interactive)" tab.

Select "Add filters" to add the following filters:

- **Status**: Select Failure, and then select Apply.

- **Application**: Enter Teams, and then select Apply.

If select each failed sign-in, you can get additional information, including a tab dedicated to "Conditional Access." Check if any of your policies is impacting the device (see Figure 8-14).

CHAPTER 8 TEAMS ROOMS AND DEVICES

Activity Details: Sign-ins

| Basic info | Location | Device info | Authentication Details | **Conditional Access** |

🔍 Search

| Policy Name ↑↓ | Grant Controls ↑↓ | Session Controls ↑↓ |

Figure 8-14. Sign-ins log checking the Conditional Access tab

8.2.22 Troubleshoot Bluetooth Beaconing

Bluetooth Beaconing (Proximity Join) for an MTR is a feature that utilizes Bluetooth signals to enhance the meeting experience. Bluetooth Beaconing allows participants to join a scheduled Teams meeting as they enter the meeting room. The MTR device emits a Bluetooth signal that can be detected by the participant's device, prompting them to join the meeting without needing to manually connect. To troubleshoot this feature, a few checks have to be executed.

- Proximity Join uses use Bluetooth Low Energy (BLE). Check on the device that the Bluetooth beaconing is enabled, as in Figure 8-15.

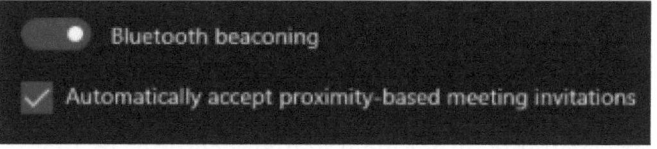

Figure 8-15. Enabling Bluetooth beaconing

- Check that there is no obstacle between the MTR compute unit and the meeting room. The Bluetooth signal must be strong to allow devices to join the MTR.
- Verify that there is no policy (like Intune) changing the behavior of the MTR's Bluetooth connection.

253

8.3 Knowledge Check

Question 1:

Which of the following steps are involved in managing Teams device settings using the Teams admin center?

1. Create and configure device configuration profiles for Android-based devices.
2. Manage Teams Rooms from the Microsoft Teams Rooms Pro Management portal.
3. Configure Intune policies for Teams devices.
4. Assign or change configuration policies.
5. Filter devices using device tags.

Question 2:

What configurations are necessary for implementing IP phone policies in Teams?

1. Set the SignInMode for devices.
2. Enable or disable Better Together mode.
3. Configure the idle timeout for hot desking.
4. Allow or disallow the Home Screen feature.
5. Enable DHCP for IP phones.

Question 3:

Which options are available under local network settings in Teams configuration profiles?

1. DHCP enabled.
2. Logging enabled.
3. Primary DNS.
4. Subnet mask.
5. Secondary DNS.

Question 4:

Which advanced calling features can be enabled for Teams phone devices with a Teams Shared Devices license?

1. Call park and retrieve.
2. Cloud-based voicemail.
3. Auto attendants.
4. Group call pickup.
5. Walkie Talkie.

Question 5:

What are the key activities involved in maintaining Teams Rooms and devices?

1. Keep the Teams Rooms app and device firmware up-to-date.
2. Configure device settings and policies through Intune.
3. Configure conditional access policies for resource accounts.
4. Configure the SIP gateway.
5. Enable advanced voice capabilities for shared space devices.

Answers
Question 1: 1, 2, 3, 4, 5
Question 2: 1, 2, 3, 4
Question 3: 1, 2, 3, 4, 5
Question 4: 1, 2, 3, 4
Question 5: 1, 2, 3, 4, 5

CHAPTER 9

MTRs Based on Windows and Surface Hub

In Chapter 8 introduced the difference between the three platforms that can be used as the base for the Teams MTR (Android, Windows, and Surface). As part of the exam preparation, you need to understand how some specific features and configuration for the Windows and Surface MTRs are managed.

In this chapter, the following required skills and exam topics are described:

Configure and manage Teams Rooms on a Surface Hub or Windows:

- Configure the authentication type during a Surface Hub out-of-box-experience (OOBE) setup
- Configure meeting room settings on a Surface Hub device
- Create and validate a Surface Hub provisioning package
- Assign a provisioning package to a Surface Hub
- Specify domain group policy exclusions for Teams Rooms on Windows
- Configure custom displays for Teams Rooms on Windows
- Customize meeting room settings by using XML files on Windows
- Configure settings for peripherals for Teams Room on Windows
- Monitor Surface Hub health with Azure Monitor
- Manage Surface Hub Updates via Update Rings

CHAPTER 9   MTRS BASED ON WINDOWS AND SURFACE HUB

Configure optional features for Teams Rooms and devices

- Configure HDMI ingest and options
- Configure a content camera
- Configure Teams casting
- Auto accept a proximity join
- Configure an intelligent speaker
- Configure Direct Guest Join
- Configure hot desking on Teams shared devices
- Configure Hotline phones

9.1 Configure and Manage Teams Rooms on a Surface Hub or Windows

Surface Hubs and Microsoft Team Rooms (MTRs) have some specific logics and configurations that you must understand to manage them properly. Having a Windows operating system as the base of your MTRs means that some aspects not used with Android (like Group Policies and configuration based on XML files) are relevant to your deployment.

9.1.1 Configure the Authentication Type During a Surface Hub Out-of-Box-Experience (OOBE) Setup

Surface Hubs are deployed with a default administrator password that is well known, which is why it is important to change the password in Settings. Go to Accounts, select Sign-in options, click Password, and then click Change. The default password is SfB. You can now update the password.

If you join the Surface Hub to the Entra ID, you can use Local Administrator Password Solution (LAPS) to manage the local administrator password.

You can also protect the hardware settings by using a password for Unified Extensible Firmware Interface (UEFI) that replaces the traditional BIOS.

The Surface Hub, for a hybrid or cloud-only organization backed by the Microsoft Entra ID, supports password-less sign-ins. Password-less sign-ins are supported by using the Microsoft Authenticator app and FIDO2 security keys provided by your organization.

9.1.2 Configure Meeting Room Settings on a Surface Hub Device

The Settings menu allows the Surface Hub to configure the parameters shown in Table 9-1.

Table 9-1. *Surface Hub Settings*

Setting	Location	Description
Device account	Surface Hub, Accounts	Set or change the Surface Hub's device account.
Device account sync status	Surface Hub, Accounts	Check the sync status of the device account's mail and calendar on the Surface Hub.
Password rotation	Surface Hub, Accounts	Choose whether to let the Surface Hub automatically rotate the device account's password.
Change admin account password	Surface Hub, Accounts	Change the password for the local admin account. This is available only if you configured the device to use a local admin during the first run.
Device Management	Surface Hub, Device management	Manage policies and business applications using mobile device management (MDM).
Provisioning packages	Surface Hub, Device management	Set or change provisioning packages installed on the Surface Hub.
Open the Microsoft Store app	Surface Hub, Apps & features	The Microsoft Store app is available only to admins through the Settings app.
Skype for Business domain name	Surface Hub, Calling & Audio	Configure a domain name for your Skype for Business server.

(*continued*)

Table 9-1. (*continued*)

Setting	Location	Description
Default Speaker volume	Surface Hub, Calling & Audio	Configure the default speaker volume for the Surface Hub when it starts a session.
Default microphone and speaker settings	Surface Hub, Calling & Audio	Configure a default microphone and speaker for calls, and a default speaker for media playback.
Enable Dolby Audio X2	Surface Hub, Calling & Audio	Configure the Dolby Audio X2 speaker enhancements.
Open Connect App automatically	Surface Hub, Projection	Choose whether projection will automatically open the Connect app or wait for user input before opening.
Turn off wireless projection using Miracast	Surface Hub, Projection	Choose whether presenters can wirelessly project to the Surface Hub using Miracast.
Require a PIN for wireless projection	Surface Hub, Projection	Choose whether people are required to enter a PIN before they use wireless projection.
Wireless projection (Miracast) channel	Surface Hub, Projection	Set the channel for Miracast projection.
Meeting info shown on the welcome screen	Surface Hub, Welcome screen	Choose whether meeting organizer, time, and subject show up on the welcome screen.
Welcome screen background	Surface Hub, Welcome screen	Choose an image to be used as the background during user sessions and on the welcome screen.
Session timeout to Welcome screen	Surface Hub, Session & power	Choose how long until the Surface Hub returns to the welcome screen after no motion is detected.
Resume session	Surface Hub, Session & power	Choose to allow users to resume a session after no motion is detected or to automatically clean up a session.

(*continued*)

Table 9-1. (*continued*)

Setting	Location	Description
Access to Microsoft 365 meetings and files	Surface Hub, Session & power	Choose whether a user can sign in to Microsoft 365 to get access to their meetings and files.
Turn on screen with motion sensors	Surface Hub, Session & power	Choose whether the screen turns on when motion is detected.
Screen time out	Surface Hub, Session & power	Choose how long the device needs to be inactive before turning off the screen.
Sleep time out	Surface Hub, Session & power	Choose how long the device needs to be inactive before going to sleep mode.
Friendly name	Surface Hub, About	Set the Surface Hub name that people will see when connecting wirelessly.
Maintenance hours	Update & security, Windows Update, Advanced options	Configure when updates can be installed.
Recover from the cloud	Update & security, Recovery	Reinstall the operating system on Surface Hub to a manufacturer build from the cloud.
Save BitLocker key	Update & security, Recovery	Back up your Surface Hub's BitLocker key to a USB drive.
Collect logs	Update & security, Logs	Save logs to a USB drive to send to Microsoft later.
Event viewer	Update & security, Logs	Launch Windows Event Viewer to see events that have happened on the Surface Hub.

9.1.3 Create and Validate a Surface Hub Provisioning Package

A provisioning package is a container for a set of configurations. Windows Configuration Designer (WCD) is software to be used on a separate PC that allows you to complete the following tasks:

- Enroll in Active Directory or Microsoft Entra ID
- Create a device administrator account
- Add applications and certificates
- Configure proxy settings
- Configure Configuration Service Provider (CSP) settings

To create a provisioning package, follow these steps:

1. On a separate PC, install Windows Configuration Designer.

2. Select "Provision Surface Hub devices" to configure common settings using a wizard (as shown in Figure 9-1).

CHAPTER 9 MTRS BASED ON WINDOWS AND SURFACE HUB

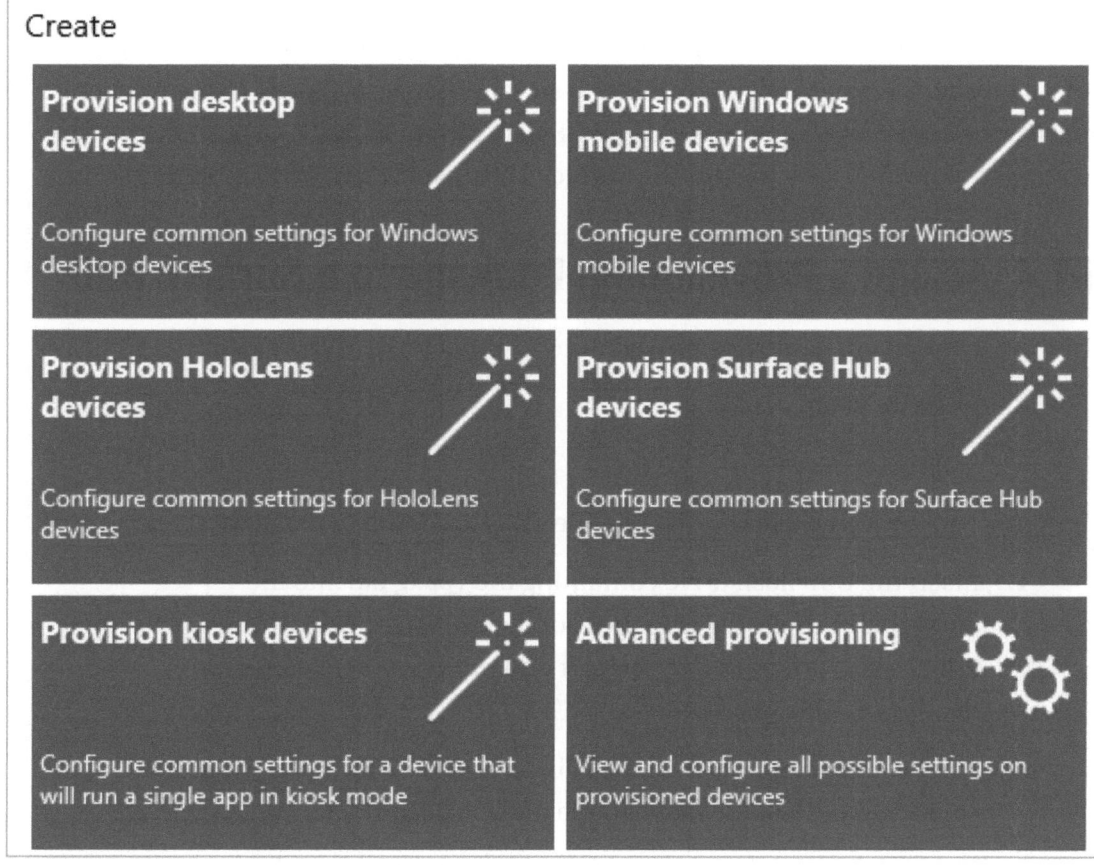

Figure 9-1. *Starting the Surface Hub Devices provisioning*

3. Create the provisioning package and save it to a USB drive.

4. Deploy the package to your Surface Hub during the first run setup or through the Settings app.

The final product of the building process is a project and provisioning package (.ppkg) file.

To finalize the package, open Windows Configuration Designer select Export select "Provisioning package." You can choose to encrypt the package and enable package signing.

Select Next to specify the output location. Windows Configuration Designer default uses the project folder as the output location. Or select Browse to change the default output location. Select Next. Select Build to start building the package. The project information is displayed on the build page. Select output location to go to the package's location to copy the .ppkg file (for the Surface Hub, usually an USB flash drive).

9.1.4 Assign a Provisioning Package to a Surface Hub

There are two ways of deploying provisioning packages to a Surface Hub:

- First run Setup
- Settings app

Apply a provisioning package during the first run by following these steps:

1. Insert the USB flash drive containing the .ppkg file into the Surface Hub. If the file is in the root directory of the drive, the initial setup program will detect it and prompt you to configure the device. Choose "Set up."

2. On the following screen, you will be asked to select a provisioning source. Choose Removable Media and click Next.

3. Pick the provisioning package (*.ppkg) you want to apply and click Next. Keep in mind that only one package can be installed during the initial setup.

4. The setup program will display a summary of the changes the provisioning package will implement. Select Yes and add it.

5. Once the device restarts for the first time, remove the USB flash drive. The settings from the provisioning package will be applied, allowing you to complete the out-of-box experience (OOBE).

6. Apply a provisioning package using the Settings app:

    - Insert the USB flash drive containing the .ppkg file into the Surface Hub.
    - On the Surface Hub, open the Settings app and enter the admin credentials when requested.

- Go to Surface Hub and select "Device management." Under "Provisioning packages," choose "Add or remove a provisioning package" select "Add a package."

- Select your provisioning package and click Add. If prompted, re-enter your admin credentials.

- A summary of the changes to be applied will appear. Confirm by selecting Yes, and add it.

9.1.5 Specify Domain Group Policy Exclusions for Teams Rooms on Windows

Joining Teams Rooms to a domain enables you to grant domain users and groups administrative rights. When you join Teams Rooms to a domain, follow these tips:

- You must create a separate organizational unit (OU) for the MTRs, with the objective to create a Group Policy Object (GPO).

- Disable all GPO inheritance (to isolate the OU from Group Policies you do not want to apply to MTRs).

- Create machine objects in the OU before joining Teams Rooms to the domain to assure that Group Policies applied to the default computer's OU aren't applied.

- Check that the group policies to be excluded do not have No Override enabled. No Override ignores the block of inheritance.

Note that even if you create a separate OU and block inheritance, there are some group policies that could cause issues if they have No Override set. A Group Policy with No Override set beats an OU with Block Policy Inheritance set. The settings in Table 9-2 are critical for meeting rooms and any group policy that modifies them should be blocked.

Table 9-2. *Policy Parameters to Be Blocked for MTRs*

Setting	Allows
HKLM\SOFTWARE\Microsoft\Windows NT\CurrentVersion\Winlogon AutoAdminLogon = (REG_SZ) 1	Enables Microsoft Teams Rooms to boot up
Power Management: On AC, turn off screen after 10 minutesPower Management: On AC, never put system to sleep	Enables Microsoft Teams Rooms to turn off attached displays and wake up automatically
net accounts /maxpwage:unlimitedOr equivalent means of disabling password expiration on the local account. Failure to do this configuration will cause the Skype account to fail logon complaining about an expired password. This impacts all local accounts on the machine, and thus failure to set this configuration will cause the administrative account on the box to eventually expire as well.	Enables Skype account to always log in

9.1.6 Configure Custom Displays for Teams Rooms on Windows

MTRs on Windows support various display resolutions. The display resolution can be set from remote or manually.

- For the remote configuration of your displays, you have to add <EnableResolutionAndScalingSetting>true</EnableResolutionAndScalingSetting> to the XML file. After you've added this line to the XML file, you can set the scale and resolution for your main display and your extended display if you have one.

- For the manual configuration of your displays, on your MTR, go to admin mode. Click Start, select Settings, select System, and select Display. Set the display resolution to as desired (including the resolution of multiple monitors if you have more than one). Next, run PowerShell as an administrator and execute the following commands:

- Powershell -ExecutionPolicy Unrestricted
- c:\Rigel\x64\scripts\provisioning\scriptlaunch.ps1 ApplyCurrentDisplayScaling.ps1

Restart the device.

9.1.7 Customize Meeting Room Settings by Using XML Files on Windows

At startup, the MTR searches for an XML file named SkypeSettings.xml located in C:\Users\Skype\AppData\Local\Packages\Microsoft.SkypeRoomSystem_8wekyb3d8bbwe\LocalState. If the file is available, the MTR applies the configuration settings indicated by the XML file and then deletes the XML file. The XML can be deployed using Group Policies or PowerShell or other methods depending on your organization requirements.

The selected method must be able to transfer files and trigger a restart on the console device. Any text editor can be used to create a settings file. If the XML has any error, the settings contained in it are applied only up to the point where the error happens.

For a list of all the elements in the XML, refer to https://learn.microsoft.com/en-us/microsoftteams/rooms/xml-config-file.

9.1.8 Configure Settings for Peripherals for Teams Room on Windows

To manage peripherals (like a content camera), once the device is connected, go to the MTR Settings, log in as Admin, and select Peripherals.

In the specific peripheral section (in our example Camera), select the peripheral you want to configure and change the settings. Select Save and exit. As we have already seen in previous configurations, using the XML file is the other option to set a peripheral on a Windows MTR.

9.1.9 Monitor Surface Hub Health with Azure Monitor

You can use the Surface Hub solution in Azure Monitor to monitor a Microsoft Surface Hub. Each Surface Hub has the Microsoft Monitoring Agent installed. The agent can send data from the Surface Hub to a Log Analytics workspace in Azure Monitor.

Use the following information to install and configure the solution.

To manage your Surface Hubs in Azure Monitor, you'll need a Log Analytics subscription (that has a cost related to the number of devices you want to monitor).

The Surface Hub solution is available as an Azure Marketplace application.

To configure the Surface Hub solution, follow these steps:

- Go to the Surface Hub page in the Azure Marketplace. Select "Get it now."

- Choose a Log Analytics Workspace. Select Create.

- Once the Log Analytics workspace is configured and the solution created, you can enroll your Surface Hub devices in two different ways:

    - Automatically through Intune

    - Manually through Settings on your Surface Hub device.

Enroll the Surface Hub device using Intune: open the Intune admin center, go to Devices, and select "Configuration profiles." Create a new Windows 10 profile, and then select templates. In the list of templates, select "Device restrictions (Windows 10 Team)."

Enter a name and description for the profile, and for Azure Operational Insights, select Enable.

You'll need the workspace ID and workspace key for the Log Analytics workspace that will manage your Surface Hubs. Enter the Log Analytics Workspace ID and enter the Workspace Key for the policy. Assign the policy to your Surface Hub devices group and save the policy.

Manually enroll the Surface Hub device: open Settings, log in as Admin, select "This device," and the under Monitoring click Configure Log Analytics Settings. Type the Log Analytics Workspace ID and the Workspace Key. Click OK to complete the configuration.

9.1.10 Manage Surface Hub Updates via Update Rings

Surface Hub uses Windows as a Service (WaaS) that enables the deployment of new features on a constant base. In WaaS we have two types of update:

- **Feature updates**: Updates that install the latest new features

- **Quality updates**: Updates that include security fixes, drivers, and other servicing updates

CHAPTER 9   MTRS BASED ON WINDOWS AND SURFACE HUB

Every new release of Windows 10 or Windows 11, including Surface Hub, is cumulative and brings the system where it is installed completely up-to-date.

There are currently three release channels for Windows:

- **The General Availability Channel**: To receive feature updates as soon as they're available

- **The Long-Term Servicing Channel (LTSC)**: Only for specialized devices (with a slower update cycle)

- **The Windows Insider Program**: To test features that will be shipped in upcoming updates

To service Windows as a service, there are different tools. Each one is a good fit for specific scenarios:

- Windows Update (stand-alone)

- Windows Update for Business (WUfB)

- Windows Server Update Services (WSUS)

- Microsoft Configuration Manager

Surface Hubs includes WUfB, and the policies can be controlled by using either Mobile Device Management (MDM) tools or Group Policy management, such as local group policy or the Group Policy Management Console (GPMC).

Deployment rings allow control on the updates rolled out to Surface Hubs. You could create a smaller group of devices used to test the newest updates, and after the required verification, deploy the same updates to the remaining devices.

Table 9-3 gives an example of deployment rings. It is important to know what the maximum deferral usable is for feature updates (180 days) and quality updates (30 days).

Table 9-3. Example of Deployment Rings for Surface Hubs

Deployment Ring	Ring Size	Servicing Branch	Deferral for Feature Updates	Deferral for Quality Updates (Security Fixes, Drivers, and Other Updates)
Preview (e.g., noncritical or test devices)	Small	Windows Insider Preview	None	None
Release (e.g., devices used by select teams)	Medium	Semi-annual channel	None	None
Broad deployment (e.g., most of the devices in your organization)	Large	Semi-annual channel	120 days after release	7-14 days after release
Mission critical (e.g., devices in executive boardrooms)	Small	Semi-annual channel	180 days after release (maximum deferral for feature updates)	30 days after release (maximum deferral for quality updates)

9.2 Configure Optional Features for Teams Rooms and Devices

All the configurations of optional features that have been explained before (as part of the MTR settings) and are listed as part of the exam syllabus are referred to in this section.

9.2.1 Configure HDMI Ingest and Options

In the Microsoft Teams Rooms Pro Management Portal, you can open an MTR device, select the Settings tab, and then select the Device submenu to check the HDMI settings. Also, two different parameters in the SkypeSettings.xml XML file are used to configure HDMI:

- **<DisableTeamsAudioSharing>**: Set to true to disable HDMI audio sharing to meeting participants in Teams meeting. The default is false.

- **<DefaultSpeaker>**: Set the device to be used to play the audio from an HDMI ingest source.

9.2.2 Configure a Content Camera

Content cameras have been used previously in this chapter as an example of configuring peripherals on a Windows MTR. For more information, refer to Section 9.1.8.

9.2.3 Configure Teams Casting

To enable casting to an MTR from a nearby device running Teams, the following steps are required:

1. Enable the Bluetooth Beaconing setting on your Teams devices (Section 8.2.22).

2. Enable the "Automatically accept proximity-based meeting invitations" setting on the Teams device for best results.

3. Your account must be signed into an account that's in the same tenant as the MTR.

9.2.4 Auto Accept a Proximity Join

Bluetooth Beaconing (Proximity Join) for an MTR is a feature that utilizes Bluetooth signals to enhance the meeting experience. For more details, see Section 8.2.22.

9.2.5 Allow Room Remote

You can control MTR devices (like camera and microphone) remotely from your personal device with the room remote in the Teams app. The room remote can be used on a mobile device with Microsoft Teams installed. By default, the room remote should be enabled on your MTR device. To enable the feature, on the device, select "More options" and then "Control room system." Then select "Turn on room remote." This setting will change only for the duration of the meeting.

The room remote can be controlled also via the XML file.

- **<AllowRoomRemoteEnabled>**: If set to true, room remote connections are allowed.

9.2.6 Configure an Intelligent Speaker

An intelligent speaker in an MTR allows you to identify the different speakers in the meeting and attribute speech to the correct person. This feature has an important role with Copilot and intelligent recaps. Certified intelligent speakers are designed to give the best results in voice recognition. It is recommended to limit the number of in-person attendees to a maximum of 10 people. People to be identified in the room need to be enrolled with their voice profile (with a maximum number of people invited with a voice profile set to 20).

The following PowerShell command can be used to enable Intelligent Speaker:

- `Set-CsTeamsMeetingPolicy -Identity PolicyName -roomAttributeUserOverride Attribute -AllowTranscription $true`

The following policies are also required:

- `roomAttributeUserOverride`: This controls the voice-based user identification in meeting rooms. This setting is required for Teams Rooms accounts.

    - `Off`: The Teams Rooms device won't send an audio stream.
    - `Attribute`: Rooms users will be attributed based on their enrollment status.
    - `Distinguish`: Teams Rooms users will be distinguished and separated.

- `AllowTranscription`: This is required for user and Teams rooms accounts. It can be set to true and false.

9.2.7 Configure Direct Guest Join

MTR devices support one-touch joining (Direct Guest Join) with meetings hosted on Cisco Webex and Zoom. BlueJeans by Verizon is also supported, only for Windows based MTRs. To enable Direct Guest Join, follow these steps:

- Allow calendar invite processing for third-party meetings. The room mailbox needs to allow external meetings and keep the message body and subject so it can see the URL needed to join the third-party meeting. Use the following steps:
    - Connect to Exchange Online PowerShell.
    - Get the user principal name (UPN) of the room mailbox.
        - `Get-Mailbox | Where {$_.RoomMailboxAccountEnabled -eq $True} | Format-Table Name, UserPrincipalName`
    - After you find the room mailbox's UPN, run the following command
        - `Set-CalendarProcessing <UserPrincipalName> -ProcessExternalMeetingMessages $True -DeleteComments $False -DeleteSubject $False`
- The meeting join link information from the third-party meeting needs to be present and readable in the meeting invite. To make sure your mail protection services do not modify the join link (if you are using Defender for Office 365 Safe Links), add the URLs to its URL rewrite exception list.
    - Cisco Webex: `*.webex.com/*`
    - Zoom: `*.zoom.us/*`, `*.zoom.com/*`, `*.zoomgov.com/*`
    - BlueJeans: `*.bluejeans.com/*`
    - If you are not using Defender, apply the same exceptions to your third-party solution.
- Enable third-party meetings on Teams Rooms on Windows.
    - On the Microsoft Teams Rooms console, select More, select Settings, and sign in as the admin. Go to the Meetings tab and select the third-party meeting provider you want to enable (e.g., Webex, Zoom, etc.).

You can also use the `SkypeSettings.xml` configuration file:

- To enable Zoom meetings, set the ZoomMeetingsEnabled XML element to True.

- To enable Cisco Webex meetings, set the WebexMeetingsEnabled XML element to True.

- To enable BlueJeans meetings, set the BlueJeansMeetingsEnabled XML element to True.

9.2.8 Configure Hot Desking on Teams Shared Devices

Hot Desking is managed using IP Phone Policies. Refer to Section 8.2.2 for more information.

9.2.9 Configure Hotline Phones

You can set up common area phones as hotline phones. For more details, see Section 8.2.12.

9.3 Knowledge Check

Question 1:
What are the steps required to configure an authentication type during a Surface Hub out-of-box-experience (OOBE) setup?

1. Set the default administrator password to SfB.

2. Change the administrator password via Settings, select Accounts. and select "Sign-in options."

3. Join the Surface Hub to Entra ID for password management.

4. Use a password for the Unified Extensible Firmware Interface (UEFI) settings.

5. Enable password-less sign-ins with Microsoft Authenticator or FIDO2 security keys.

CHAPTER 9   MTRS BASED ON WINDOWS AND SURFACE HUB

Question 2:

Which configurations are essential for setting up meeting room settings on a Surface Hub device?

1. Set the device account in Surface Hub select Accounts.

2. Manage policies and business applications using mobile device management (MDM).

3. Configure Skype for Business domain name under Surface Hub and select Calling & Audio.

4. Choose an image for the welcome screen background in Surface Hub and select Welcome screen.

5. Set the maintenance hours for updates in "Update & security" and select Windows Update.

Question 3:

What are the necessary steps to create and validate a Surface Hub provisioning package?

1. Install Windows Configuration Designer on a separate PC.

2. Configure common settings using the "Provision Surface Hub devices" wizard.

3. Save the provisioning package to a USB drive.

4. Deploy the package during the first run setup or through the Settings app.

5. Encrypt the package and enable package signing during export.

Question 4:

What configurations are involved in enabling Direct Guest Join for Teams Rooms?

1. Allow calendar invite processing for third-party meetings.

2. Add URLs to Defender for Office 365 Safe Links exception list.

3. Enable third-party meetings on Teams Rooms via the console.

4. Use the `SkypeSettings.xml` file to enable Zoom meetings.

5. Set the room mailbox to allow external meetings and retain message body.

CHAPTER 9   MTRS BASED ON WINDOWS AND SURFACE HUB

Question 5:

What steps are required to configure and manage Teams Rooms on a Surface Hub or Windows?

1. Configure the authentication type during OOBE setup.
2. Assign a provisioning package to the Surface Hub.
3. Specify domain group policy exclusions for Teams Rooms on Windows.
4. Customize meeting room settings using XML files on Windows.
5. Monitor Surface Hub health with Azure Monitor.

Answers

Question 1: 2, 3, 4, 5
Question 2: 1, 2, 3, 4, 5
Question 3: 1, 2, 3, 4, 5
Question 4: 1, 2, 3, 4, 5
Question 5: 1, 2, 3, 4, 5

CHAPTER 10

Prepare the Network for Teams and Troubleshooting Calls

The main topics for this chapter are preparing the network for deploying Microsoft Teams and troubleshooting call failures and session quality. Proper planning of the network quality is crucial for providing an optimal user experience in Microsoft Teams. Poor network quality can result in choppy audio and pixelated video, significantly disrupting clear communication during calls and meetings. Low latency and minimal packet loss are essential for real-time interactions in Teams, ensuring that conversations and meetings proceed smoothly.

Troubleshooting calls and quality in Microsoft Teams is an important task and can be complex due to the variety of issues users might face, the numerous tools required for troubleshooting, and the necessary understanding of media flows and voice and meeting configuration. Users may encounter a range of problems, from missing dial pads to voice and video issues, which require different troubleshooting methods.

It is required to understand how Teams handles media streams, including codecs and encryption, to diagnose and fix issues effectively.

In this chapter, the following required skills and exam topics are described:

Prepare the network for the deployment of Teams

- Perform a network analysis by using the Microsoft Teams Network Assessment tool
- Determine network readiness for Teams
- Determine Enterprise Content Delivery Network (eCDN) requirements for Teams live events and town halls.

- Specify the network configuration for certified devices
- Determine network requirements by using the Network planner for Teams
- Specify the optimal network architecture for Teams
- Specify Teams Quality of Service (QoS) requirements and policies
- Validate local internet breakout strategy for client media optimization
- Validate VPN split tunneling
- Validate DNS resolves to the nearest point of entry in Microsoft 365
- Configure Teams for QoS
- Configure Media Bit Rate (MBR)
- Create and assign a network roaming policy
- Configure the network topology
- Configure tenant data upload for the Microsoft Call Quality Dashboard
- Configure Microsoft Power BI reports for the Microsoft Call Quality Dashboard
- Configure reporting labels for Call Analytics

Troubleshoot call failures and session quality

- Troubleshoot a missing dial pad
- Troubleshoot voice & meeting issues by using self-help diagnostics in the Microsoft 365 admin center
- Troubleshoot Entra ID sign-in issues for Teams phones
- Interpret Teams media flows
- Troubleshoot tenant dial plans by using regular expressions and PowerShell
- Interpret E.164 normalization rules to resolve dialing issues
- Interpret reverse number lookup to resolve caller ID issues

- Diagnose call failures
- Troubleshoot dynamic emergency address by using client debug logs
- Troubleshoot Teams client media issues by using the Microsoft Remote Connectivity Analyzer for Teams
- Troubleshoot calls by using Advanced Call Analytics
- Troubleshoot calls by using the Microsoft Call Quality Dashboard
- Inspect PSTN usage reports for SIP call failures

10.1 Prepare the Network for the Deployment of Teams

If your organization has already optimized the network for Microsoft 365, Microsoft Teams should be able to run correctly. That said, there are additional tools and configuration that could be required to improve the performances and quality of Teams. This section is focused on some of them.

10.1.1 Perform a Network Analysis by Using the Microsoft Teams Network Assessment Tool

The Microsoft Teams Network Assessment tool is used to test the connectivity to various Teams servers deployed in the Microsoft Azure network. The tests are used to validate Teams calling. There are two different sets of tests available:

- **Network performance**: Streams packets to the nearest edge site and back for a configurable amount of time.
- **Network connectivity**: Verifies network and network elements between the test location and the Microsoft network are correctly configured to enable communication to the IP addresses and ports needed for Microsoft Teams calls.

Download Microsoft Teams Network Assessment Tool from Official Microsoft Download Center.

The default installation path is `C:\Program Files (x86)\Microsoft Teams Network Assessment Tool`. Running the NetworkAssessmentTool app executes the following tests:

- Connectivity check for source port range 50000–50019
- Service connectivity check

10.1.2 Determine Network Readiness for Teams

There are different elements that must be considered to verify that your organization's network is ready for Teams. The Microsoft Teams Network Assessment tool is the basic one that gives you feedback about the readiness status. In addition to this tool, you can use the Teams Network Planner to assess and plan your network requirements and the Call Quality Dashboard (CQD) to monitor call quality and performance metrics through the CQD to identify and address potential network issues. These tools will be explained in this chapter.

10.1.3 Determine Enterprise Content Delivery Network (ECDN) Requirements for Teams Live Events and Town Halls

Enterprise content delivery networks (eCDNs) are specialized networks designed to optimize the distribution of a large amounts of data, such as video. eCDNs reduce network congestion and improve performance by caching content closer to the end users within the enterprise.

Teams can leverage Microsoft eCDN or third-party eCDNs for streaming events like this:

- Town halls
- Live events
- Large meetings with more than 1,000 participants

Microsoft Teams events use a unicast stream (every viewer gets a video stream from the Internet). ECDN platforms create local distribution points using one of the viewers of the event to relay the stream to other peers, reducing the bandwidth usage and improving the quality of the stream.

CHAPTER 10 PREPARE THE NETWORK FOR TEAMS AND TROUBLESHOOTING CALLS

Microsoft Teams is compatible with Microsoft eCDN (included with a Teams Premium license) and solutions from Microsoft's partners like Hive Streaming, Kollective, and Ramp.

To enable eCDN, open the TAC and go to Meetings. Click "Live events settings." As shown in Figure 10-1, to enable eCDN, follow these steps:

- Toggle the Video distribution provider to On.

- Choose an eCDN provider using the drop-down list.

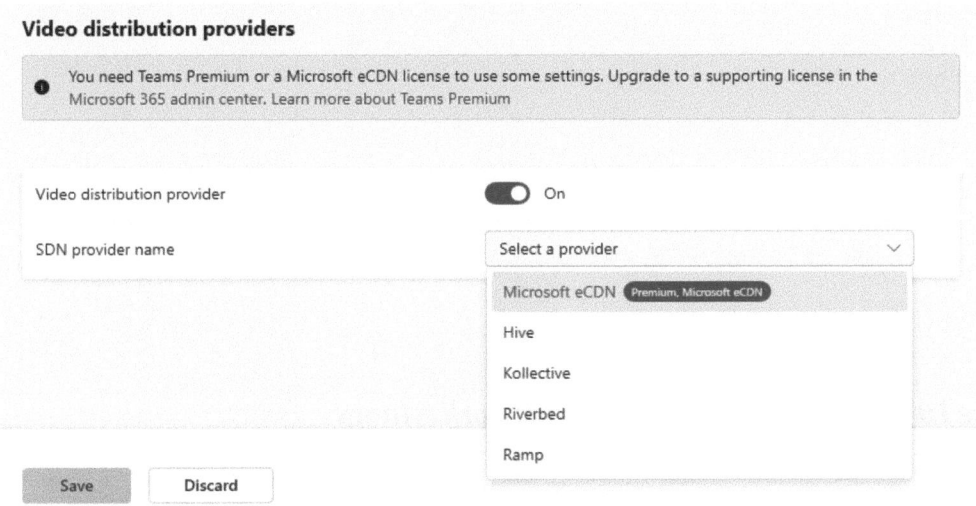

Figure 10-1. Enabling eCDN providers

10.1.4 Specify the Network Configuration for Certified Devices

In Section 8.2.1 we talked about Teams configuration profiles for devices to manage Teams-certified devices. As part of the configuration profile, you have also a Network settings part that allows you to configure parameters like IP address, default gateways, and so on (as shown in Figure 10-2). This is useful to manage basic network settings without using additional tools like Intune.

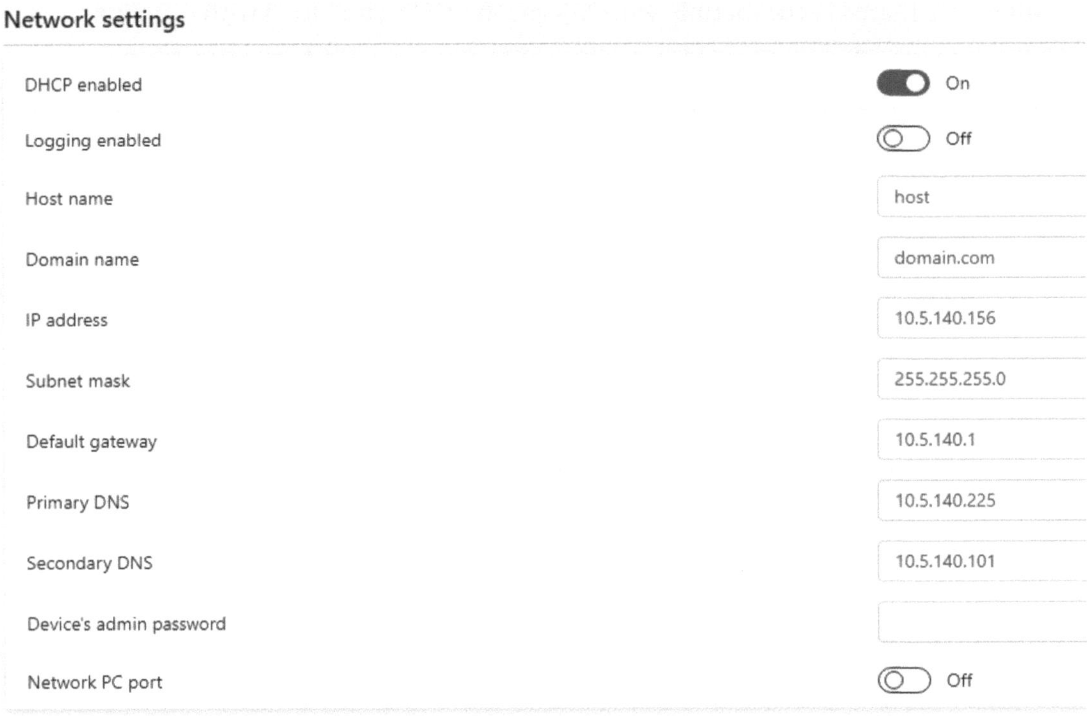

Figure 10-2. Configuration profile's network settings

10.1.5 Determine Network Requirements by Using the Network Planner for Teams

Network Planner is a tool that is available in the TAC. Select Planning and then "Network planner." In Network Planner it is possible to define the requirements to connect your organization to Teams, based on different personas (the default type are Teams Rooms on Windows, Remote worker, and Office worker) and providing your network information in the "Network plans" tab. In the network plan you must add the network sites and network users for each site that you want to evaluate. Additional information required will include ExpressRoute, Connected to WAN, Internet egress, Internet link capacity, and PSTN egress.

Whan all the required sites are added, you can click the Report tab and select "Start a report." You must select a name for the report and the number of personas for each type that are going to be used in the evaluation. Click "Generate report" when ready (see Figure 10-3).

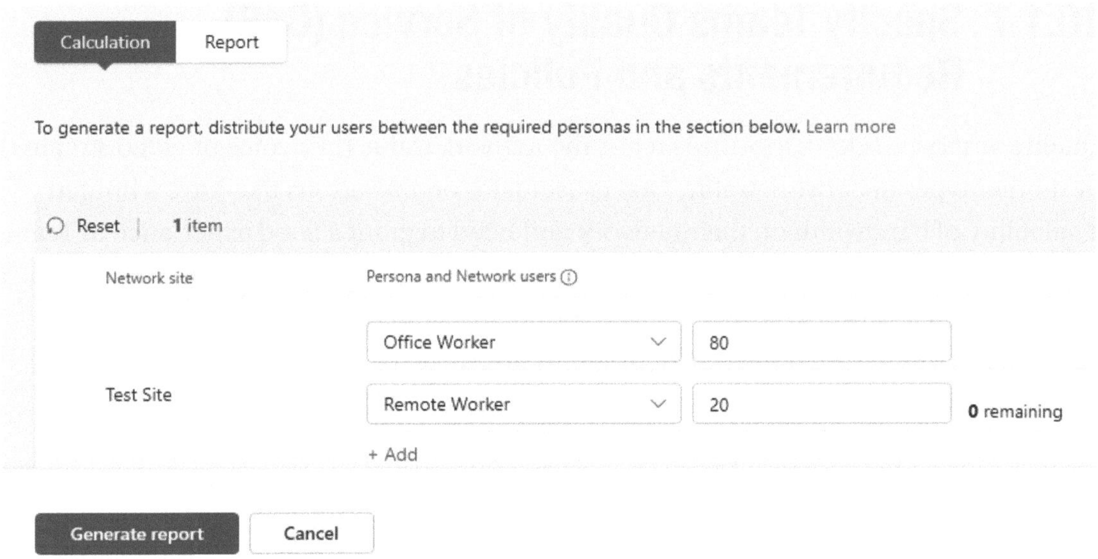

Figure 10-3. Parameters for Network Planner report generation

The report generator will ask what percentage of the available bandwidth can be used for real-time traffic. Click "Run report" and the amount of required bandwidth for Audio, Video, Screenshare, and so on will be displayed.

10.1.6 Specify the Optimal Network Architecture for Teams

The network architecture should be optimized to send Teams real-time traffic from the corporate network to a local Internet connection. All over the world Microsoft exposes "Distributed Service Front Door infrastructure" that are local ingress point whose purpose is to offer a path to the cloud services as short as possible. Optimizing your network to connect to the Internet locally to each site is called "local egress direct Internet network architecture." It is possible to validate your strategy using the `Microsoft 365 connectivity test` at https://connectivity.office.com/.

The tool tests the connection from a selected network location to the nearest Microsoft 365 service front door. A file named `Connectivity.[guid].exe` will be downloaded to the test client to run the report.

10.1.7 Specify Teams Quality of Service (QoS) Requirements and Policies

Quality of service (QoS) prioritizes real-time network traffic (like voice or video streams) over other types of network traffic. QoS is useful for organizations that have a limited availability of bandwidth on their network and need to grant a good experience in Teams calling and meetings for their users. Without QoS, a congested network could experience issues like Jitter, packet loss, and delayed round-trip time (RTT). QoS depends on network devices having queues with different priorities for the different types of traffic. Without QoS a network device has only one queue, and all data is treated as first-in, first-out.

You can implement Teams QoS using Differentiated Services Code Point (DSCP) that mark each network packet with an identifier number, depending on the type of traffic. The following are supported methods:

- **Port-based Differentiated Services Code Point (DSCP) tagging at router**: Your network's router examines incoming packets to determine which range of ports are used. If a QoS policy exists, the router tags the packet with the correct tag and puts it in the defined queue.

- **Client inserted DSCP markers in IP packet headers**: DSCP markers are added when the network traffic leaves the client.

Endpoint marking in windows is managed by Group Policy. The best practice is to manage the traffic from Windows with client-inserted DSCP and control all the remaining network traffic with an access control list (ACL) to apply port-based DSCP at the router/switch level. The implementation of QoS is limited to the internal network. The Internet traffic removes the DSCP tags.

To apply client-inserted DSCP QoS for Windows, you must use Group Policy, sign in to a computer with Group Policy Management installed, open Group Policy Management, and in Group Policy Management locate the container where the new policy should be created.

Right-click, select Create a GPO in this domain, and link it here.

In the New GPO dialog box, type a name for the new Group Policy object, and then click OK.

Select Edit, expand Computer Configuration, expand Windows Settings, right-click Policy-based QoS, and then select "Create new policy" (as shown in Figure 10-4).

CHAPTER 10 PREPARE THE NETWORK FOR TEAMS AND TROUBLESHOOTING CALLS

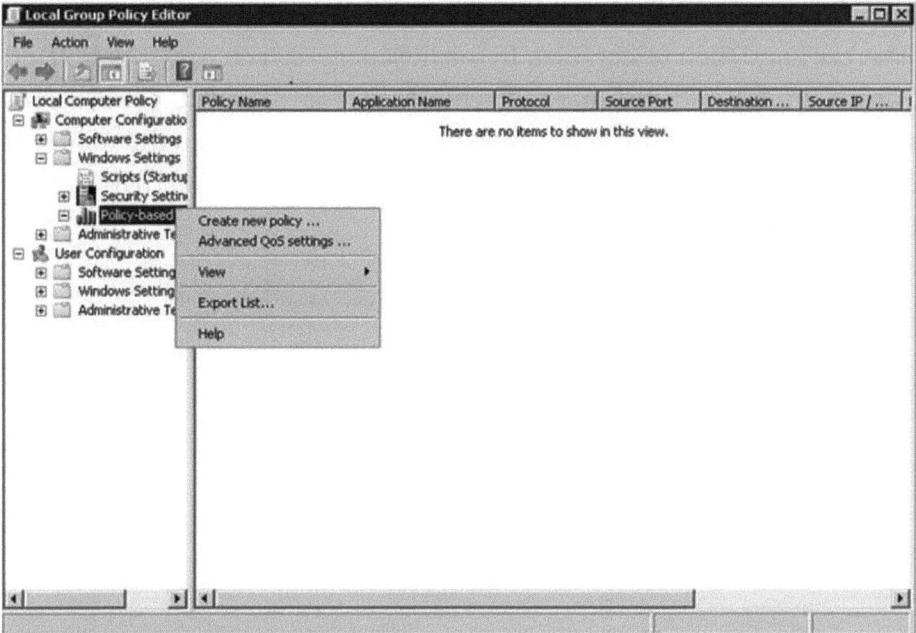

Figure 10-4. *Adding policy-based QoS*

Type a name for the new policy, select Specify DSCP Value, set the value to 46, and then click Next (as in Figure 10-5).

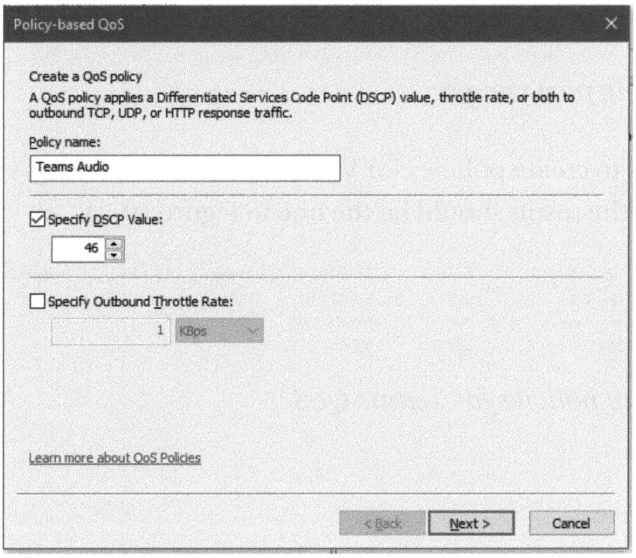

Figure 10-5. *DSCP value configuration*

On the next page, select "Only applications with this executable name," enter the name Teams.exe, and then select Next. In the next page, select "Any source IP address" and "Any destination IP address" and then click Next. For "Specify the protocol and port numbers," select TCP or UDP from the drop-down menu; for "From this source port or range," use one of the set of values in Table 10-1 (for example, the UDP audio values added in Figure 10-6). Click Finish.

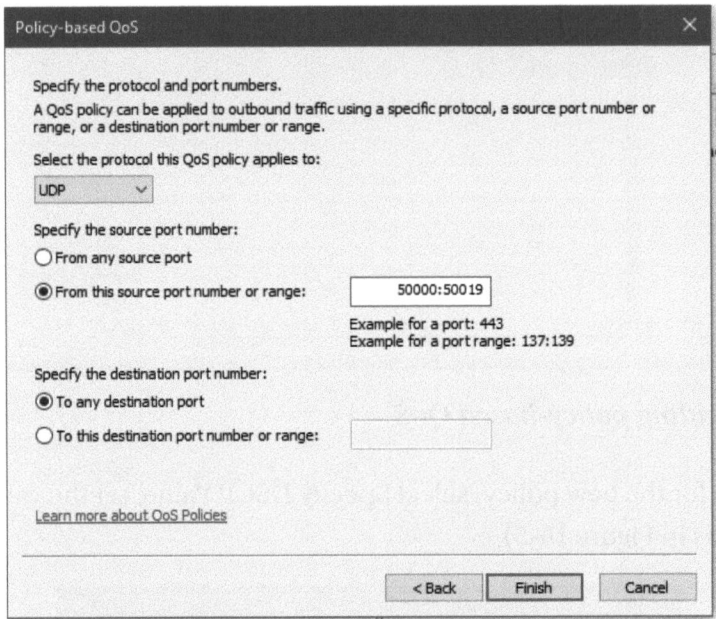

Figure 10-6. Setting port ranges

Repeat the steps to create policies for Video and Screen Sharing, substituting the appropriate values (the result should be the one in Figure 10-7).

Policy Name	Application Name ...	Protocol	Source Port	Destination ...	Source IP / ...	Destination ...	DSCP Value	Throttle Rate
Teams Audio	teams.exe	UDP	50000:50019	*	*	*	46	-1
Teams Video	teams.exe	UDP	50020:50039	*	*	*	34	-1
Teams Application-Screen Sharing	teams.exe	UDP	50040:50059	*	*	*	18	-1

Figure 10-7. Group policies for Teams QoS

10.1.8 Validate Local Internet Breakout Strategy for Client Media Optimization

Implementing a local egress direct Internet network architecture is key for Microsoft 365 services, such as Exchange Online, SharePoint Online, and Teams (as described in Section 10.1.6).

To ensure that your local egress direct Internet network architecture is optimized for Microsoft 365, it is possible to validate your strategy using the Microsoft 365 connectivity test.

The Microsoft 365 connectivity test is a diagnostic tool that assesses the connection from a selected network location to the nearest Microsoft 365 service front door.

The test measures parameters like the following:

- Latency measurement
- Route tracing
- Bandwidth testing
- DNS configuration
- Service endpoint accessibility

10.1.9 Validate VPN Split Tunneling

An organization could use virtual private networks (VPNs) to encrypt network data and create a private network over a public network from the corporate laptops and devices to the internal network. This method has downsides when it comes to services that are accessed via the Internet (like Teams) because all the traffic is sent in the VPN encryption tunnel to the internal corporate network and then (eventually) to the Internet. VPNs are typically not designed to support real-time communication software, like Teams, and this architecture does not align with the best practices that require using the shorter path between the client and the Microsoft network. Also, VPN adds an encryption payload that consumes network bandwidth and computational resources.

Split tunneling is a solution that allows you to define a set of resources to be accessed directly from the client, without using the VPN (that is still the default route for the remaining traffic).

Traffic for Microsoft 365 should be excluded from the VPN tunnel directly from the user to the service over their local Internet connection. The specific VPN client settings depend on the VPN software used on the clients. The `Microsoft 365 network connectivity test` can be used to validate the spilt tunnel configuration. The test results are shown in "Virtual private network (VPN) you use to connect to your organization."

10.1.10 Validate DNS Resolves to the Nearest Point of Entry in Microsoft 365

As explained previously, the DNS and Internet egress are critical for ensuring that user connections are made to the nearest point of entry to Microsoft 365 services. Microsoft 365 front-end servers are distributed in different locations around the world. By configuring internal DNS servers to provide local name resolution for Microsoft 365 endpoints, network traffic destined for Microsoft 365 can connect to front-end servers as close as possible to the client.

The `Microsoft 365 network connectivity test` can be used to validate the DNS configuration and the resulting egress location. The test results are shown in the following parts of the report:

- Network egress location (the location where your network connects to your ISP)
- Your distance from the network egress location
- Time to make a DNS request on your network
- Your distance from and/or time to connect to a DNS recursive resolver

10.1.11 Configure Teams for QoS

To configure QoS for Teams, you start configuring the client source port range. Table 10-1 shows the recommended initial port ranges.

CHAPTER 10   PREPARE THE NETWORK FOR TEAMS AND TROUBLESHOOTING CALLS

Table 10-1. *Default Port Ranges and DSCP Values*

Media Traffic Type	Client Source Port Range	Protocol	DSCP Value	DSCP Class
Audio	50,000–50,019	TCP/UDP	46	Expedited Forwarding (EF)
Video	50,020–50,039	TCP/UDP	34	Assured Forwarding (AF41)
Application/Screen Sharing	50,040–50,059	TCP/UDP	18	Assured Forwarding (AF21)

To configure QoS in the TAC, go to Meetings and select "Meeting settings." You must toggle "Insert Quality of Service (QoS) markers for real-time media traffic." The packets are marked based on the originating port and should respect the setting applied the client port ranges (see Figure 10-8).

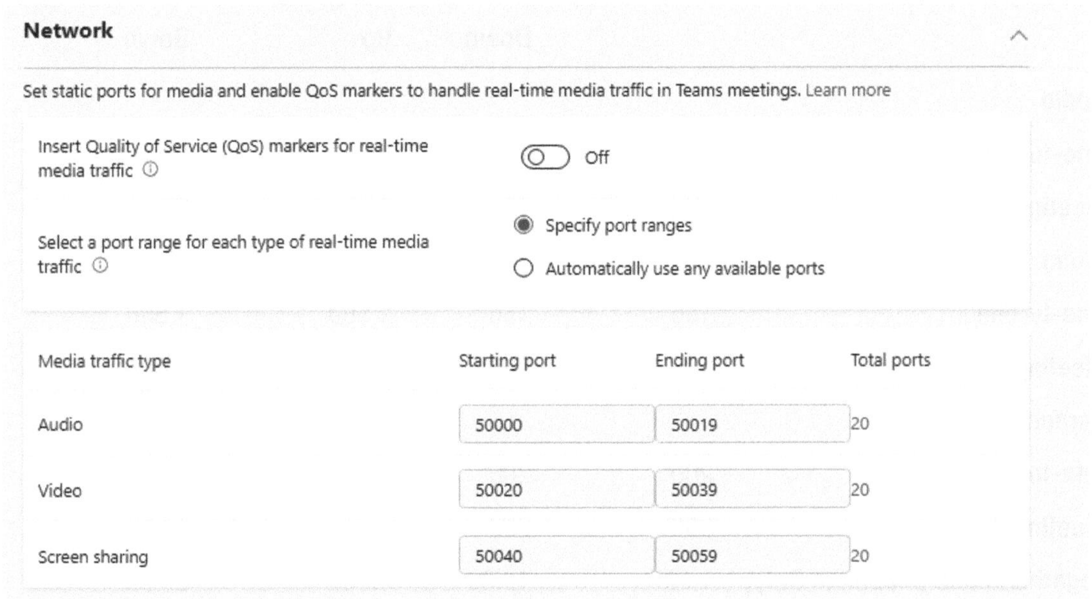

Figure 10-8. *Enabling QoS in TAC*

10.1.12 Configure Media Bit Rate (MBR)

In Microsoft Teams, the average media bit rate (MBR) for calls and meetings refers to the amount of data transmitted per second during audio or video communication. This bit rate can vary depending on several factors, including network conditions, the quality of the call, the number of participants, and whether the communication is audio-only or includes video.

By using a parameter in the meeting policies, it is possible to limit the average bit rate (the setting is about the average combined media bit rate for audio, video, and video-based app sharing in both meetings and peer-to-peer calls). The media bit rate applies to both inbound and outbound to the Teams client and to the Teams service. The default MBR is 50,000 Kbps, which on the single client practically corresponds to applying no limit. Table 10-2 shows the minimum and recommended MBR values for the various Teams modalities.

Table 10-2. Minimum and Recommended MBR Values

Modality	Minimum Up	Minimum Down	Recommended Up	Recommended Down
Audio				
One-to-one	10	10	58	58
Meetings	10	10	58	58
Video				
One-to-one	150	150	1,500	1,500
Meetings	150	200	2,500	4,000
Screen sharing				
One-to-one	200	200	1,500	1,500
Meetings	250	250	2,500	2,500
Together Mode (Meetings Only)	1,000	1,500	1,500	2,500

To configure the MBR value, open the TAC, go to Meetings, and select "Meeting policies." Navigate to "Media bit rate (Kbps)" and set the value desired.

10.1.13 Create and Assign a Network Roaming Policy

You can control the use of IP Video and MBR outside the meeting policies in a dynamic way by using Network Roaming Policies (TeamsNetworkRoamingPolicy).

With a TeamsNetworkRoamingPolicy policy, the Teams client dynamically picks up the settings based on which network site it connects. The roaming policy overwrites the meeting policies; however, if there's no policy assigned to the site, the values set in the meeting policy are used.

TeamsNetworkRoamingPolicy is managed by using the following PowerShell cmdlets:

- Get-CsTeamsNetworkRoamingPolicy
- New-CsTeamsNetworkRoamingPolicy
- Set-CsTeamsNetworkRoamingPolicy
- Remove-CsTeamsNetworkRoamingPolicy

The parameters are as follows:

- AllowIPVideo: Controls if video can be turned on in meetings hosted by a user and one-on-one and in group calls started by a user
- MediaBitRateKb: Defines the total average media bit rate for audio, video, and video-based app sharing transmissions in calls and meetings for the user

For example, when you need to control bandwidth usage and video availability dynamically, you can use the following command:

- Set-CsTeamsNetworkRoamingPolicy -Identity BandwidthSiteLow -AllowIPVideo $true -MediaBitRateKb 500
  - -Identity LowBandwidthSite: Specifies the identity of the BandwidthSiteLow policy.
  - -AllowIPVideo $true: Enables video (IP Video) for meetings and calls.
  - -MediaBitRateKb 500: Sets the total average media bit rate to 500 kbps

CHAPTER 10   PREPARE THE NETWORK FOR TEAMS AND TROUBLESHOOTING CALLS

10.1.14 Configure the Network Topology

If your organization is deploying Location-Based Routing for Direct Routing (see Section 5.5.1) or dynamic emergency calling (see Section 6.11), you must set the network settings to enable those features. For a description of the required steps, refer to Section 6.14.

10.1.15 Configure Tenant Data Upload for the Microsoft Call Quality Dashboard

The Microsoft Call Quality Dashboard (CQD) shows call and meeting quality at the organization level. CQD captures both the individual calls and the quality of all the calls made using Teams and gives a quick overview of the trends for call quality, server-client streams, client-client streams, and voice quality. To properly use the CQD, Microsoft recommends uploading the tenant and building data. There are two types of tenant data files: building and endpoint (the templates for both files can be downloaded from https://download.microsoft.com/download/0/b/9/0b9c1610-d421-489a-a3f9-d1ae703c9f1b/locations-template.zip). The first time visiting CQD, you'll be asked to upload building data. You can select Upload Now to quickly navigate to the Tenant Data Upload page.

Otherwise, from the CQD Summary Reports dashboard, go to Settings (click the gear icon in the upper-right corner) and select Tenant Data Upload. On the Tenant Data Upload page, select Browse and select a data file. Specify Start date and then click Upload.

10.1.16 Configure Microsoft Power BI Reports for the Microsoft Call Quality Dashboard

Microsoft offers some templates to use the data in the CQD data via Power BI.

The latest reporting template for Teams calls quality is called Quality of Experience (QER).

Copy the content of the CQD-Power-BI-query-templates.zip file in the C:\temp folder.

The report requires Power BI Desktop to be installed (Download Power BI tools and apps). The QER also requires a Power BI Connector for Microsoft Advanced CQD.

Copy the `MicrosoftCallQuality.pqx` file from `C:\temp` in the `%username%\Documents\Power BI Desktop\Custom Connectors` folder. Open Power BI Desktop, click File, and select "Options and settings." Then go to Options and Security. Under Data Extensions, select "(Not Recommended) Allow any extension to load without validation or warning." Click OK and restart Power BI Desktop. Open File, click "Open report," and select "Browse reports." Browse to the folder where you put `QER v4.7.pbit` in `C:\temp`. Sign in with your Teams admin credentials, open the template, and you will be connected to CQD.

10.1.17 Configure Reporting Labels for Call Analytics

Reporting labels are used to indicate the physical locations of offices, buildings, or organizational sites. In the TAC, go to Analytics & Reports, Under "Reporting labels" you can upload a file (`.csv` or `.tsv`) that has a list of physical locations and their associated network subnets.

The file will be used by Call Analytics for generating reports.

The report labels and locations must be provided as is in a single data structure, with no way available to edit the single entries.

10.2 Troubleshoot Call Failures and Session Quality

Troubleshooting Teams calling, depending on the specific issue, requires working on different levels of the Teams infrastructure, including licensing, Teams devices, client software, and so on. Here we will focus on the most common problems that could happen.

10.2.1 Troubleshoot a Missing Dial Pad

If the user doesn't see a dial pad in their Teams client, you can try these techniques:

- Check the assigned licenses. The user needs a Teams license and a Teams Phone license. (They could be part of a bundle already assigned to the user.)
- Check if the user is enabled to Enterprise Voice.
- Check that a voice routing policy (or calling plan) has been assigned.

CHAPTER 10   PREPARE THE NETWORK FOR TEAMS AND TROUBLESHOOTING CALLS

You can also execute a quick test of the Teams PSTN Calling dial pad using the Remote Connectivity Analyzer.

10.2.2 Troubleshoot Voice & Meeting Issues by Using Self-Help Diagnostics in the Microsoft 365 Admin Center

In the Microsoft 365 admin center, Teams diagnostics are available to help administrators manage the top support issues for Teams. Sign in to the Microsoft 365 admin center and open Support. Select "Help and support" and on the right part of the screen a tab will open "How can we help?." An administrator can input the description of an issue to get support. In our example (Figure 10-9), asking to troubleshoot a missing dial pad opens an additional field where we can input the name of the affected user and then select Run Tests.

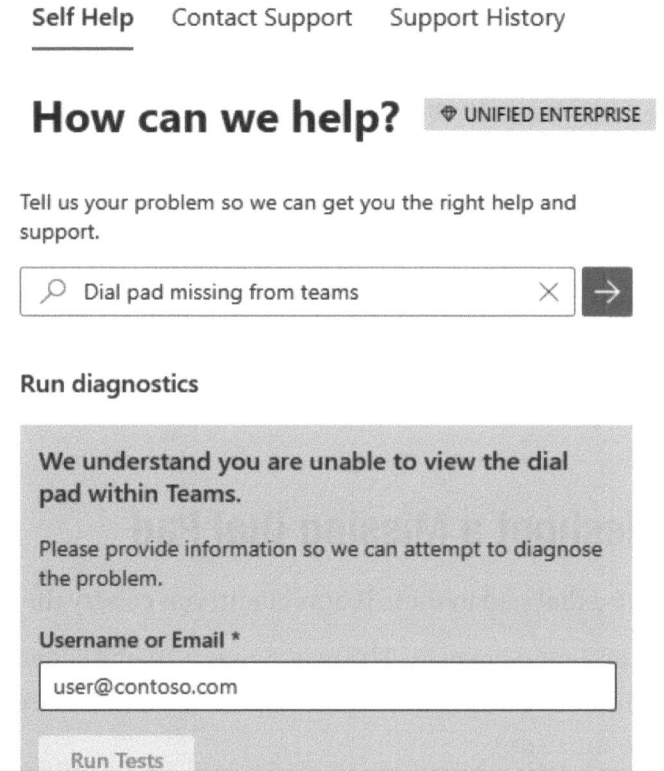

Figure 10-9. Self Help interface in the Microsoft 365 admin center

10.2.3 Troubleshoot Entra ID Sign-in Issues for Teams Phones

One of the most frequent scenarios with sign-in issues for Teams Phones is related to Conditional Access. Teams Phones are considered Android devices, so if any Conditional Access rule is applied to the Android operating system, that could impact the Teams phones too. You could see symptoms like the following:

- The devices can't sign in to Teams.
- The devices get stuck in sign-in loops.
- The devices automatically sign out of Teams randomly.

The quickest way to troubleshoot these issues is to check the sign-in log in Entra. To check the logs, open the Entra admin center. In the search bar, type "Sign-in Logs" and open the page that opens.

Select "Add filters" to add the following filters:

- Status: Failure.
- Application: Teams.

The result is shown in Figure 10-10.

Date	Request ID	User	Application	Status	IP address
15/08/2024, 13:16:57	99a0d31a-b9ff-4040-...		Microsoft Teams	Failure	
15/08/2024, 13:12:42	2cca73c1-6183-46e1-...		Microsoft Teams	Failure	
15/08/2024, 13:07:40	49f66e5c-dd21-4064-...		Microsoft Teams	Failure	
15/08/2024, 13:01:49	7e1e7f9f-db80-4502-...		Microsoft Teams Web...	Failure	
15/08/2024, 12:35:55	285aa394-185e-46c2...		Microsoft Teams Web...	Failure	

Figure 10-10. Entra sign-in logs filtering

Opening one of the lines, there are additional information including Basic info, Location, Device info, Authentication Details, and Conditional Access. If the error is a failed Conditional Access policy, you can review the policy settings.

The Remote Connectivity Analyzer could be used to execute some sign-in tests from the Internet (Microsoft Remote Connectivity Analyzer: Test Input).

10.2.4 Interpret Teams Media Flows

In Section 5.5.2, we have talked about the difference between the media traffic and the signaling traffic, both required for a Teams call or meeting. While signaling traffic always routes through the Microsoft Cloud and contributes minimally to overall network usage, media traffic is handled differently depending on whether Direct Routing is configured with or without Media Bypass. Teams Media Bypass is a feature that allows media traffic to flow directly between users' devices and the on-premises phone system, bypassing the Microsoft Cloud. This shortens the path of media traffic and reduces the number of hops in transit with a positive impact on Teams call quality. Since media traffic consumes significantly more bandwidth, optimizing its flow is critical. Within the Microsoft Cloud, two components can be involved in the media traffic path: media processors (MPs) and transport relays (TRs). The involvement of these components depends on our specific configuration.

Media processors:

- Will always be used in a nonbypass scenario.
- Will be always used for voice applications like auto attendant and call queues

Transport relays:

- Will be used only if the public IP of the SBC is not reachable
- Will always be used for scenarios with media bypass

There are some additional principles that must be considered to better understand the way media flows in Teams:

- A Microsoft Teams conference is hosted by Microsoft 365 in the same region where the first participant joined.
- A Teams media endpoint in Microsoft 365 in the cloud could be used, based on media processing needs and not based on call type. The media traffic sent from a client to the media endpoint may be routed directly or use a Transport Relay in Microsoft 365 if required due to customer network firewall restrictions.
- Media traffic for peer-to-peer calls takes the most direct route that is available
- Signaling traffic always goes to the Microsoft 365 server closest to the user.

CHAPTER 10   PREPARE THE NETWORK FOR TEAMS AND TROUBLESHOOTING CALLS

You can see how the media flow for Teams happens in the different network scenarios at https://learn.microsoft.com/en-us/microsoftteams/microsoft-teams-online-call-flows.

10.2.5 Troubleshoot Tenant Dial Plans by Using Regular Expressions and PowerShell

In Section 6.1, we have seen how dial plans are implemented in Teams and how they affect the dialing experience of Teams Voice users. The main issue could be that the dialed number is formatted in a way that is not coherent with the Teams standards or with the location where the user is. The first step to troubleshoot the issue is to check the dial plan applied to the user. If the dial plan is the expected one, debugging the various normalization rules is the next step. In the TAC, you can visualize what each rule does inside a dial plan. For more complex rules, you can use online tools that analyze regular expressions like regex101, as shown in Figure 10-11.

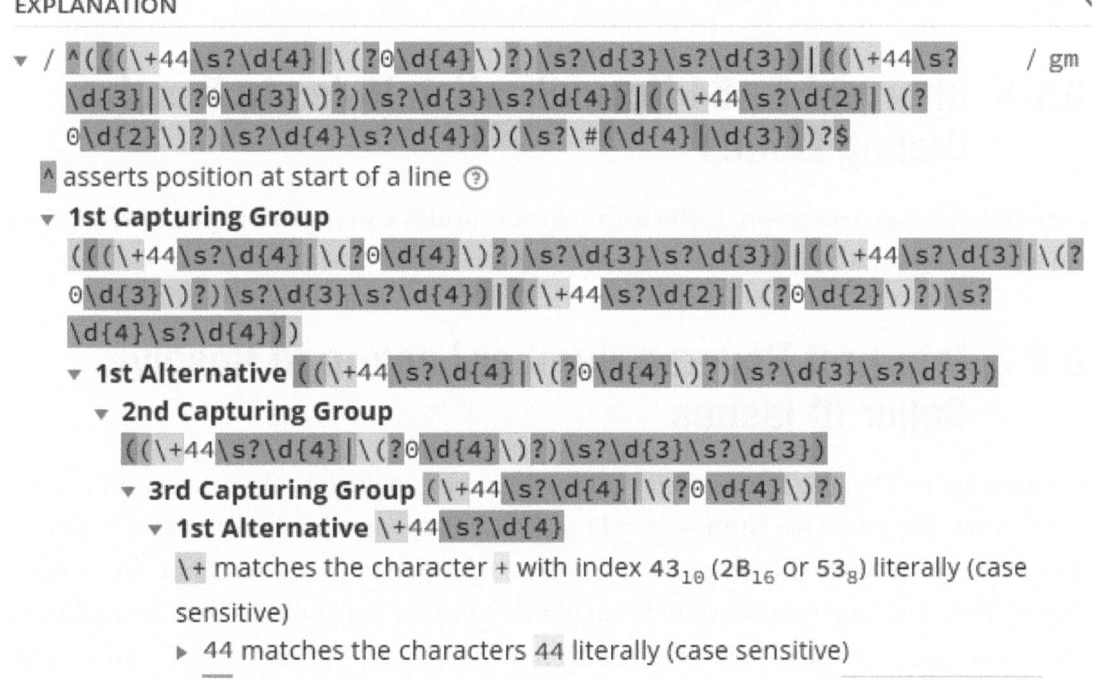

Figure 10-11. Examining a regular expression for UK numbers

To use PowerShell in your debugging, you can refer to what was explained in Section 6.1.1. For the tenant dial plan, it is possible to use the `Test-CsEffectiveTenantDialPlan` command, which is used to test the dial plan and how it will impact a specific dialed number. For example, we can test what happens when the user `Lisa@M365x07896792.onmicrosoft.com` dials the number 0207357XXXX.

- `Test-CsEffectiveTenantDialPlan -DialedNumber 0207357XXXX -Identity Lisa@M365x07896792.onmicrosoft.com | fl`
- The result is as follows:
    - `MatchingRule: Description=GB Long Distance Dialing`
    - `Rule;Pattern=^0(\d+)$;Translation=+44$1;Name=GB Long`
    - `Distance;IsInternalExtension=False`
    - `TranslatedNumber: +44207357XXXX`

So the matching rule "GB Long Distance Dialing" adds the +44 to a national call as required for the E.164 standard.

10.2.6 Interpret E.164 Normalization Rules to Resolve Dialing Issues

As for the previous paragraph, E.164 normalization rules use regular expressions and are managed in the same ways we have already seen.

10.2.7 Interpret Reverse Number Lookup to Resolve Caller ID Issues

For incoming PSTNs, the Teams client shows the incoming external phone number as the caller ID using Reverse Number Lookup (RNL). If the number is associated with a user or contact in Microsoft Entra ID or a personal contact, the Teams client shows the caller ID based on that information. If the phone number isn't in Microsoft Entra ID or a personal contact, the telco-provided display name is shown if it's available. If the display name looks wrong, check the Entra directory, the user's Teams contacts, or Outlook contacts for a match.

10.2.8 Diagnose Call Failures

Call failures are usually caused by a wrong configuration (in which case the issue is reproducible) or to a temporary disruption on one of the parts of the Teams voice deployment.

Call Analytics is the main tool used to troubleshoot a failed Microsoft Teams call or meeting quality at the single user level.

Call Analytics includes information about devices, networks, connectivity, and call quality.

Call Analytics examines each leg of the call (meaning, all the users and phone numbers that joined a call) but doesn't show information on users who don't fully join a call or meeting.

Call Analytics is available in the TAC. Go to Users and select "Manage users." Here you can select a user and then open the "Meetings & calls" tab on the user's profile page. Here you can find all the calls and meetings that the user participated in for the last 30 days.

Click the specific meeting or call to have an overview of the call and the call experience for each participant (see Figure 10-12).

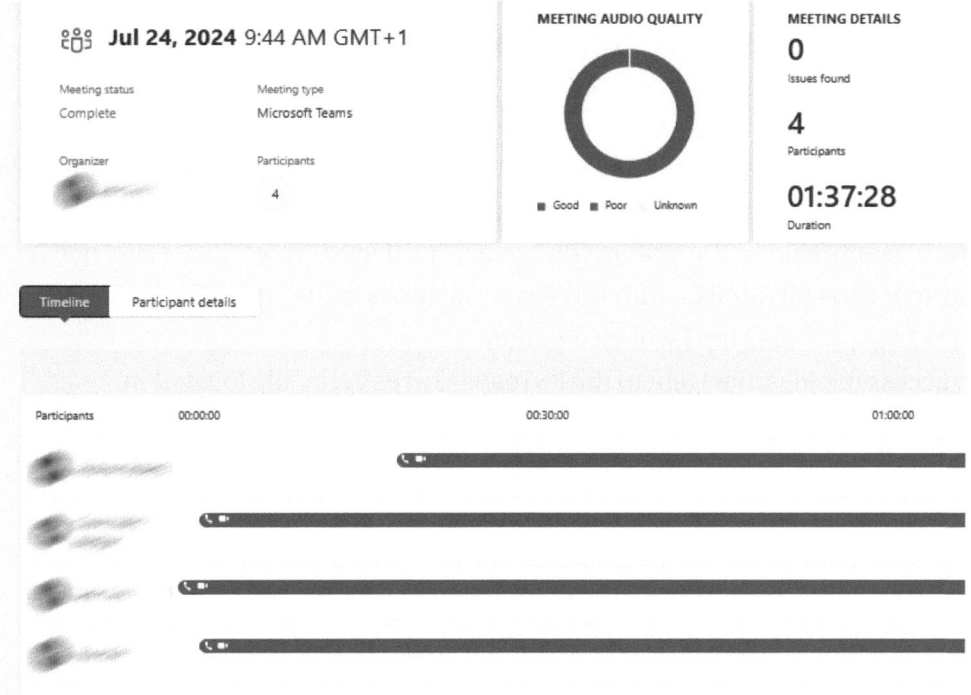

Figure 10-12. Call analytics for a meeting

CHAPTER 10   PREPARE THE NETWORK FOR TEAMS AND TROUBLESHOOTING CALLS

By opening the "Participants details" page, it is possible to examine details about each user in the call and use them for troubleshooting. In Figure 10-13, by opening a participant's details, we can see that the call quality was poor due to a not-optimal network connection.

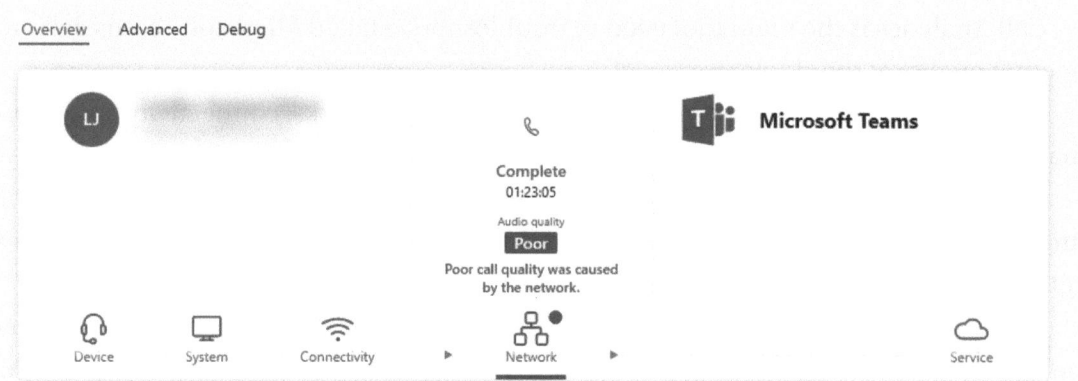

Figure 10-13. *Poor call quality flagged for a participant*

10.2.9 Troubleshoot Dynamic Emergency Address by Using Client Debug Logs

We talked about dynamic emergency calling in Section 6.11. The Teams client diagnostic logs can help in troubleshoot dynamic addresses. To collect Teams client logs, click the Microsoft Teams icon in the system tray, select "Collect support files" (alternatively, use the shortcut Ctrl+Alt+Shift+1 with the Teams client in focus). A folder named MSTeams Support Logs [timestamp] will be created.

To access the logs, navigate to the MSTeams_latest.log file located in %userprofile%\AppData\Roaming\Microsoft\Teams\logs.txt.

10.2.10 Troubleshoot Teams Client Media Issues by Using the Microsoft Remote Connectivity Analyzer for Teams

We have already talked about the Remote Connectivity Analyzer in Section 8.2.19. In this chapter, we also explained that the Microsoft 365 network connectivity test can be used to validate the connectivity between your network and the Microsoft 365 services. These tests could point out if any of the required services is not reachable and to other Teams client issues.

10.2.11 Troubleshoot Calls by Using Advanced Call Analytics

As we said before, Call Analytics is available inside the user management interface in the TAC under Users (select "Manage users"). The Advanced tab has additional information that allows for a more comprehensive troubleshooting compared to the Overview page. In Advanced we have a complete summary of the inbound and outbound streams information, system, connectivity, and network. Any parameter in the call or meeting that was not a match with the expected requirements will be flagged as a potential source of an issue (like Jitter in Figure 10-14).

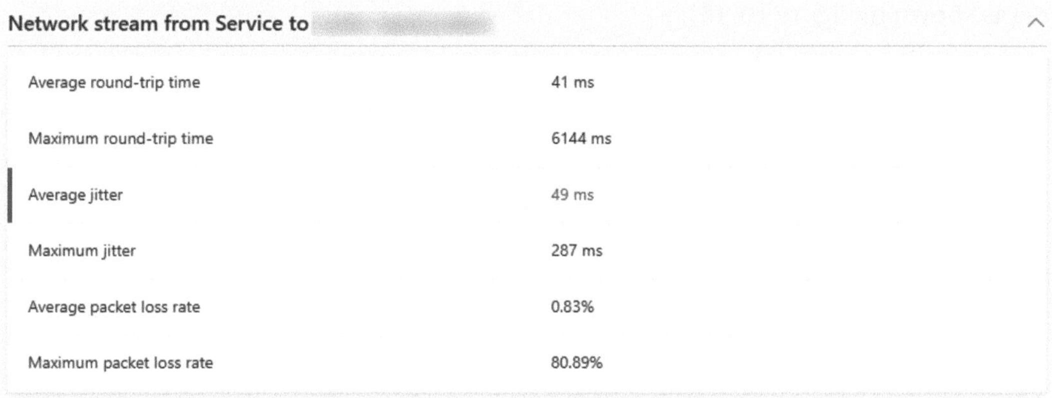

Network stream from Service to	
Average round-trip time	41 ms
Maximum round-trip time	6144 ms
Average jitter	49 ms
Maximum jitter	287 ms
Average packet loss rate	0.83%
Maximum packet loss rate	80.89%

Figure 10-14. Average Jitter flagged as a potential issue

10.2.12 Troubleshoot Calls by Using the Microsoft Call Quality Dashboard

Previously in this chapter we talked about the Call Quality Dashboard. When troubleshooting poor quality in Teams calls, CQD allows you to analyze data at both an organizational and individual level. If you notice that a specific user is experiencing poor call quality, you can dive deeper by using CQD data in combination with per-user call analytics. This approach helps you determine whether the issue is isolated to that user or is part of a broader network problem affecting multiple users. For instance, after identifying a call quality issue through per-user call analytics, CQD can reveal whether the problem stems from a network condition impacting several users. By analyzing the data, you can see if the issue is related to network congestion, packet loss, or other factors that might degrade call quality. This insight is crucial for taking corrective action, whether that involves adjusting network configurations, improving bandwidth allocation, or addressing specific hardware issues.

10.2.13 Inspect PSTN Usage Reports for SIP Call Failures

In the TAC section, select "Analytics & reports" and then "Usage reports." It is possible to create different reports about different aspects of Teams in the tenant, including Teams calling. The "PSTN and SMS (preview) usage" report is helpful in identifying trends and issues (as shown in Figure 10-15).

CHAPTER 10   PREPARE THE NETWORK FOR TEAMS AND TROUBLESHOOTING CALLS

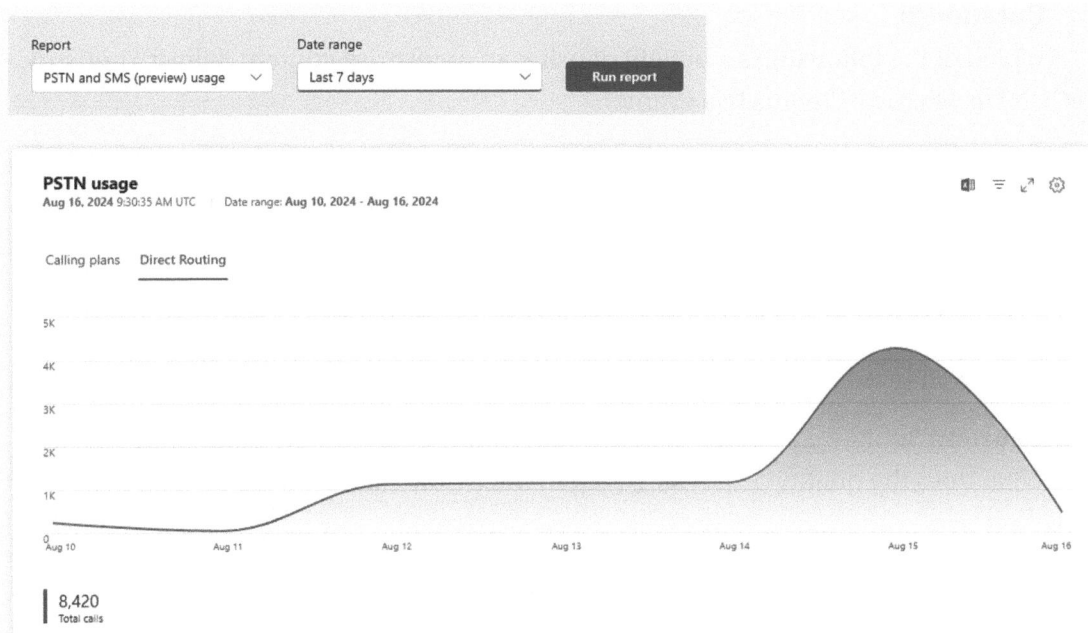

Figure 10-15. *PSTN and SMS (preview) usage report*

It is possible to export the data in a .csv file and filter the calls in different ways, including "Event type" and "Final SIP code." For example, an SIP code 404 or 487 could identify a failed call.

10.3 Knowledge Check

Question 1:

Which of the following tools is used to assess the network's readiness for Microsoft Teams?

1. Microsoft Teams Network Planner.

2. Microsoft Teams Network Assessment Tool.

3. Microsoft Power BI.

4. Microsoft Remote Connectivity Analyzer.

CHAPTER 10 PREPARE THE NETWORK FOR TEAMS AND TROUBLESHOOTING CALLS

Question 2:

Which of the following is a benefit of using an enterprise content delivery network (eCDN) in Microsoft Teams live events?

1. Increases the number of participants in a meeting.
2. Reduces network congestion by caching content closer to end-users.
3. Improves audio quality by filtering background noise.
4. Enhances video resolution by increasing bandwidth usage.

Question 3:

What does the quality of service (QoS) in Microsoft Teams primarily help to prevent?

1. Unauthorized access to network data.
2. Increased latency during file downloads.
3. Jitter, packet loss, and delayed round-trip time.
4. Overuse of data storage capacity.

Question 4:

Which method is recommended for applying quality of service (QoS) settings for Microsoft Teams traffic in a Windows environment?

1. Editing the Windows Registry.
2. Adjusting the firewall settings.
3. Using Group Policy to insert DSCP markers.
4. Manually tagging each packet in the Teams application.

Question 5:

What is the purpose of validating DNS resolves to the nearest point of entry in Microsoft 365?

1. To improve email security.
2. To block unauthorized access to Teams meetings.
3. To enhance data encryption during transmission.
4. To ensure user connections are made to the nearest Microsoft 365 service front door.

CHAPTER 10 PREPARE THE NETWORK FOR TEAMS AND TROUBLESHOOTING CALLS

Answers

Question 1: 2

Question 2: 2

Question 3: 3

Question 4: 3

Question 5: 4

Index

A

ABR, *see* Adaptive bitrate streaming (ABR)
Activity log, 34, 35
Adaptive bitrate streaming (ABR), 62
Ad-hoc Meetings, 17
Admin policies, 154
Advanced configurations and design principles, Direct Routing
    configuring SBA, 127–129
    designing and configuring LBR, 121
    designing and configuring LMO, 122–124
    on-network conferencing, 126, 127
AllowPSTNConferencingDialOutType value, 146
Always Bypass, 124
Amazon Web Services (AWS), 107
Analog devices
    ATA, 95
    Direct Routing, 96
    operator, 97
    SIP Gateway, 96
    solutions, 95
    specific scenarios, 95
Analog Telephone Adapter (ATA), 95
Android Teams Rooms, 214
APP, *see* Intune app protection policies (APP)
APP data protection framework, 241
Assigning policies
    methods, 33, 34
    status check, Activity log, 34, 35
    users' effective policy, 32
        direct assignment, 33
        global policy, 33
        group assignment, 33
Assigning policy packages, 37, 38
ATA devices, 95
ATA, *see* Analog Telephone Adapter (ATA)
Audio & video, 29, 30
Audio conferencing bridge
    assigning phone number, 52, 53
    audio conferencing policies, 55
    conference bridge settings options, 53, 54
    configuration settings, 52
    description, 52
    dial-in numbers, 52
    function, 52
    managing with PowerShell, 56
Audio conferencing policies, 55, 56
Audio conferencing PSTN calls, 145, 155
Audio traffic, 122
Auto attendants
    business requirements, 172
    configuration steps, 175
    features, 171, 172
    holiday call settings, 186
    holidays, 184
    implementation steps, 174
    Microsoft 365 Groups, Voicemail, 183, 184

INDEX

Auto attendants (*cont.*)
    PowerShell, 177–179, 188, 189
    prerequisites, 173, 174
    resource accounts, 182, 183
        licenses, 182
        phone number, 182
    Teams Phone, 171
    voice application policies, 188
AWS, *see* Amazon Web Services (AWS)
Azure communications gateway, 85
Azure Monitor, 267, 268

B

Bluetooth Beaconing (Proximity Join), 253, 271

C

Call Analytics, 299, 301
Call delegation, 198, 199
Caller ID policies, 187
    block incoming Caller ID, 141
    CNAM, 141
    components, 140
    End User Control, 141
    inbound Caller ID options, 141
    parameters, 139, 140
    PowerShell commands, 141, 142
    PSTN caller ID, 140
    restrictions, 141
Call failures, 299, 300
Call hold policies, 202
    configuration, 143
    description, 143
    PowerShell commands, 143–145
Calling features, Teams Phone
    users
        audio conferencing settings, 199–201
        call delegation, 198, 199
        call forwarding, 197
        call hold policies, 202
        dial-out from meetings policy, 201
        Group call pickup, 195–197
        shared calling, 202, 203
        simultaneous ring, 197, 198
        voicemail, 193–195
Calling line ID (CLID), 140, 166
Calling party name (CNAM), 140, 141, 166
Calling policies, 113
    key features, 135, 136
    PowerShell commands, 136, 137
Call Park policies
    description, 138
    parameters, 138
    PowerShell commands, 139
Call Quality Dashboard (CQD), 280
    Power BI reports, 292
    tenant data upload, 292
    Troubleshoot Calls, 302
Call queues
    business requirements, 172
    caller ID policies, 187, 188
    ConferenceMode, 184
    configuration steps, 177
    custom Music on Hold, 186, 187
    deploy channel-based, 179–181
    features, 171, 172
    implementation steps, 176
    Microsoft 365 Groups, Voicemail, 183, 184
    PowerShell, 177–179, 188, 189
    prerequisites, 173, 174
    resource accounts, 182, 183
        licenses, 182
        phone number, 182
    routing methods, 184

INDEX

Teams Phone, 171
voice application policies, 188
voice-enabled Teams channel, 181
Calls flow
    calling policies, 113
    configuration, 114, 115
    voice route, 113
    voice routing policies, 114
CAPs, *see* Common area phones (CAPs)
CCSEs, *see* Collaboration communications systems engineers (CCSEs)
Channel meetings, 16
CLI, *see* Command-line interface (CLI)
CLID, *see* Calling line ID (CLID)
Cloud Video Interop (CVI), 207, 223
Collaboration communications systems engineers (CCSEs), 2
Command-line interface (CLI), 10
CommonAreaPhonePolicy, 233
Common area phones (CAPs), 245, 246
Communications credits, 51, 88, 89
Compliance recording policies, 155
Compliance voice recording
    APIs and SDK requirements, 99
    communications admins, 98
    definition, 98
    licenses, 98
    policies, 99
    PowerShell commands, 99, 100
    RecordedUsersPolicy policy, 100
    solutions, 98
Conditional Access policies, 234, 235
Configuring dynamic emergency calling
    calling locations, 158
    calling scenarios, 157
    LIS, 162–164
    policies, 159–161
    validation, 164, 165
Configuring Teams Phone policies
    caller ID policies, 139–141
    call hold policy, 143–145
    calling policies, 135–137
    Call Park policies, 138, 139
    compliance recording policies, 154–156
    dial plans, 132–135
    inbound call blockiing, 148–150
    outbound call restrictions, 145–148
    policy packages, 151–154
    unassigned number routing, 150, 151
Connect Model, 100
Content cameras, 271
Content sharing, 25, 26
Coordinated meetings, 222
CQD, *see* Call Quality Dashboard (CQD)
Creating webinars
    attendee pre-webinar steps, 41
    co-organizers, 40
    during webinar, 41
    external presenters, 40, 41
    post-webinar actions, 41
    Public, 40
    scheduling and registration, 42
    Teams client, 40
    webinar preparation, 41
CRM, *see* Customer relationship management (CRM)
Customer relationship management (CRM), 80
Customizing audio conferencing, 56–58
Custom meeting templates
    options, 65, 66
    parts, 66
    settings, 65
    Teams Premium, 65
Custom policy packages, 36
CVI, *see* Cloud Video Interop (CVI)

INDEX

D

Data Loss Prevention (DLP), 242
DDIs, *see* Direct dial-ins (DDIs)
Dedicated numbers, 52
Default audio conferencing number, 52
DHCP, *see* Dynamic Host Configuration Protocol (DHCP)
Dial-in numbers, 52
Dial mask, 161
Dial-out from meetings policy, 201
Dial plans
    adding, 133
    definition, 132
    normalization rules, 133, 134
    PowerShell commands, 134, 135
    Teams clients, 133
    types, 132
Differentiated Services Code Point (DSCP), 284, 285, 289
Direct dial-ins (DDIs), 79, 81
Direct Guest Join, 223, 273, 274
Direct Routing, 81, 89, 90
    additional configurations (*see* Advanced configurations and design principles, Direct Routing)
    calls flow, 113–115
    interoperability solutions, 105
    PSTN calling flow, 105
    SBCs (*see* Session Border Controllers (SBCs))
    SIP trunks, 106
DLP, *see* Data Loss Prevention (DLP)
DSCP, *see* Differentiated Services Code Point (DSCP)
Dynamic emergency calling, 300
Dynamic emergency calling scenarios, 157
Dynamic Host Configuration Protocol (DHCP), 97, 98, 233, 248, 254

E, F

eCDNs, *see* Enterprise content delivery networks (eCDNs)
Education_Teacher policy package, 39
Emergency call routing policies, 159, 160, 162
Emergency dial string, 161
EnableUserOverride parameter, 141
Enduser PSTN calls, 145
Enterprise basic data protection, 241
Enterprise content delivery networks (eCDNs), 62, 280, 281
Enterprise enhanced data protection, 241
Enterprise high data protection, 241
E.164 standard, 132
Event groupss, 58
Event hotline management, 80
The Exchange Online mailbox, 225
External App/Device Production, 72

G

Get-CsOnlineDialInConferencingBridge, 56, 126
Get-CsOnlineDialInConferencingUser, 57
GetCsOnlineDialOutPolicy, 146
Get-CsOnlinePSTNGateway, 116
GetCsTeamsCallHoldPolicy, 144
GetCsTeamsCallingPolicy, 137
Get-CsTeamsIPPhonePolicy command, 232
Get-CsTeamsMeetingBroadcastPolicy, 63, 64
GetCsTenantDialPlan PowerShell command, 135
Global Live Event policy, 61
GrantCsCallingLineIdentity, 142, 144

INDEX

Grant-CsGroupPolicyPackage Assignment, 39
GrantCsTeamsCallHoldPolicy, 144
GrantCsTeamsCallingPolicy, 137, 148, 193
Grant-CsTeamsComplianceRecording Policy, 100
Grant-CsTeamsMeetingBroadcast Policy, 63
Grant-CsTeamsMeetingPolicy, 32
Group call pickup, 195–197
Group package assignment, 38
GUID, see Globally unique identifier (GUID)
Group policy assignment, 33, 64, 192, 193, 202

H

Hive streaming, 63, 64, 281
Hot Desking, 79, 157, 232, 233, 254, 274

I, J

Inbound call blocking
    features, 148
    PowerShell commands, 149, 150
    PSTN number, 149
Inbound Caller ID Options, 141
Integrating third-party call centers with Teams
    advanced features, 101
    Connect Model, 100
    elements considerations, 101
    Extend Model, 101
    Power Model, 101
Intelligent speaker, 272
Intune, 80, 227, 268
Intune app protection policies (APP), 241
Intune Configuration Profiles, 243, 244
IP phone policies, 232, 233

K

Key SIP messages, 119
Kollective, 63, 281

L

LAN, see Local area network (LAN)
LBR, see Location-based routing (LBR)
Live events, 20
    creating and delivering steps, 70–72
    definition, 58
    interactive features, 58
    organizer checklist, 59, 60
    platforms, 70, 72
    policies, 60–62
    PowerShell commands, 63, 64
    production modes, 72
    roles, 58, 59
    settings, 61, 62
    video distribution providers, 62, 63
LIS, see Location information service (LIS)
LMO, see Local media optimization (LMO)
Local area network (LAN), 95
Local media optimization (LMO)
    network topologies, 123
    SBC's current firmware supports, 124
    trunk translations rules, 125, 126
    voice quality enhancement, 122
Local media optimization with centralized SBC, 106, 122, 123
Local media optimization with proxy SBC, 124

INDEX

Location-based routing (LBR), 106, 121, 130, 292
Location information service (LIS), 132, 162–164

M

MAC address, 246, 247
Maintain Teams Rooms and devices
    activities, 230
    add Android device MAC address, 247
    Android devices, 246, 247
    Android devices configuration profiles, 240
    BitLocker, 243
    CAPs, 245, 246
    conditional access policy MFA exception, resource accounts, 234
    configure device settings, 230–232
    create and manage teams device tags, 246
    Generate verification code, 247
    Intune Configuration Profiles, Windows MTRs, 243
    Intune Policies, 241, 242
    IP phone policies, 232, 233
    Local Network Settings, 233
    Monitor Teams Device Health, 248
    MTR Home screen
        configuration and operations, 239
    Pro Management Portal, 240
    security and updates, 233
    settings
        Surface Hubs, 235
        Windows, 235
    shared space devices
        advanced voice features, 244
        enable Hotline, 244
        sign-in, 253
        SIP Gateway, 248
        Teams devices panel, 231
        troubleshoot bluetooth beaconing, 253
        troubleshoot remote provisioning issues, 252
        troubleshoot update issues, 251, 252
        user phones, 246
        VFD, 244
MBR, *see* Media bit rate (MBR)
MDM, *see* Mobile device management (MDM)
Media Access Control (MAC) IDs, 246
Media bit rate (MBR), 290, 291
Media Bypass, 122, 124
Media bypass for home office and mobile users, 124
Media ports (UDP), 117
Media processors (MPs), 296
Media traffic, 122, 123, 289, 296
Meeting engagement, 24, 25, 66, 67, 216
Meeting join & lobby, 23, 24
Meeting options
    default options, 68
    settings, 68
Meeting policies
    audio & video, 29, 30
    content sharing, 25, 26
    default policies, 20
    deployment methods, 21
    management, 20
    managing with PowerShell, 31
    meeting engagement, 24, 25
    meeting join & lobby, 23, 24
    meeting scheduling, 21, 22
    recording & transcription, 27, 28
    watermark, 31
Meeting registration, 18

INDEX

Meetings, 16
    additional features, 18
    channel meetings, 16
    private meetings, 16
    scheduled meetings, 17
Meeting scheduling, 21, 22
Meeting themes
    description, 67
    features, 67, 68
    Teams Calendar, 68
Meeting types, 15, 49
"Meet now" meeting, 17, 18
MFA, *see* Multifactor
    authentication (MFA)
Microsoft 365 E5/A5/G5 Plans, 79, 102
Microsoft 365 network connectivity test, 287, 288
Microsoft 365 resource accounts, 225
Microsoft Azure network, 279
Microsoft calling plans, 81, 86–88
Microsoft Cloud, 296
Microsoft Exchange Online Resource Account, 225–227
Microsoft Surface Hub 3, 220
Microsoft Teams
    administrative interfaces, 7
    administrative tools, 7
    definition, 5
    features, 5, 6
    meeting room technologies, 7
    SharePoint and OneDrive integration, 7
Microsoft Teams certified hardware
    certified devices, 91, 92
    devices and peripherals, 90
    key characteristics, 90
    selection, key factors, 92
    types, 91

Microsoft Teams Network Assessment tool, 279, 280
Microsoft Teams Phone Mobile, 81
Microsoft Teams PowerShell module, 7
Microsoft Teams Rooms(MTR), 79, 209
    components, 209
    Surface Hub (*see* Surface Hub)
    Windows (*see* Windows)
Microsoft Teams Rooms Pro Management Portal, 7, 209, 270
Microsoft Teams Shared Devices, 79
Microsoft Teams Shared Devices license, 229
Mobile device management (MDM), 241
Monitor Teams Device Health, 248, 249
MPs, *see* Media processors (MPs)
MS-721 exams
    communication specialists, 1
    preparation, 2
    Teams-focused, 1
MTR, *see* Microsoft Teams Rooms (MTRs)
Multifactor authentication (MFA), 234

N

Network Planner, 280, 282, 283
NewCsCallingLineIdentity, 141–143
New-CsGroupPolicyAssignment, 39, 64
NewCsTeamsCallingPolicy, 137
New-CsTeamsComplianceRecording Policy, 100
New-CsTeamsIPPhonePolicy, 232
New-CsTeamsMeetingBroadcastPolicy, 63, 64
New-CsTeamsMeetingPolicy, 31, 32
NewPolicyName Teams meeting broadcast policy, 64
Number Translation Rules, 125

313

INDEX

O

Only for Local Users, 124
On-network conferencing, 126, 127
Operator Connect, 81–84
Optimal network architecture, 283
Outbound call restrictions
    audio conferencing call restrictions, 145
    definition, 145
    PowerShell commands, 146, 148
    types, 145
    user's settings, 146

P

PBX, *see* Private Branch Exchange (PBX)
Pearson VUE, 2
Per-organizer and per-user Policy, 21
Per-organizer policy, 21
Personal devices, 93
Per-user policy, 21
Plan and design teams-certified device solutions
    Android MTRs *vs.* Windows MTRs features, 214, 215
    architectural requirements, 211
    coordinated meetings, 222
    CVI, 223
    Direct Guest Join, 223
    enrollment requirements, Microsoft Intune, 227, 228
    Microsoft Exchange Online Resource Account, 225–227
    The Microsoft Teams Rooms Pro Management Portal, 209, 210
    requirements, room size, 211
    rooms capacity, 210
    rooms standards, 210
    Shared Devices, advanced features, 229
    Surface Hub, 220
    Teams Devices Certification Program, 220, 221
    Teams panels, 221, 222
    Teams Rooms Basic and Teams Rooms Pro features, 211, 212
    Teams Rooms Certified Components, 221
    update strategy, Teams Meeting Room devices, 224, 225
    workloads and teams licenses, 230
PLAR, *see* Private line auto ringdown (PLAR)
Policy-based recording, 98, 154
Policy management, 32
Policy packages, 32
    assigning, 37, 38
    assigning to group, 153
    assigning to multiple users, 153
    assigning to user, 152
    custom policy packages, 36
    definition, 151
    managing with PowerShell, 39
    permissions and capabilities allocation, 35
    policies, 35
    PowerShell commands, 153, 154
    professional roles, 35
    TAC/PowerShell commands, 36
    Teams packages, 152
    Teams policies, 152
PowerShell, 178–180, 188, 189, 191, 193
PowerShell module, 10, 11
Private Branch Exchange (PBX), 86
Private line auto ringdown (PLAR), 244
Private meetings, 16
Provisioning Server URL, 97

PSTN, *see* Public Switched Telephone Network (PSTN)
PSTN audio conferencing
  communications credits, 51
  licenses, 50
  meeting organizer, 50
  phones, 50
  service numbers, 50, 51
PSTN calls only, 148
PSTN connectivity
  minimum requirements, 76
  requirements, 77
PSTN connectivity options
  acquiring new phone numbers, 82
  communications credits, 88, 89
  Direct Routing, 81, 89, 90
  Microsoft calling plans, 81, 86–88
  Microsoft Teams Phone Mobile, 81
  Operator Connect, 81–84
  porting existing phone numbers, 82
  Teams Phone Mobile, 84–86
PSTN usage record, 161
Public Switched Telephone Network (PSTN), 75

Q

QER, *see* Quality of Experience (QER)
QoS, *see* Quality of service (QoS)
Quality of Experience (QER), 292
Quality of service (QoS), 122
  client source port range, 289
  DSCP, 284
  DSCP value configuration, 285
  DSCP values, 289
  group policies, 286
  network devices, 284
  organizations, 284
  policy-based, 285
  real-time network traffic, 284
  setting port ranges, 286
  TAC, 289
  Teams, 288

R

Ramp OmniCache, 63
RecordedUsersPolicy policy, 100
Recording & transcription, 27, 28
Recording types, 154
Remote Connectivity Analyzer, 295, 301
RemoveCsTeamsCallHoldPolicy, 145
Reporting labels, 293
Reverse Number Lookup (RNL), 298
Riverbed, 63
RNL, *see* Reverse Number Lookup (RNL)
Room remote, 271

S

SANs, *see* Subject alternative names (SANs)
SBA, *see* Survivable Branch Appliance (SBA)
SBCs, *see* Session Border Controllers (SBCs)
Scheduled meetings, 17
SendSipOptions parameter, 116
Service numbers, 50, 51
Service-scoped dial plans, 132
Session Border Controllers (SBCs), 117
  Azure Marketplace, 108
  cloud-based *vs.* On-prem, 108, 109
  configuration, 111, 112
  deploying, 112, 113
  description, 107

INDEX

Session Border Controllers (SBCs) (*cont.*)
    SBA for Direct Routing, 109, 110
    supported SBC, 107
Session Initiation Protocol (SIP), 75, 247, 248
SetCsCallingLineIdentity, 142
Set-CsOnlineDialInConferencing Bridge, 56
Set-CsOnlineDialInConferencingUser cmdlets, 57
Set-CsOnlinePSTNGateway command, 126
SetCsTeamsCallHoldPolicy, 144
SetCsTeamsCallingPolicy, 137
Set-CsTeamsIPPhonePolicy, 232
Set-CsTeamsComplianceRecording Policy, 100
Set-CsTeamsMeetingBroadcastPolicy, 63
Set-CsTeamsMeetingPolicy, 31, 32
Set-CsTeamsTranslationRule command, 125
Shared calling policy, 202
Shared numbers, 52
Shared space devices, 93
Shared Space Devices
    advanced voice features, 244
    enable Hotline, 244
Signaling traffic, 122
SIP, *see* Session Initiation Protocol (SIP)
SIP-compatible device, 247
SIP devices, 97, 98
SIP Device support, 94
SIP Gateway, 96, 248
    compatibility, 93
    configuration, 94
    definition, 93
    features, 93
    primary function, 93
SIP signaling (TCP/UDP), 117
SIP signaling port, 113
Split tunneling, 287
Stream, 72
Subject alternative names (SANs), 112
Subnets, 162
Supported SBC, 107
Surface Hub, 220
    advantages, 220
    Azure Monitor, 267, 268
    deployment rings, 269, 270
    disadvantages, 220
    hybrid/cloud-only organization, 259
    meeting room settings, 259
    OOBE setup, 258
    provisioning package
        building process, 263
        create, 262, 263
        first run setup, 264
        Settings app, 264
    settings, 235
    WaaS, 268
    WUfB, 269
Survivable Branch Appliance (SBA), 110, 127
    Azure IP ranges and service tags, 128
    clients, 110, 128
    configuration, 128, 129
    distributable code, 127
    firewall configuration, 127
    logical schema, 110
    prerequisites deployment, 127
    PSTN calling, 109
    PSTN calls, 110
    Teams PowerShell cmdlets, 128

INDEX

T

TAC, *see* Teams admin center (TAC)
Teams admin center (TAC), 7, 10, 112, 133
Teams administrators, 249
Teams Android-based MTRs, 227
Teams Calling Plan, 190
Teams deployment
    CQD
        Power BI reports, 292
        tenant data upload, 292
    eCDNs
        providers, 281
        streaming events, 280
    MBR, 290
    Microsoft 365
        DNS configuration, 288
    minimum and recommended MBR values, 290
    network analysis
        Microsoft Teams Network Assessment Tool, 279, 280
    network configuration, certified devices, 281, 282
    network readiness, 280
    Network Requirements
        Network Planner, 282, 283
    network topology, 292
    optimal network architecture, 283
    policies, 284–286
    reporting labels, call analytics, 293
    requirements, 284–286
    TeamsNetworkRoamingPolicy, 291
    Teams, QoS, 288
    validate local internet breakout strategy
        client media optimization, 287
    VPN split tunneling, 287, 288
Teams devices, 230, 231
Teams Devices Certification Program, 220, 221
Teams Essentials, 78, 79
Teams licensing, 7, 8
Teams Media Bypass, 296
Teams meetings
    interactive features, 47
    settings, 47
TeamsNetworkRoamingPolicy, 291
Teams Phone
    auto attendants (*see* Auto Attendants)
    calling features (*see* Calling functionalities, Teams Phone)
    call queues (*see* Call queues)
    features, 76
    licensing options, 78
    usage scenarios, 80
    users (*see* Users, Teams Phone)
Teams Phone Devices
    personal devices, 93
    shared space devices, 93
    Teams Devices Certification Program, 90
Teams Phone Mobile, 84–86
Teams Phones, 110, 128, 295
Teams Phone SIP Gateway, 93, 95
Teams Premium, 49
Teams Premium license, 49
Teams Premium licensing, 42
Teams Production, 72
Teams Rooms and Devices
    optional features configurations
        content cameras, 271
        Direct Guest Join, 273, 274
        HDMI ingest and options, 270
        Hot Desking, Teams Shared Devices, 274

INDEX

Teams Rooms and Devices (*cont.*)
    hotline phones, 274
    intelligent speaker, 272
    Proximity Join, 271
    room remote, 271, 272
    teams casting, 271
  plan and design teams (*see* Plan and design teams-certified device solutions)
Teams Rooms Basic, 79, 211
Teams Rooms Basic License, 212
Teams Rooms Pro, 79
Teams Rooms Pro License, 212
Teams usage scenarios, 80
Teams uses configuration profiles, 231
Teams webinars
  creation (*see* Creating webinars)
  definition, 39
  key features, 39, 40
TenantLevel control, 148
Tenant-scoped dial plans, 132
TestPolicy meeting policy, 39
TRs *see* Transport relays (TRs)
Transport relays (TRs), 296
Troubleshoot call failures and session quality
  average jitter as potential issue, 301
  Call Analytics, 301
  CQD, 302
  diagnose call failures, 299, 300
  dynamic emergency calling
    client debug logs, 300
  E.164 normalization rules to resolve dialing issues, 298
  entra ID sign-in issues, Teams Phones, 295
  interpret teams media flows, 296, 297
  missing dial pad, 293
  PSTN usage reports, SIP call failures, 302, 303
  Remote Connectivity Analyzer
    Teams client media issues, 301
  RNL to resolve caller ID issues, 298
  self-help diagnostics, Microsoft 365
    admin center, 294
    meeting issues, 294
    voice issues, 294
  Teams infrastructure, 293
  tenant dial plans
    regular expressions/powershell, 297, 298
Troubleshooting Direct Routing
  certificate issues, 117
  firewall issues, 117
  investigating and diagnosing calling issues, 119, 120
  SBC connectivity, 117–119
  validating SBC connectivity, 116
Trunk translations rules, 125, 126
Trusted IP addresses, 162

U

Unassigned number routing
  commonly used solutions, 150
  PowerShell commands, 151
  routing rules, 150, 151
User blocking, 148
Users, Teams Phone
  assign calling policies, 192, 193
  assign phone number
    Microsoft Teams Admin Center, 190, 191
    PowerShell, 191
  dial plans, 190
  standard license, 190

steps, 189
Teams Calling Plan, 190
verified emergency address location, 191
voice routing policy to direct routing user, 193

V

VFD, *see* Virtual Front Desk (VFD)
Video distribution providers, 62, 63
View-only meeting experience, 19
Virtual Front Desk (VFD), 244, 245
Virtual private networks (VPNs), 287, 288
Voice application policies, 188
Voice over IP (VoIP), 75
Voice routes, 113–115
Voice routing policies, 104, 114, 115, 127
VoIP, *see* Voice over IP (VoIP)
VPNs, *see* Virtual private networks (VPNs)
VPN split tunneling, 278, 287

W, X

WAN, *see* Wide area network (WAN)
WaaS, *see* Windows as a Service (WaaS)
Watermark, 31
WCD, *see* Windows Configuration Designer (WCD)

Webex Meetings, 224, 274
Webinars, 3, 13, 15, 19, 39–43, 48, 49, 60
Wide area network (WAN), 96
Windows
    Customize Meeting Room Settings, XML Files, 267
    Teams Rooms
        custom displays, 266
        domain group policy exclusions, 265
        peripherals, settings, 267
        policy parameters, 266
Windows as a Service (WaaS), 268, 269
Windows Configuration Designer (WCD), 262–264
Windows MTR devices, 228
Windows Teams Rooms, 214, 230
Windows Update for Business (WUfB), 269
WUfB, *see* Windows Update for Business (WUfB)

Y

Yammer, 70, 72

Z

Zoom Meetings, 224, 274, 275

MIX
Papier aus verantwortungsvollen Quellen
Paper from responsible sources
FSC® C105338

If you have any concerns about our products,
you can contact us on
ProductSafety@springernature.com

In case Publisher is established outside the EU,
the EU authorized representative is:
**Springer Nature Customer Service Center GmbH
Europaplatz 3, 69115 Heidelberg, Germany**

Printed by Libri Plureos GmbH
in Hamburg, Germany